## *Praise for Dan Jackson's* Old Bug

"There are books—and then there are books. The first category includes 99% of your average Barnes & Noble stock, while the second is made up of the paradigm-shifters, the perspective granters, the wonder-inducers—books that, once met, never leave you. *Zen and the Art of Motorcycle Maintenance* is in this lovely group, along with the works of Vonnegut and Sagan, Bill Bryson and Lewis Thomas. Now add Dan Jackson's *Old Bug*, a love-child of Pirsig and Joseph Campbell with a dash of Bryson, a deeply engaging blend of travel through the inner and outer worlds of one thoughtful and thought-filled man. His journey across the country in an uncertain vehicle is the perfect metaphor for the spiritual trek he takes in a vehicle no less temperamental—the questing and questioning mind. It will stick to your hands until you've finished, and stick to your mind long afterward."

— Dale McGowan, author of *Parenting Beyond Belief*
and *Calling Bernadette's Bluff*

"A remarkable and engrossing true story... I loved reading about two middle-aged men taking a voyage of self-discovery in an old Beetle. It is filled with funny episodes and quite touching moments. A great read that I just couldn't put down. From the cover to the last word, this is one book I'm sure is destined for a hit."                    — Jessica Roberts, *BookPleasures.com*

"Recounting a cross-country road trip between the author and a friend who have barely seen each other in thirty years, *Old Bug* is as much about a lingering question in the soul as it is about the journey, namely, "If I don't believe in traditional religion, then what do I believe in?" Pondering God, morality, mortality, meaning, and the mysteries of life itself, *Old Bug* recounts confronting inner demons long buried even as it mirthfully recounts the hassle of struggling to keep a '69 VW Beetle running smoothly in the 21st century. A gentle, thoughtful read of discovery and larger-than-life quandaries."

— *Midwest Book Review*: Reviewer Choice

Old Bug

# Old Bug

The spiritual quest of a skeptical guy
on a road trip across America
with a long lost friend
in a beat-up Beetle

## DAN JACKSON

END RUN PRESS

The author would like to thank Paul Bradley, Liliana Cruz, Esmé Jackson, Suzanne Eblen, Cindy and Tom Muro, Marion Jackson, Marcy Kaplan, Alan Bardsley, Dolores Rider, Kathleen Corr, John Kweder and, of course, Richard.

For information contact End Run Press:
info@endrunpress.com

ISBN-10: 0-9794463-0-9
ISBN-13: 978-0-9794463-0-6
Library of Congress Control Number: 2007925579

Book design by Michael Kellner

Photos by RMK

Published by End Run Press
www.endrunpress.com

3.0

# For Esmé,
## WITH LOVE AND SQUALOR

Only that day dawns
to which we are awake.

—HENRY DAVID THOREAU

# PREFACE

This is the story of a self-proclaimed spiritual journey, taken by a not-particularly-spiritual person, at the dawn of the 21$^{st}$ century. It is not a spiritual journey in the tradition of a pilgrimage to Jerusalem or a *hajj* to Mecca or Siddhartha's sitting under the Bodhi tree in search of enlightenment. There are no saffron robes or burning bushes, no talking animals or gauzy vestal virgins. There are no visions in the sky or voices in the night.

It's a spiritual journey taken in an age of interstates and fast food franchises, of cell phones and Internet connections; a time where most notions of the spiritual are either quaintly nostalgic or cloyingly pretentious; a time when people don't do things like take spiritual journeys. For me, that was the whole point. I wanted to know if such a thing was even possible anymore.

In an age polarized between those who accept without question a God of Scripture and those who condemn religion as dangerous delusion, I wanted to find some middle course, to search for something greater than myself, something that I could believe in wholeheartedly without having to turn a blind-eye to five centuries of science and discovery. I wanted to quiet an old bug that had been buzzing around my spirit, like an unresolved note, like an unanswered question, for much of my life.

And so I accepted an invitation from a friend I hadn't seen in years, climbed into a 32-year-old-Volkswagen, and set off on a crazy road trip home.

1

## THE BUZZING

I t began with a brief e-mail from an old high school friend of mine, a man I had not seen in over ten years and not spent any significant time with in almost thirty.

His name is Richard. We were in the same class at a Catholic high school in South Jersey, from 1969 until 1973. Richard never graduated. He was expelled during our senior year under what are still, to me, mysterious circumstances, involving a minor altercation at a cafeteria vending machine. He was called to the principal's office and never returned. The stuff of legend. Last I'd heard, he was living in Portland, Oregon, somehow involved in computers, possibly married, something about a teenage stepson. His brief message had the subject line: *R U There?* It read:

> *Dan this is Richard calling…. are you*
> *still at this e-mail??*

There are certain people with whom we remain inextricably

linked, despite lives that go in separate directions, despite the corrosive effects of time and distance. People whose numbers we keep in our address books even though we haven't spoken to them in years. People whom we ask about when we run into old friends. People who, consciously or not, shaped the person we have become. For me, Richard was one of those people.

We first met when we were both 14, high school freshmen in a class of roughly 300—the uniformed product of Catholic elementary schools from a handful of fading small towns strung along the Jersey side of the Delaware River, across from Philadelphia. We were in English class together—*Our English Literary Heritage*—a yearlong slog from Beowulf to Chaucer to, hopefully, someone who wrote comprehensible English.

At age 14, I was not someone who stood out in a crowd. I had no discernible talents. The only boy in a family of younger sisters and doting aunts, I entered high school clueless about everything from Bob Dylan ("who?") to guy talk ("what's an RBI again?") to sex ("homosay*what?*"). Blessed with childhood asthma, an overprotective mother and Catholic guilt, I was easily winded, quickly intimidated and too well-behaved for my own good. I was physically limp and socially shy. Another nondescript face in the crowded hallways of high school.

Our English teacher, Miss Bergen, had a fondness for writing assignments. Once or twice a week, she'd have us take a shot at some arcane form of poetry. Iambic pentameter. Dactylic and anapestic couplets. A Petrarchan sonnet. A haiku. To my surprise, I discovered I had a flair for this sort of exercise. I could pop out short verse with grace and ease. And even better, it was funny. Kids laughed. And no one laughed harder than Richard. I would write things just to see how hard I could make him laugh.

One day, Miss Bergen announced that there was going to be a school wide drama competition. Each English class had to select and produce a short play to perform during a school assembly. Our choices were limited to the admittedly short library shelf of Catholic youth-appropriate drama. Emboldened by my new-found talent, I was eager to try my hand at something longer than a handful of lines. With Richard's encouragement, I asked if it would be all right if we wrote our own play. She thought it was a great idea. Then, on second thought, "Just let me read it first."

That weekend, I sat down at my mother's manual typewriter and painstakingly pecked out, off the top of my head, a one-act play. One draft, no rewrites, typos caught on the fly, if at all. I titled it, using two words plucked at random from the diction-ary, "Pickled Zarf." It was about three families: one living in the past, one in the future, one in the present. Its most memorable bit was a single, recurring line. After each family member delivered a brief soliloquy declaring their deepest desires, they capped it off by saying: "And then I'd be happy." It was off-the-wall kooky in an early-'70s adolescent kind of way. Richard nearly peed his pants reading it.

Miss Bergen was impressed, but insisted we let the class decide. So the next day, Richard and I read it aloud. The class listened, and laughed, and we were in business. As writer, I also got to be director. Richard took on the role of impresario, overseeing casting, the building of props, the begging and borrowing of cos-tumes. In the weeks that followed, we both became deliriously engrossed in the process of turning the ragtag script into a ragtag production.

The *Pickled Zarf* premiered before an assembly of the entire freshman class. Pitted against a dozen competitors, ours was the only original work, and by far the most elaborately produced. It drew laughter, loud applause and first prize.

That won us the chance to compete against the upper-class winners, this time performing before the entire student body. As the runts, we went first. I can remember standing in the wings with Richard, hearing the words I had written, listening to the packed auditorium roar with laughter, thinking to myself, "Can you believe we actually did this? That this is actually happening?" It was one of the defining moments of my life.

In the end, we took second place to the seniors (performing, as I recall, an excerpt from *The Crucible*), but for me the whole experience had a profound impact on my sense of what was possible. Of what I could do. Of who I was. And Richard was an essential part of that. Without his encouragement, his enthusiasm, his laughter, it would never have happened. At a crucial moment, when I had the opportunity to bloom into something, Richard supplied the sunlight. I doubt he was even aware of this contribution to my emerging sense of self, but it is a debt I have always felt I owed him.

So when I got his e-mail, I responded immediately:
*"Hell yeah I'm here. How are you? What's up?"*

The next day, he replied:
*"Better than ever. Here's a deal for you. How would
you like to drop everything you are doing and drive to
New Jersey?"*

The last time I'd been in contact with Richard was perhaps a year earlier, when I e-mailed him for advice about buying memory chips for a computer. Though it was never clear to me if he actually worked for a computer company, he did seem to know a lot about the subject.

The last time I'd actually seen him in person was nearly a decade before that, when a job took me to Portland, Oregon. I called him, and we went out for dinner. At that time, he was deeply embroiled in some sort of grassroots campaign to overthrow the Microsoft Windows operating system, diligently beta testing the latest version of IBM's OS/2 on several computers he'd cobbled together from donated parts.

Richard, from what I could tell, had spent much of his life drifting. Adulthood had fallen on him like an avalanche. The spring before he'd been expelled from high school, his father had died. Not long after that, for reasons I never quite understood, he moved out of his mother's house in a fit of rancor and rented a seedy little garden apartment off Route 130. To pay the rent, he got a job at Sears Tire Center, fetching tires off the wall racks. He spent much of his free time and cash consuming more than his fair share of pot and acid. The summer after high school, he fell off a ladder at work and somehow injured his back. I can remember being in his apartment, the curtains always drawn, watching him sit ramrod-stiff in a straight back chair, smoking yet another joint, the simple act of inhaling sending waves of suppressed pain across his face. At the time, he was 18 years old.

Not long after that, we lost touch. I was off to college. Richard hung around South Jersey for another year or so, then moved to Tulsa, Oklahoma. Over the years, I heard through the grapevine that he was back in Jersey, then back to Tulsa, then in Dallas, then Salt Lake City. I heard he was processing microfiche. Working the night shift. Then I heard he was driving trucks cross-country.

For my part, I managed to get through college and landed in Washington, D.C., where I lucked into a gofer job for a documentary film producer. Over the next few years, I gradually climbed my way up the career ladder to editor, then writer, then director of educational films, corporate videos, local commercials and various and sundry forms of non-broadcast television. When I turned 30, I made an impulse move to Los Angeles, to find, as they say, my fortune.

One day, not long after I'd arrived in L.A., Richard called me out of the blue to say he was in town, riding shotgun on a semi-load of frozen food, and had two hours to spare while the trailer was being unloaded. I picked him up at some vast cargo center near the airport. Not sure where else to go, I drove him down to the beach to show him the Pacific Ocean.

We stumbled upon a film crew who turned out to be shooting a music video for Tiffany, the teenage pop diva of the moment. For background, they had a staged a Frankie Avalon-style beach party, bonfires blazing, bouncing Ken and Barbie types tossing beach balls and Frisbees, lots of tan skin and finely honed bodies, cameras on cranes, growling generators hooked to a battery of lights, Tiffany's disembodied voice blaring intermittently out of a tower of speakers. Tiffany was nowhere to be seen, no doubt still in her trailer, waiting in the wings for everyone to get their act together so she could fake sing at the fake beach party. It was one of those "Only In L.A." moments.

Richard and I stood around like middle-aged tourists, he in worn khaki work clothes rumpled from sleeping in a truck cab, me with my trying-to-act-like-I'm-part-of-L.A. attitude, both of us searching for something to say. He didn't much care what I'd been up to. He'd lost touch with most of our old friends. He'd given up on Tulsa and Dallas. Salt Lake City had had nice mountains, but too many Mormons.

Driving a truck seemed for him a comfortable way of being nowhere on a sustained basis. He stared out past all the lights and the circus hubbub, at the dark ocean slapping the shore in the distance, and let out a long, inexplicable sigh.

"Life's a bitch and then you die." He looked at his watch and said he needed to get back. "Miles to go. Miles to go."


Four years later, when I had dinner with him in Portland, he seemed happier. He'd moved to Oregon a few years earlier, in pursuit of a job that hadn't worked out "for reasons I'd prefer not to go into." But he liked Portland. Something about the place felt right, "like I'm home." He'd plugged into the geek underground and was excited about whatever he was doing with computers. He was living in an apartment building that he was managing for some guy he called "Little Caesar". Halfway through the conversation, he mentioned that he'd met a woman he really liked. "I'm actually going out with somebody. Imagine that."

For the first time since high school, I could see some of his old spark, a glimpse of that kid I'd stood back stage with many years before, listening to the laughter, basking in the sunlight of the possible.

That was more than ten years ago.

Since then, I'd heard he'd gotten married and was living with his wife and her son. I'd heard they bought a house recently. But beyond those barest details, I knew little else about what was going on in his life.

\* \* \*

A few years after landing in L.A., I was fortunate enough to catch a wave of re-enactment reality shows. When that subsided, I caught another wave of cable documentaries: Discovery Channel, History Channel, VH1. To quote a cameraman friend of mine, it wasn't exactly all blondes and blowjobs, but it was work that I very much enjoyed. A career I loved. By then I was married, with a daughter, a house, a dog, two cars, cable TV, a retirement plan, more credit cards than I knew about; settled down, my tent pegs driven deep into the bedrock of America.

My first reaction to Richard's e-mail invitation was no. The idea of dropping everything to drive across the country seemed impossible at best. I suppose most people would have had the good sense to let it go at that.

For starters, the logistics involved in stepping away from my hectic life for a week seemed insurmountable. At the time, I had no lack of activity. I was in the thick of producing a documentary cable series for one of the many Discovery channels. Producing television is an endless process of crisis management. From finding a usable story to approving the credit roll, every step is riddled with ever-shifting priorities and random disasters. It's like trying to lead a parade of butterflies.

When I was not working, I was doing the usual head-of-household stuff: picking up, paying bills, helping with homework, walking the dog, taking out the trash – all while trying to work my way through the never-ending list of things that needed repair or attention. There was rarely a moment I did not have some obligation, real or imagined, to attend to. The Forties had become, for me at least, the Maintenance Decade. Life is all about keeping what we'd managed to accumulate and assemble from falling apart.

In the coming month, things weren't going to get any less crazy. My 11-year-old daughter, Esmé, was about to graduate from elementary school and we had family coming to town for the occasion. My wife, Liliana, was up to her ears overseeing the school's end-of-the-year fiesta and silent auction.

So "drop everything" seemed a laughable request.


And that wasn't even my primary reason for saying no.

In our last two brief encounters, Richard and I had barely been able to sustain an hour of conversation. It seemed odd that he would ask *me*, of all people, to spend a week in a car with him. Why me? What would we talk about? How quickly would we get on each other's nerves? Was he operating under some fantasy that we could click back into the people we were 30 years ago? What if he'd morphed into a certifiable nutcase? I flashed on long lectures about letting Jesus into my life, or arguments about the reality of extraterrestrials. I envisioned a Fear-and-Loathing tote bag full of psychedelics, uncorking a torrent of *Sturm und Drang* that climaxed at a rest stop in North Dakota. In the rain. At 3 a.m…. "Get out of the car."

Then there was the question of rationale: What's the point? Why drive 3,000 miles for no real reason? I had no pressing desire to go back to New Jersey. I suppose I could visit my parents. That might be good for a day or two, but beyond that, there was no one I particularly wanted to see, and nothing I particularly wanted to do. And once I got there, the demands of work and Esmé's impeding graduation would mean I'd need to get back as soon as possible. So why get involved in such an apparently pointless, potentially dull, possibly dangerous journey?

But I didn't say no. At least not right off the bat.

For one thing, I was intrigued. What was he up to? Why was he taking this trip? Why was he asking me to join him?

For another thing, I felt I owed Richard a kind of karmic debt that I had never made any effort to repay. When he was down, I had never made much of an effort to help him out.

And, the thought of taking a brief break from the ceaseless drip of responsibility was sure tempting.

So, after a few days of pondering, I wrote him back:

> *I'd love to, but I'm so knee-deep in responsibility that it'd be tough to pull off. What's the mission?*

Richard responded the next day:

> *I am driving to NJ leaving June 2 to arrive June 6. Will stay for 5 days and then return. I have the time, the desire and a new car. I need a road trip to help me crystallize some ideas and a coast to coast christening for the car will give me plenty of time to think...plus I haven't been back there in 14 years.*
>
> *I am fine to do this myself but on a trip like this it is just as much fun to have a decent traveling companion. That is the mission...to have a prime cross-country adventure and extract maximum spiritual benefit.*

It all sounded reasonable enough. I sensed no brooding demons or bizarre agendas hidden between the lines. And there was even a motivation that hadn't occurred to me: "to extract maximum spiritual benefit."

Until that came up, I'd been seeing this hypothetical drive more along the lines of a vacation. A break from the routine. A chance to take off the backpack, to relax and have some fun. Not that there's anything wrong with that.

Vacations are fine. Just not now. I preferred to take vacations when projects ended. When things were all buttoned up. When I no longer had anything to worry about. Taking a week off in mid-madness meant risking the whole parade coming to a grinding halt. Deliveries delayed, deadlines missed. And as vacations went, I could think of many more relaxing, fun and adventurous options than being stuck in a car for five days with somebody I barely knew anymore.

But the notion of a spiritual journey cast the trip in a different light. A spiritual journey was not a vacation. A spiritual journey was a test. Not necessarily of one's faith in God, but at least of one's faith in something. Of one's faith in the beliefs, whatever they may be, that propel him or her through the forests and freeways, the diapers and dishes, the carpools and corridors of life. For reasons that I could not quite put my finger on, that idea appealed to me.

I was not totally clear on what might constitute a "spiritual journey" for a chronic ex-believer like myself. It was not something I had ever attempted before, at least not consciously. I'm not exactly the spiritual journey type.

Let me explain. I have little patience for, much less belief in, any form of organized religion. I suppose I fall into the category of lapsed Catholic. As I've said, I was educated in parochial schools and grew up believing in the invisible empire of God the Father, Jesus Christ, the Blessed Virgin Mary and a large supporting cast of saints and angels. Midway through high school, faced with the well-documented doubts raised by science, philosophy, history and common sense, it occurred to me that I didn't have to remain aboard Catholicism's leaky ship if I didn't want to. And so I jumped.

I can remember the precise moment it happened. One spring morning when I was fifteen, I was walking to school. Along my route there was an old oak tree that had been hit by lightning sometime the previous winter. The tree had fallen, taking with it a section of the cyclone fence that bordered the school's outer athletic fields, creating a convenient shortcut that saved me from hauling myself and my armload of schoolbooks another three blocks to the street gate.

That particular morning, my head tangled in I-can't-remember-what adolescent turmoil, I climbed up on that fallen tree and found my balance, high enough to see the school in the misty distance. That's when it hit me. A realization as bright and stunning as an unexpected firecracker:

Belief is a choice. And I could choose not to believe.

Rather than continue trying to resolve the many conflicts between what I had been brought up to believe and what I was discovering about the world around me, I could simply stop believing. Stop trying to strain experience through the sieve of religion.

And so, that's what I did. I snuffed the fading candle out. As I jumped off that uprooted tree, I felt a rush of exhilaration, like a trapped bird finding its way free of a dark barn. My life was now mine.

And that was that.

I've never gone back. After years of sampling from the buffet table of alternatives, from Baptist to Buddhist, I was happy to be released from the considerable manipulations and occasional hypocrisy of organized religion. After trying to wrap my head around conceptions of God ranging from the classic bearded grandpa to a vague creative force, I was left with no desire to climb aboard the bus of any of the many spiritual traditions I'd encountered to date.

So why would someone like me be attracted to the possibility of a "spiritual journey?" I wasn't sure myself. But for starters, it might have been the suspicion that I was missing something.

It is the oft-acknowledged plight of the once Catholic, from James Joyce to Madonna, to have experienced the awe and wonder, the strength and the humility that come from belief in a higher power, then lost the belief that inspired those emotions. The believer inside us, like the child inside us, never quite dies. Call it the residue of lost faith. I was still stirred by sacred places, by the silence of cathedrals, by the meditative trance of a medieval chant, by the ancient power of ritual, the smell of incense, the flicker of candlelight, the crack of dawn.

I would see the calm assuredness in the eyes of the wise believer, hear tales of spiritual guidance and strength, and I'd wonder: maybe there *is* something to all this. Maybe in my efforts to unmask religion, I'd been struck by a kind of blindness. Maybe, in my eagerness to flee religion's grip, I'd denied myself the comfort of its embrace. Maybe, behind all the smoke and mirrors, behind all the righteousness and the hypocrisy, behind all the charlatans and shenanigans, there was something there that might be of value to me.

This suspicion kept me hovering at the peripheries, circling the tent, reading Otto and Armstrong and Durkheim, listening to Bach and admiring Michelangelo. It kept me from closing my ears to all discussion of spirituality and signing on as a full-fledged atheist, impatiently explaining how religion was just a con game for the dimwitted masses, studiously picking apart the philosophical arguments offered over the years for God's existence, getting all indignant over school prayer and the Pledge of Allegiance.

For some reason, I just couldn't go there.

I mean, come on: every human society ever known (as far as I am aware) has practiced some form of religion. Throughout history, in every corner of the world, multitudes of people have considered their faith in God—or at least in a spiritual power beyond the surface of reality—to be at the core of their very being. Something has to be driving that impulse. Even if you dismiss what's on the surface—all those Sacred Heart of Jesus pictures and happy Buddha statues and Holy Day yarmulkes—I cannot accept that there's not something to it, something deep down in common core of what it means to be human.

To dismiss a billion worshippers, a million houses of worship, holy books and statues and candles flickering beyond count, as merely the artifacts of millennia-long mass delusion, anachronisms left over from a simpler time, felt more like hubris than wisdom. Like I was somehow missing the point.

What that point was, I did not know. But I was not willing

to deny the possibility of its existence.

The idea of a spiritual journey re-awakened a question that had been buzzing in my head, on and off, for much of my adult life. Not in any debilitating, neurotic way. And not all the time. Just occasionally. Like a housefly on a summer's night when you're trying to sleep, circling unseen in the darkness, buzzing.

The question was this: if I don't, or can't, or won't believe in the core assumptions of religion, namely that the world was created and is controlled by an unseen power called God, who has revealed himself to us in holy scriptures, who expects us to live by certain rules, and who passes judgment over us in this life and in the next, then what do I believe?

Religion, whatever its downsides, personal or historical, brings certain benefits to the believer. It provides community, ethical guidance, strength in the face of adversity, consolation in the face of death, a basis for hope, a path to forgiveness, a sense of higher purpose, and a connection to something beyond one's self, to something infinite and eternal.

The nonbeliever's predicament, at least in my case, was that once you cancel the policy, you also lose the benefits. And life without religion does not mean life without quandaries. I still had my moral dilemmas, my struggles to forgive, my moments of despair, my fear of death. Faced with suffering, I still sought hope. I still yearned for the reassurance of meaning and purpose. I still wanted to feel part of something greater than myself. Who doesn't?

But where do I turn for answers?

Science, which played a considerable role in undermining

the basic foundations my faith, provided little to replace them. Science is basically a process of coming to conclusions that are free of individual bias and political agenda. It's a method for getting to the truth by way of observation, hypothesis and experiment (versus superstition, rhetoric and reliance on sacred texts.)

Overall, science has had an incredible success rate, revolutionizing the world and the way we live. In a thousand ways, it has allowed the human race to harness the earth to a breathtaking degree. It has cured diseases, fed the multitudes, offered up a wealth of solutions for our every basic—and not so basic—need. It has vastly expanded the horizons of perception, from the nucleus of an atom to the edge of the universe.

Over the last five hundred years, science has almost entirely usurped religion's role of explaining how the world works. When the theories of science have butted heads with the assertions of religion, from heliocentric vs. geocentric to evolution vs. creationism, science has always gotten my vote.

But there is one thing that science lacks: In its desire to be objective, science tends to avoid things it can't measure—like the stuff that goes on inside our heads. Scientists avoid theories about the meaning and purpose of life, about good and evil, about how to endure injustice and suffering, about how to find hope or face death... the hard-to-quantify, subjective experience of being human. Science is not much help in navigating inner life's troubled waters. When it comes to matters relating to that part of experience variously referred to as the soul, the spirit, the heart, science has never succeeded in finding substitutes for religion

So where is a seeker supposed to turn, when neither science nor religion have all the answers?

I suppose I was lucky. Unlike earlier generations who struggled with similar issues, I didn't feel lost in some godless abyss. I wasn't metaphorically wandering alone on a cold, existential beach moaning in despair, as I stared up at the God-shaped hole in the gathering darkness.

Overall, I felt pretty grounded. I was able to function in society with reasonable success. I'd managed to find a fairly reliable moral compass. My life didn't seem to be without meaning. Granted, I hadn't been tested by grave tragedy, injustice or suffering. I'd had my occasional dark day, but I was able to dig myself out of it, more or less capable of confronting the subjective challenges of being human.

Which, I suppose, is why the question of what I believed in didn't buzz with more urgency. Clearly, I had some core, foundational beliefs. I just wasn't sure what they were. I was content to live the unexamined life. I just kept going, day to day, easily distracted by the rattle and hum of modern life. As long as the house stays standing, why bother squirming down in the crawlspace to understand why? Why take the risk of opening up the hood and tinkering with the engine when the car seems to be running just fine? Such efforts usually only lead to trouble. If it ain't broke…

Nonetheless, there was that buzzing, that fly in the night that I could never quite get rid of. A few months before Richard's invitation, something happened that made it buzz even louder.

It was a question my daughter Esmé asked me. She was ten at the time. We were driving home from school one spring day. Somehow, the conversation turned to religion. She mentioned that she had a friend who was a Christian, and another friend who was Jewish. She asked me what the difference was. I tried my best to explain what people of each of those faiths believed. She mulled over for a minute what I had to say, then asked me another question.

"What are we?"

"What do you mean?"

"Are we Christian, or Jewish, or something else?"

"We're not any religion."

"We're not?"

"No."

"Why not?"

"Because there isn't any religion that your mother or I can honestly say we believe in. And I didn't want to tell you something was true if I didn't believe it myself."

"Then what do we believe?"

I doubt that my fumbling response made anything any clearer to her, but it did make something clear to me. Though I knew I believed in *something*, I was unable to easily put those beliefs into words. Here my own daughter was asking me what I believed, what *we* believed, and I couldn't tell her.

Until then, it hadn't occurred to me that what I believed mattered to other people. We live in a culture where core beliefs have become increasingly private, where people are more comfortable talking about sex then about religion. What you believe is something you keep to yourself.

My wife and I had made a conscious decision to not raise our daughter with any religion. And until then, the subject had rarely come up. But when it did, it made me realize that my daughter would not escape life's quandaries any more than I had. As a father who had chosen to abandon the beliefs of his own childhood, I felt I had a duty to pass along *something*, to make an effort to articulate what I *did* believe.

But what was that? What was my answer to all those basic

questions: Who made the world? Why am I here? What makes something right or wrong? Why is life unfair? What gives it meaning? What happens when you die?

It made me want to take a few days to just sit and think, to step outside the routine of my life so I could get a good look at it, open the hood so I could better understand what made it go. A spiritual journey seemed just the ticket.


In the end, my decision came down to a dinner conversation I had had 25 years earlier, on the first day of my first cross-country trip. When I was 20, I'd hitchhiked, alone, across the United States, from New Jersey to California. It was the culmination of a crisis in my life.

The year before, I'd received a substantial scholarship to attend a college in Boston to study filmmaking. Coming at the end of a depressingly long and dull senior year of high school, I looked forward to being revitalized, to meeting people who shared my interests, to doing things I'd never done.

But that's not what happened. I couldn't get into any decent courses. The concerns of most of my classmates seemed limited to getting wasted, finding a decent local therapist or coming out of the closet. That year, Boston was hit with an especially long and frigid winter. It all left me feeling miserable.

By the end of the school year, I was gripped by a visceral urge to flee. The day I left for summer break, I knew I would never return. My parents reacted with a stunned "What do you mean, you're not going back to college?" This ramped up to hyperventilating panic when I announced what I was going to do instead: hitchhike across the country. To nowhere in particular. Just west.

At the time, I couldn't put into words why I was doing it. My every fumbling attempt was met with a checklist of logical reasons not to: I was throwing away my education, walking away from a scholarship; I was wasting a critical year of my life; I was scarring my future résumé; I could get killed.

To me, even then, the idea of hitchhiking across the country seemed more symbolic than practical. An initiation rite, like an aboriginal walkabout. I wanted to prove to myself that I could do it.

In the end, to my parent's credit, they accepted my decision. I left one weekday morning in early September, the first week of the new school year. I remember my two younger sisters were silently eating Cheerios. My mother was washing dishes, keeping her anxiety to herself. I hefted my overloaded pack onto my back, said a low-key goodbye and walked out the back door. With few plans and $200 in my pocket, I hiked out to Route 130 and stuck out my thumb. The first ride I got was from a guy whose face was covered with cold cream.

After eight hours and four rides, I'd only made it to the western suburbs of Philadelphia. Around four o'clock, after a ride-less hour watching school buses and carloads of kids headed home after what was for them just another routine day, a pickup slid to a stop in the shoulder ahead of me. The driver was a guy in his thirties, who turned out to be a schoolteacher named John. Hearing my story and seeing all my gear, he asked where I was planning to spend the night. When I told him I had no idea, he invited me to camp in his backyard.

His house was on a large wooded lot. He led me to a clearing in the trees, where he left me to pitch my tent. After maybe half an hour, a little girl whom I assumed to be his daughter, four or five years old, came out to watch.

"What are you doing?"

"Your dad said I could camp out in your backyard."

"Why?"

"Well, I'm traveling across the country and I need someplace to spend the night."

"Won't it be cold?"

"Maybe."

"Are you all by yourself?"

"Yeah. Just me."

"Aren't you scared?"

"Not yet."

"Why?"

"I'm not sure. I'm just not."

A few minutes later, her mother came down to check me out. At first glance, she seemed to be a back-to-nature type, all earth tones and wild hair, with a look-you-in-the-eye straightforward-ness about her. Hippie-turned-mom.

"I see you've met Isabelle. She likes to ask questions. Isn't that right, Isabelle?"

"Are we camping, too?"

"No, dear."

She picked up Isabelle and she introduced herself as Sandy.

"John said you were heading across the country."

"Yeah."

"Where to?"

"Not sure exactly. Maybe San Francisco."

"Hmm."

She stood there for a few minutes, watching me struggling to hammer in a tent peg without a hammer.

"You're welcome to join us for dinner if you like."

"Thanks. That'd be great."

"Come up in about an hour."

"OK."

She headed back to the house with Isabelle under one arm. I glanced at my watch. It was just after five. When the tent was finally standing, I climbed inside and unrolled my sleeping bag. For the next hour, I lay there, at first trying to read, then just staring up at the orange nylon roof as the daylight waned. It was the first real moment of reflection I'd had since leaving home that morning. Until then, my mind had been occupied by the business of hitchhiking. Getting a ride. Talking to people.

But now that I had no such distractions, doubt started buzzing like a persistent mosquito in my head: hard to snag, but also hard to ignore, ever there, threatening to bite. There I was, lying on a sleeping bag in some stranger's backyard while the rest of the world went on without me. What the hell was I doing?

At five to six, I got out of the tent and walked up to the house. John greeted me at the back door. "I see you've got yourself all set up back there."

"Yeah. Thanks."

Their home was '70s rustic. Lots of wood and mismatched second-hand furniture. Shelves of well-thumbed paperbacks, home-processed 8-by-10 black-and-whites of Isabelle, a modern-day version of a potbelly stove radiating heat from the living room.

"I hope you like brown rice," John said, as he set a big bowl of it on the table. Sandy was stir-frying vegetables in a large iron skillet on the stove. Carrots. Peppers. Zucchini. Alfalfa sprouts. Tofu chunks. She drizzled tamari sauce and stirred intently with a wooden spoon. John lifted Isabelle into her wooden booster chair.

I took a seat at the table. "Smells great."

Sandy poured the vegetables onto a serving plate and joined us. It was the first vegetarian dinner I'd ever eaten. It was a little strange, but not bad. More than anything else, it gave me the feeling that I had entered new territory, that my journey had begun.

As we settled into eating, Sandy turned her grilling skills on me: where was I from, why was I doing this, what motivated me? One thing you discover hitchhiking is that you have to keep telling and re-telling your story. This is a task we rarely face in other circumstances in life: having to put into words, over and over, what we're doing and why.

One thing I soon discovered was that my story is not a given. It doesn't come polished and published. At that time, mine was, at best, a rough draft. When the questions came on an undercurrent of doubt or suspicion, I became disturbingly aware that my motivations, my ultimate goals, even my feelings, were not clear, even to me. My story was full of holes. And Sandy knew it.

"I don't get it. What was so terrible about this college you were going to?"

"It's hard to say really. I just didn't feel like I belonged there."

"Maybe you just didn't give it enough time." Maybe. When I didn't answer, the inquisition continued. "I think that people have these romantic notions that running away is the answer. Dropping out is the answer. But I don't think that's true. I think sometimes the answer is sticking it out. Hanging in there. Making the effort to try to get the most out of the here and now, instead of giving up and running away."

Giving up and running away? Is that what I was doing? I poked at my brown rice, searching for a response to her unwavering righteousness. The mosquitoes of doubt buzzed furiously in my brain, drowning out half-formed rebuttals.

Mercifully, John rose to my defense, "I'm not sure I agree with that." Sandy turned to him like an army facing an attack to its open flank—a not entirely surprise attack. He calmly wiped his mouth with a napkin while she reloaded her rhetorical rifle. "In fact, I kind of wish I'd done the same thing when I was your age."

"What are you talking about?" she jumped in to cut off the challenge.

"Nothing. I'm just saying that I can understand why he's doing it."

"And why is that?"

"I think, at some point, you need to take charge of your own life. Life can be…like a bus ride. You find yourself sitting there being driven by somebody else's agenda: School. Work. Whatever. Somebody else's idea of where they think you should be going. I think it takes a lot of guts to get off the bus. To begin your own journey. To set your own course. To take hold of the steering wheel of your own life. Am I right?"

I was amazed. He was exactly right. His words gave instant focus to the blurry feeling I'd been trying to grab hold of for months: the steering wheel of my own life.

"Yeah. Right."

Sandy just shook her head, recognizing an argument she'd rather avoid, and mumbled in retreat, "just be careful you don't drive off the road." John grinned as he bent down to pick up the rice and carrots Isabelle had dropped all over the floor. "Oh, go ahead. Drive off the road."

It had been a while since I had driven off the road. Maybe that's what it takes, sometimes, to transform the buzzing in one's head into words and deeds.

My earlier trek cross-country had been a trip west, a journey into the future, into the unknown, following the great American tradition of pioneer wagons and Dust Bowl émigrés. The idea of going with Richard seemed the opposite: a journey east. A journey back, into the past, into the known, into my own history. A return to a world I'd thought I had left behind.

I mentioned the invitation to my wife and she said, without hesitation, "Go for it. You've been working hard. You need a break." The next day at work, I pondered my giant schedule board and realized that, if I planned it right, I could delegate and rearrange the tasks at hand so that the battle could go on without me for a week. I floated the idea to my boss and he said, "Go for it. You've been working hard. You need a break."

So that night, I e-mailed Richard.

"I'm in."

# 2

# CAPTAIN KARMA

Six weeks later, I was in the heavens, gazing down at the top-sides of clouds and the stark mountains of the California coast. The plan was for me to fly from L.A. to Portland on the first Saturday in June. Richard would pick me up at the airport, I'd stay at his place overnight and we'd leave the next morning. The goal was to get to South Jersey by the following Thursday. I'd spend that weekend with my parents and fly home Monday; all told, a quick, ten-day road trip with a spiritual-journey twist.

The month and a half between decision and deed had given me time to reflect on what that twist ought to entail for an old skeptic like myself. What did "spirituality" mean to me? What would it take to realize a goal I only vaguely grasped for this cross-country drive? What attitudes should I go into it with? What behaviors should be encouraged?

First off, I conceded a distinction between religion and spirituality. Religion refers to institutions, or at least formal traditions:

Catholicism, Buddhism, Seventh-day Adventism, Hare Krish-
naism, Scientology. Religion entails an established set of core
beliefs, mythologies, rituals, rules, hierarchies and sacred texts
that the believer is expected to accept, on faith, as parts of the
whole; a total turnkey package. The faithful are generally discour-
aged from tweaking with the fundamentals or asking too many
questions. The upside is that they don't have to tweak with the
fundamentals or ask too many questions.

Spirituality, on the other hand, connotes one's relationship to
a realm beyond the material world; what Mircea Eliade called the
realm of the Sacred (as opposed to the realm of the visible, day-
to-day Profane). This spirit world is not something we can see, or
measure, or even prove exists. Our perception of it depends upon
a gut feeling, an instinctive sense that there is something more to
life than what appears on the surface, that there exists a reality
beyond perception. This sense of the spiritual, common throughout human history, is probably what got religion going in the first
place. The Holy Hunch.

Though this spiritual realm cannot be perceived directly,
it can manifest itself in many ways: in sacred places, in holy
objects, in ritual acts, in music, in art, in the mysterious atmosphere of feeling and imagination, in the human "spirit" that en-
livens us and keeps us going. It is the source, for many, for meaning and purpose, moral courage and human compassion, hope and
strength. It is both airy nothing and eternal everything.

Religion gives form and substance to this unseen realm, popu-
lating it with gods and angels, saints and souls, ghosts and devils,
and a mixed bag of other supernatural beings and cosmic forces;
a clear and colorful story that makes the misty spiritual concrete—an alternate reality that is far easier to conceive of,

to relate to, and to live with. But religion also casts the spiritual in the mold of a particular time and culture, rendering it somewhat inflexible to change.

It is possible to have an experience of spirituality outside the context of a particular religion. As religions have evolved from being universal institutions, where everyone embraced a single faith, into a growing collection of diverse denominations, many have chosen to chart their own spiritual course. Unable to accept at face value all the fixed assumptions of any particular creed, they prefer to pick and choose from a buffet table of ideas about God, the afterlife, divine justice, creation and whatever else they feel ought to be included on their plate of spiritual beliefs.

Was I among them? Did I buy into the basic premise that there is something more to life than what appears on the surface? Did I believe in an alternate reality — or, at least, in some invisible force implied by the words "human spirit"?

Science would say no. If you can't see it, if you can't measure it, it doesn't exist. I accepted that science, as a basic method of getting to a reliable answer, is the way to go in the material, measurable world. If I wanted to fix my car or figure out the thermodynamics of heat flow in my house, I was totally on board with the scientific solution.

But, to me, science provided no means for addressing life's less tangible questions. There was no machine for measuring the human spirit. There was no unified theory of the meaning of life. No pharmaceutical for hope (at least not yet).

These things seemed to come from someplace else, someplace beyond the surface. To science, a Gregorian chant or the Hallelujah Chorus are just so many sound waves. Ayers Rock is just geology. The Cathedral at Chartres is just engineering. But I

could see something more. To me, all these things had a power
beyond the surface. They embodied something... sacred.

Like a billion humans before me, I too could feel that Holy
Hunch. I was intrigued to know what that something sacred was.
Though these instincts were at best vague, I wanted to open
myself up to the possibility that there was a spiritual realm, an
unseen power; I wanted to make that leap of faith, if only for the
duration of the drive, to see where it took me.

But how? What should I do?

For someone of a more traditional religious bent, going on a
spiritual journey would most likely entail following a long-es-
tablished set of procedures. Muslims who go to Mecca adhere to
a centuries-old itinerary that prescribes precisely what to wear,
where to be when, what to do. I didn't have that. All I had was a
vague hunch that "spiritual journey" could still mean something
in an adamantly secular world. But after declaring that objective,
what exactly was I supposed to do?

What did other people do? Did the tradition of spiritual journeys offer any common elements that I might adapt?

One possibility was the idea of going on a retreat. As I understood it, a retreat, be it for Catholic monks or corporate
moguls, was about getting away from the hubbub of daily routine
so that one could reflect on the bigger picture. To step out of
one's life in order to see it with greater clarity, like climbing to
the top of a mountain to get a better view of the terrain. To me,
having never been on one, retreats connoted a few days of quiet
reflection, strolling through the forest, mediating on the lawn,
closing my eyes and listening to the wind slip through the leaves.
Basically allowing the stirred up sediment of daily life to settle
down so the spiritual essence could become clear.

That sounded like a viable strategy. I had a bad habit of living in my distractions, frittering away entire days mucking with minutia: tick-tick-ticking away on the keyboard, making lists, mending malfunctions, rearranging the deckchairs on my desktop, stuck in surface mode. The idea of retreating from the details, shutting off the distractions and tuning out the chatter, held a definite appeal. I liked the idea of getting to know myself by getting away from myself. This seemed a valid, time-tested technique for approaching the spiritual.

So I decided that one of the guiding principals of this road trip would be to take a break from being me. Turn off the cell phone. Resist the temptation to download e-mail. I resolved to put work, and anything else that was on the great to-do list in my mind, on hold for a week. To retreat.

But I also realized that the journey I was about to embark on would not neatly fit my idea of a retreat. I would not be taking quiet strolls across verdant lawns to commune with nature. I would be stuck in a car driving along interstates. In my experience, truck stops and motels weren't the best places to find quietude. Granted, there can be something meditative about long-distance driving, but not when there's someone else in the car.

Perhaps a more appropriate parallel would be a pilgrimage. I'd read recently about the revival of a medieval pilgrimage along the Camino de Santiago, a trail that starts in southern France and crosses much of Spain to a cathedral in Compostela. Getting from one end of the trail to the other takes weeks. The point is not so much the destination as the journey. It is not meant to be easy. It is not a vacation. It is meant to be a test. This sounded familiar.

I have done my fair share of traveling and I have learned that it can be tricky. Traveling, especially with someone who doesn't share your routines, invariably forces the traveler out of his or her comfort zone: having to eat lunch an hour late, having to listen to someone else's music. These little ripples in the routine create a grating friction between expectation and reality.

I wanted to avoid that rut. Taking the attitude of a pilgrim offered an out. Pilgrims did not complain when the blister appeared. They were thankful for whatever food and shelter they were given. Because the point of a pilgrimage was not personal gain, not entertainment value, not relaxation. The point was to surrender to the journey in order to transcend oneself, to experience a oneness with something greater, even if you had no idea what that "something greater" might be.

So my second resolution was to surrender to the journey, to go with the flow, to embrace the discomfort, to accept the nerve wracking, the irritating, the dumbfounding, the boring, the torturous, all as potentially positive parts of the experience, opportunities to confront my own boundaries. I resolved to go into this trip without expecting to be entertained, or relaxed, or amused.

I also resolved to keep things simple. The day before my flight to Portland, I packed for the trip, trying to predict what June might be like in Montana. Normally, my instinct would be to cover all options, just in case. I've been caught in enough unseasonable heat waves, freak cold spells, and torrential downpours to have learned the value of having the right clothing. But in the spirit of retreats and pilgrimages, I didn't want to overdo it. Less is more.

I piled everything I would normally take onto the bed and began eliminating. Do I really need a sweatshirt? A second pair of shoes? A comb? Toothpaste? A razor? Clean underwear, every day? Well, maybe.

I suppose if I were really serious, I would have taken nothing.

Just shown up with the clothes on my back. But that seemed a little extreme. In the end, I restricted myself to what I could jam into a standard carry-on bag: two changes of clothes, a waterproof jacket, and minimal toiletries.

The morning of the first Saturday in June, Liliana and Esmé drove me to the airport.

"Have a good time." My wife stood by the curb while I took my bag out of the trunk. I hadn't told her—or anybody else—about the whole spiritual journey thing, preferring to spin this trip as a much-needed break.

"Thanks."

"Don't forget to send the postcards," my daughter reminded, sticking her head out the open back seat window. I'd told her I would send a postcard from each state we passed through.

"I won't forget."

"Bye."

And I was off.

An hour later, I was in the sky. From my window seat, I could see the tops of clouds. Below, the blue Pacific washed onto a curving ribbon of shoreline. We flew north, over the coastal mountains, blanketed in early summer green, the bare rock underneath bursting through at the summit.

So here I was. Off on my so-called spiritual journey, the hypothetical now a reality. Crammed into seat 27-F, staring out the window, the whole idea seemed sort of silly. What was I thinking? I gazed at the passing clouds for a sign of something sacred, maybe even a hint of angels, but all I could see was weather.

I wondered what a medieval monk would make of such a sight, what St. Augustine or Dante would think if they were looking through my eyes. Would they think they were seeing the world from God's point of view? Or would they figure the devil was playing a trick on them? Would it be some affirmation of their beliefs? Or would they just flip out?

For me, it was all atmosphere and earth. No big surprises. The sacred had become the mundane. The guy beside me was asleep. The stewardess was passing out peanuts. This potentially miraculous spectacle was merely something to be endured.

I landed in Portland just before noon. It was a brilliant, crisp spring day. The plan was to phone Richard when I arrived and he'd come pick me up at the airport, which he said was "right around the corner." In no particular hurry, I wandered into a gift shop and bought an Oregon postcard and some stamps. I continued through the terminal, passed the clusters of fellow travelers gathered around the baggage carousel, exiting through the sliding doors to the sidewalk outside, where the cabs and rental car shuttles gathered.

I called Richard on my cell phone. His line was busy. Just as I was about to hang up, I heard the buzz of an incoming call. It was Richard.

"You here yet?"

"Yeah. I just called you. The line was busy."

"I was just calling you."

"I guess that means we're in sync."

He laughed. "Where are you?

"Outside USAir baggage."

He said he'd be there in a minute.

A few weeks earlier, I'd picked up a copy of Stephen Ambrose's *Undaunted Courage* on the discount table at Costco. It was a popular history of Lewis and Clark and, browsing the maps, I realized that, coincidentally, they had crossed the country along a route that paralleled the one we would be taking, ending up not far from Portland. Two guys on a trip cross-country. I was curious to learn how much had changed in 200 years.

At the dawn of the 19th century, Thomas Jefferson appointed his private secretary, Meriwether Lewis, to organize and lead an expedition into the recently-purchased Louisiana Territories. Lewis recruited William Clark, an officer whom he met while in the Army, and a ragtag crew of 25 men he dubbed the Corps of Discovery. They journeyed by boat up the Missouri River with the goal of making their way across the continent to the Pacific, becoming the first explorers to chronicle the uncharted American West. Near the end of their voyage, they passed by the place that would one day become Portland.

That was in the fall of 1805. They were paddling down the Columbia River in canoes they'd made by hollowing out tree trunks, facing a blistering sea wind and nonstop downpour. It had taken an inconceivable effort to get here. They'd pushed against hundreds of miles of river current, crossed snow-covered mountains on foot, faced off against grizzly bears and hostile natives. It had taken a year and a half to make it one way.

It had taken me only a few hours and the mild discomfort of an airline seat. From the airport sidewalk, I watched the ebb and flow of modern travel, a near-effortless experience compared with even 100 years ago. I wondered if it were even possible for a journey across the country to qualify as an adventure anymore.

Then I heard a voice: "Dan. Dan! Over here!"

Up the street, wedged between unloading SUV's and taxis, I saw Richard, standing beside a faded blue, very used Volkswagen Beetle.

Not wanting to leave the car, he waved me over, with a huge grin on his face. "You made it. Great."

"Here I am."

As I got closer, he walked towards me, eagerly shaking my hand with both of his. "Welcome to Portland, man."

"Good to be here."

This was the first I'd seen him in nearly a decade. If anything, he seemed younger. He had always been a big guy, a few inches over six feet. All the time I had known him growing up, he'd been overweight, hauling around his big body like so much excess baggage. No more. He was now lean and muscular, light on his feet, his face bright and clear-eyed. Though his hair had receded a bit and he had a goatee sprinkled grey, my first impression was that he seemed more like a kid than when he was a kid.

It also became evident just how different our lives had become.

"You know, I live fifteen minutes from here and this is the first time I've ever been to this airport."

"Really. Where do you fly out of?"

"Nowhere. I've never been on an airplane in my life."

Never been on an airplane in his life? How was that possible? "Are you serious?"

"It's not my preferred form of transportation," he said, leading me back towards the car. "This is my preferred form of transportation."

The little bug sat there like the setup to a bad joke.

"What do you think?"

In one of his e-mails, Richard had mentioned that he had "a new car." He hadn't mentioned that it was a near-antique VW Bug. Then again, I hadn't asked.

"What year is it?"

"1969."

The year we had started high school.

"Is this what we're driving across the country in?"

"Absolutely. It's perfect."

Right.

While Richard slid into the driver's seat, I opened the passenger door. The seat bottom was ripped, and the stuffing, trying to escape, was held back for now by a desiccated piece of duct tape. There was no place for my carry-on bag to go but the backseat. So I pulled at a lever on the side of the passenger seat to tilt it forward. It didn't work. I pulled harder, and when that didn't work, I tried shaking the seat to loosen the latch.

Richard leaned over from behind the wheel. "It gets stuck sometimes."

Raise, pull, raise harder, pull harder. Jiggle the seat. Raise, pull. Nothing.

"Hang on. I'll get it."

Richard climbed out of the car and walked around to the passenger side. I stepped back and let him take over. With one swift yank, like a chiropractor cracking a joint, he lifted the latch and eased the seat back forward.

"There you go."

I sensed a smirk on the car's face as I shoved my bag, which suddenly seemed the size of an indulgent steamer trunk, into the cramped backseat, pushed the seat back into place, and got in.

For those of you who have not experienced the view from inside a classic Bug, I encourage you to try it. You have no idea how lulled you've become by the comforting security of a long and substantial engine compartment standing guard between you and that inebriated driver whose oncoming Suburban has just crossed into your lane. Not to mention those airbags and shoulder belts.

A '69 VW Bug has none of that. The car seems designed to maximize the damage caused by a head-on collision. The engine is in the back, turning the rounded nose of the hood into a large, empty can. Which hardly matters, as from inside the car, you can't see it anyway. You get the comforting impression that it's just you, a thin layer of glass and the road.

"So this is it, huh?"

"Yep. Pretty good shape for an old girl, huh?"

The interior seemed to have been stripped of what few non-essential items it once possessed. The floor was bare metal. The ceiling liner had been removed. Even the cigarette lighter was an empty hole.

"I can't remember the last time I was in one of these."

"This is my sixth. No, it's my seventh." He counted out with his right hand: "'63, '65, '71, '72, '70, '71, '69. That's seven. Only kind of car I've ever owned."

"Really."

"Well, I briefly drove a 1966 Chevy Bel Air. But it wasn't mine."

Come to think of it, the last time I'd been in a Bug was with Richard just after high school. I wasn't even that impressed back then.

"So what's the appeal?"

"Low cost. Reliability. Simplicity. They're getting to be hard to find."

That's because Volkswagen stopped selling them in the U.S. in the mid-'70s. Don't be fooled by those recent incarnations. Those are highly sophisticated Jettas with a retro body. Not even the same species. The classic Bug is the Everyman Car, the most popular single model in automotive history, famed for being dirt cheap and so simple that it could be maintained with a screw-driver, a wrench and a cursory knowledge of the internal combus-tion engine. It got started as a pet project by, of all people, Adolf Hitler, who back in the '30s asked Ferdinand Porsche to design a "people's car," the German version of Ford's Model T. A factory was built in 1938, but it was converted to war production before it got around to making any cars. In 1945, the British, impressed with Porsche's design, decided to reopen the bombed-out plant and started cranking out Bugs. They kept on cranking them out, with little modification, until 1978. Close to 20 million. The last place they were in production was Mexico, where, unlikely as it may seem, most of them were used as taxis.

The fact that this particular Bug was built the year Richard and I first met was not lost on me. We would be traveling into the past in a vehicle from the past. There seemed a certain poetic correct-ness to that. If this was a novel and we were characters, I could see putting us in a '69 Bug. But this was not a novel. This was a real car that two real people hoped to drive for a real 3,000 miles.

"How many miles has it got on it?"

"No idea." The odometer had been disconnected years ago. But, figuring 10,000 miles a year, it had to be over 300,000. On a four cylinder engine. In rainy Oregon. The fact that it was running at all was a minor miracle.

"I bought it about two months ago. Pure luck. I saw this little baby parked in some guy's front yard with a *For Sale* sign, just after the floor fell out of my '71. Totally rebuilt engine. It was like finding gold."

I played with the radio volume knob, hoping against hope that it would turn into a fake faceplate hiding a CD player. No such luck.

"No radio huh?"

"I had it disconnected."

"Why?"

"Less commercials."

"So no music."

"No music."

It's funny the things in life we can and can't do without. The creature comforts we forego easily, versus the ones we hang onto with a death grip. For me, driving and listening to music were synonymous. One and the same. I can't drive a mile in L.A. without something coming through the speakers. I'd gotten through many a long distance trip by filling the time with music. To that end, I'd brought along CD's of Beethoven symphonies, figuring they'd be a fitting soundtrack for our spiritual road trip. It had never occurred to me that we'd be driving in silence.

Sensing myself slipping into panic mode, I took a deep breath and reminded myself of my quickly-forgotten resolutions for this mission. I wasn't here to pass judgment on Richard's choice in cars. I wasn't taking this trip to enjoy the comforts of some luxury edition, climate controlled, nine-speaker-sound-system SUV. This was not a vacation. This was a pilgrimage, a spiritual journey. And spiritual journeys are meant to be a test. They're meant to take us out of our comfortable world of habit, to expose us to situations we're not accustomed to, to strip us of the armor we use to protect ourselves from exposure to reality. To test our mettle. To see what we're made of. Like boot camp.

So I decided to knock off the whining and deal with it. Three thousand miles in a senile, old death trap with only the roar of the wind and the wheezing of the engine? What the hell? Why not?

I shifted the conversation to catching up.

"I heard that you got married and bought a house?"

"I've been married for awhile. Eight years now."

"What's your wife's name?"

"Meg. She's great. Best thing that ever happened to me. We just bought this house we're in, year before last. It's the perfect house for me."

"And I also heard you had a son now? Or she has a son?"

"Kevin. Yeah. He's seventeen. In fact, we're about to pass by his high school. Right there."

"What year is he? Senior?"

"Yeah. Just graduated last week."

"Wow. Richard with a kid out of high school. Look at you."

"I've come a long way, baby."


Richard lived in a bungalow on the outskirts of town. What was left of his old VW was parked on the lawn next to the driveway, a bumper resting in the front seat. Sure enough, the floor had rusted away.

"Welcome to my little piece of heaven."

As he dug out his keys and unlocked the front door, he told me that he'd bought this house sight unseen. His wife, Meg, saw it, loved it, called him at work to tell him it was perfect, and that's all the information he needed. "That's how well that woman knows me."

We stepped into a small, dark living room. An obese cat purred from a chocolate brown sofa covered with cat hair. Richard scooped it up like a small child, cuddled it to his face and proudly introduced me.

"This is Ravi."

The room had an intense feline scent drifting, vaguely visible, through the air, suggesting Ravi was not an only child. Sure enough, as Richard escorted me from room to room, each had its own cat, all looking vaguely related, some sharing Ravi's weight problem.

In the master bedroom, a final cat lay on the bed. As we entered, it tensed up, eyeing me with a bored suspicion that didn't rise to the level of moving. Richard explained that this was his "baby."

He picked the cat up and laid it on his shoulder. "Two months ago she'd never let me do this." The cat looked around nervously as it found its balance and climbed behind Richard's head to his other shoulder. "She used to be terrified of people. Now look at her."

What was meant to be a dining room contained piles of overloaded cardboard boxes. Richard capped off the animal tour by pulling the cover off a terrarium filled with a half dozen white rats. He lifted one out.

"Check this out." He looked up towards the ceiling, and then took the rat he was holding and laid it directly onto his upturned face. It stood there a moment, getting its footing, then nervously shifted around, trying to figure out where it was. Richard acted like the rat was a warm washrag. "Ahhhh."

As it crawled up to his forehead, he began explaining to me

what incredible creatures rats were. "I never thought you could let a rat do this. But it's amazing how tame they can be."

My question was: what the hell have I gotten myself into?

I am, by nature, an optimist. I like to think of myself as someone who acts impulsively, who trusts in people's good nature. Rather than wringing my hands, weighing the good against the bad, losing sleep over possibilities for disaster, I prefer to just act, just do it. As a result, I've gotten myself into many situations I've later regretted: bought bad clothing, made dumb investments, gotten lost on back roads. At that moment, as I stood in Richard's musky dining room, watching a white rat crawl over his face, it occurred to me that I'd done it again.

All of what I was experiencing in my first hour in Portland – the deathtrap car, the obese cats, Richard with a rat sitting on his face – could easily be written as the opening act of a National Lampoon Vacation movie. And my first instinct was to see it that way.

But the truth, I reminded myself, now fully engaged in internal debate, was that it could also be seen as the first few steps of a quasi-mythic quest. The ancient vessel in which we are to sail. The strange creature guarding the portal of the cave. The eccentric traveling companion possessed of weird wisdom.

I could feel myself balanced on a fence between these two alternate versions of reality, these two stories, these two emotional reactions. What it boiled down to was this: which story did I want to be in? I had a choice. Was this going to be an overblown farce, with me standing at a detached distance, laughing at the absurd ridiculousness of it all while gathering goofy anecdotes? Or was it going to be a 21$^{st}$ century version of a spiritual journey, in which I ducked under the protective police tape of sarcasm, and surrendered to the experience, simply letting it be, hoping that I might encounter some small revelation, some tiny ray of enlightenment, some hint of epiphany?

And so again, I shifted gears. I smiled to myself as Richard lifted the rat off his face and gently laid it back in its terrarium. I smiled and thought, bring it on.

And bring it on he did. The next stop on the tour was Richard's "inner sanctum," a bedroom converted into what appeared to some sort of hacker's bunker. Those of you who have followed the emergence of the Internet as a force in Western culture are aware of an underworld of people, presumably pale 20-something guys locked away in small rooms in their parents' homes, who dedicate their lives to uploading files to newsgroups and message boards and FTP sites, like millions of digital ants hauling grains of data to construct a veritable mountain range of information. A world of dedicated individuals whose idea of a good time is ferreting out bugs in Microsoft's latest software or networking together computers that use different operating systems. A world where paying for anything, from a Pentium processor to a spreadsheet program, is considered a sign of impurity.

And here it was. Along two walls, tables and benches held a cobbled-together array of computers, monitors, keyboards, disk drives, printers: all, as Richard proudly explained, networked together. My first reaction was that I'd stumbled upon the source of all those e-mails I kept getting from highly-placed Nigerian officials offering to park their millions in my bank account.

"Wow."

"Five years in the making. Twelve processors. Three different operating systems. Fifty gigabytes of storage. High speed Internet access."

"What do you do with it all?"

"Nothing. And everything."

Richard explained that a group of fellow travelers came over once a week to push the envelope a little further out into cyberspace. They had aspirations of forming a consulting company, but beyond fixing friends' computers, it was pretty much just a hobby.

"So are you involved with computers at work?"

"I don't work. At least not in the past six months. I much prefer living life outside the tentacles of commerce and the corrosive influence of money."

Easier said than done. Until last winter, he explained, he'd had a job at a bank, something to do with data storage. But the job soured, and he was now in the final months of unemployment. "Which is why I need to take this trip now. Now is when I have the time and the money." His plan, when he returned from the trip, was to turn this computer group into something that generated a little cash. Or get another job.

But enough shop talk.

"Smile."

He pointed to the eye of a small digital camera, attached to the top of a monitor. I smiled, and a moment later my befuddled image appeared on the screen, puffier and more disheveled than I'd imagined. Richard explained that he wanted to send our friends back east evidence of my arrival. With a few clicks, my mug took off into cyberspace.

In the few weeks after I'd decided to join him on this trip, Richard had been e-mailing old friends back in Jersey, who had in turn been e-mailing each other, stirring up talk of a mini-reunion among the old crowd. Our mutual friend, Paul, had taken the reins, searching out people I hadn't heard from in years, coaxing others to drive in from out of state, even borrowing a large house with a pool and big backyard for a get-together the following Sunday afternoon. It gave our trip the benefit of a deadline. We were heading east for a reunion.

I had gotten caught up in it myself. One afternoon, about a week before leaving, I impulsively tried locating a few of the old crowd who were rumored to live not far from our hypothetical route across the country. Nothing serious, just a few harmless Internet searches.

Like Mars Churchfarm. As I remembered him, a brainy kid, thin, pale, wild hair, ever willing to climb out on an existential limb; Sartre, Jr. I'd always had a soft spot for the guy. I'd lost touch with him years ago. After high school, he had gone to a university in the Midwest. Last I'd heard, he'd graduated with a Ph.D. in some obscure corner of algebra and was last seen teaching in Fargo, North Dakota. My first Internet search turned up an e-mail address for a professor at a Fargo college. I figured, "what the hell?" and shot him a message, asking if he was Mars from Jersey, informing him that Richard and I might be passing through Fargo the first week in June.

An hour later, he replied:

> *I'm looking forward to seeing both of you! It is however somewhat dependent on when you arrive in Fargo...I must leave about 2pm on Friday to drive to Ft. Collins. Otherwise my only obligations involve me from 9am – 2pm at work.*

Inspired by this success, I tried finding another friend, Bill, who, rumor had it, now lived in Cincinnati. A 411 search yielded half a dozen phone numbers. I picked one at random and got a message machine with a kid's voice on it. I started leaving a message: "If you're the Bill who went to Holy Cross..." when someone picked up the phone. It was Bill.

"Dan?"

"Bill?"

We were both in disbelief. Tracking him down, after 30 years, had taken all of about two minutes. He hadn't heard from any of the old gang since just after college. I explained the planned drive cross-country, and asked if he minded us stopping to see him in Cincinnati. He was so up for the idea, he said he might even join us for the final leg and come to the reunion.

It felt like some weird magic was being performed to make all this happen. The unexpected trip, the emergence out of the blue of all these old spirits, all converging so effortlessly. It was the kind of stuff that someone of a more religious bent would point to as proof of a higher power. I started calling Richard "Captain Karma".

"Time to celebrate."

Richard opened a drawer and pulled out a small wooden pipe and tin box from which he extracted a nugget of hash. As noted earlier, Richard was an early convert to the healing powers of pot. Even back in high school, he considered it more than just a means of getting high. For him, it seemed to be a sort of passkey to an underground pothead society. A secret handshake. A ritual that triggered an us-against-them sense of community amongst fellow travelers. The fellowship of the leaf.

As for me, a childhood plagued by asthma had left my lungs with little tolerance for smoke of any kind. Not wanting to be a social wet rag, I would usually take part in the joint passing. But after a hit or two, I'd inevitably break into the hacking cough of a true novice. On the rare occasion the pot had any noticeable effect, it only made me drowsy. So I'd always felt like an outsider in Potville.

Apparently, neither of us had changed much on this subject. Richard carefully loaded the bowl like a priest preparing communion. He offered it and, in the spirit of the moment, I gave it a try. As usual, it made me cough. Sensing my discomfort, Richard asked if I'd prefer a beer. I said sure. He took a final hit, then put the pipe and tin back in its drawer.

I followed him into the kitchen, where he opened the refrigerator and began fishing in the back of the shelves. On the kitchen table, I noticed a giant plastic bag of raw almonds. In the corner, the obese cat stared at an empty food bowl.

"We don't drink much beer. I think Meg brought home a six pack last Christmas. It's still in here somewhere."

He found it and handed me a bottle of local brew. Then he grabbed a couple almonds and popped them in his mouth.

"These are for the trip. Want some?"

I took a couple.

"You know you can live on almonds," he informed me as he wandered back to his inner sanctum to check his e-mail. Nothing new in the past 5 minutes.

"I've got our route all planned out."

He pulled out an old Rand McNally road atlas that had no cover and a permanent vertical fold, and paged to an interstate map of the lower 48.

"If we take 84 up into Washington, hit 90 through Idaho, Montana, South Dakota, Minnesota, Wisconsin, all the way to

Chicago, then hit 80 to Jersey. Boom. Figure 800 miles a day, we'll be there Thursday afternoon."

This was our first conversation about the route and the first indication that we had slightly different expectations about the pace and course of this journey. For openers, I'm not a big fan of flat-out, never-stop-for-nothing, 16-hour driving days. Second, I had told Mars that we'd stop by Fargo and Bill that we'd pick him up in Cincinnati.

"What about Mars and Bill?"

"Oh, right." In two words, Richard fully summed up his lack of enthusiasm for these side trips of mine. "Where are they again?"

"Mars is in Fargo. And North Dakota is one of the few states I've never been in."

"Me neither."

I grabbed the map. "Look. We could easily jump on 94, go through North Dakota, then drop down through Minnesota."

"I guess."

"Bill's in Cincinnati. We could head south from Chicago, then take 70 to the Pennsylvania turnpike."

Richard wasn't liking this one bit. "That's another couple hundred miles.'

"So what? It'll be good to see him. And he wants to come to the reunion with us." It was a plan I'd made without consulting Richard, and before I knew about the Bug. "Though I'm not sure if he'll fit in your car."

"Oh, he'll fit."


About an hour later, Meg arrived home. She wore unassuming office clothes, low maintenance hair and the easy-going manner of a working mom. "Hi. I'm Meg. Sorry I'm a little late. I stopped to buy you guys something."

She hoisted a large shopping bag onto the kitchen chair and pulled out a pair of beaded seat covers. She explained, clearly speaking from experience, "You're gonna be damn glad you have these. Keeps the circulation going."

She took a large bowl of pasta salad out the fridge and offered me some. We sat around the kitchen table, eating and talking, while Richard left to give his rats their medicine. She seemed very down to earth and straightforward. I liked her immediately.

She said she was surprised when Richard told her I'd agreed to go on this trip. "I can't think of anyone from my high school I would call to have lunch with much less asking them to drive across the country." I replied that I was a little surprised myself by how the whole thing had come together.

I'd asked if she'd ever been to New Jersey. She said no. She'd never been to the East Coast. Though she and Richard had been together for more than 10 years, she'd never met any of his family. "He hasn't been back there himself in all the time I've known him."

I recalled him saying this in his e-mail, but it only now struck home. I assumed his mother was still alive, but I wasn't even sure of that. It seemed odd that he'd gotten married and raised a son and had not once gone back to introduce them to his own family. They hadn't seen him in longer than I had.

Richard walked into the room, holding a rat.

"Richard, you really haven't been back to Jersey in 14 years?"

"Nope," he said, forcing an eyedropper filled with blue liquid into a rat's mouth.

"Is your mom still there?"

"Yep." The yep/nope treatment. I recognized it from my Jersey youth. It meant "You ain't gettin' nothin' outta me, buddy. This subject is not open for discussion." But like a pesky pollster, I kept right on knocking.

"Has she ever come out here?"

"Nope." He left the room to return the medicated rat to its terrarium.

I called after him. "Are your brothers and sisters still back there?"

"Some are, some aren't." The door opened a crack, "My oldest sister got married and moved to upstate New York. My younger brother lived in Florida last I heard."

"Do you stay in touch with any of them?"

He came back into the room, screwing the dropper cap onto the bottle of medicine and placing it back on a shelf in the refrigerator door. "Not really. Beyond a couple letters, I haven't seen any of them since the late '80s." There was not the faintest overtone of regret or bitterness in his voice. His attitude seemed to express a simple acceptance that this was just the way things were.

I couldn't remember, back when we were in high school, ever having been to Richard's house or ever meeting his mother. I knew he was oldest of five kids, but beyond that, all I knew about his family was that his father had died, and that, not long after he'd been expelled, he'd moved out of the house because he and his mother didn't get along. Apparently, they still didn't.

"Do they know you're coming?"

"Yeah. I've called my sister a couple of times. She told my mom. They're supposedly planning some kind of get-together on Saturday."

"But you haven't talked to your mother directly?"

"No. My mom and I don't talk much." He closed the fridge door. I hadn't realized that Richard's relationship with his family was still so tenuous. What was that all about? And what, if anything, did it have to do with this trip? It seemed reasonable to assume that a get-together with a family you had barely spoken to in fourteen years might come with a fair share of emotional baggage. But if so, Richard showed no sign of it. Before I could find out more, two teenage boys burst from the basement steps.

Meg did the introductions.

"This is Kevin. And Tommy." Kevin was a big kid with a teenager's lumbering shrug and monosyllabic vocabulary. Tommy was apparently a friend.

"Kevin, this is your dad's high school friend from L.A."

"You were in high school?" Kevin couldn't resist poking his father.

"Shut up, you mutthead," Richard tossed back.

I held out my hand. "Dan. Good to meet you."

"Hey."

As Kevin filled a cereal bowl with pasta salad, Richard gave him a parental grilling about his short list of chores. "I'm not going to be here for almost two weeks and I need you to step up to the plate. Homework. Garbage. Somebody's got to give the rats their medicine."

"And feed them," Meg was quick to add, "And clean the cage."

"Yeah, yeah."

Kevin described a new video game they'd been playing as he wolfed down the last of his pasta salad. From what I could tell, the three of them had a comfortable ease with one another, none of the undercurrent of suspicion and stress found in many

---

53

families with teenagers. They seemed to feel no need to impress or to prove anything.

Before the sun went down, Richard insisted we take a ride up to a nearby overlook called Rocky Butte. As we drove, I pried a few more details out of him.

"Meg seems great."

"Yeah. She's a true soul mate. I'm very lucky to have found her."

"How long have you guys been married?"

"Coming up on eight years. We were together a couple years before that."

"How old was Kevin when you met? Like four or five?"

"Seven. He's seventeen now. He's a great kid. Great kid."

"You and he seem to get along."

"Yeah, we get along well. I see a lot of myself in him."

"Is his biological father in the picture anywhere?"

"Not really. He pretty much ran off."

We reached a narrow road that wound up the side of a small mountain.

"I hike up here every morning, rain or shine. It takes me about an hour and half to get up and back."

"I was going to say: you look like you're in great shape."

"A hundred sit ups. Fifty push-ups. Three-mile walk. Everyday. That's my regime." His military attitude seemed in sharp contrast to his fondness for computers and pot. "Been doing it for two years now. Rain or shine, I'm up this hill every day."

Rocky Butte was no small hill. The road climbed steeply through the trees, passing increasingly upscale homes as the view improved. At the top, the trees opened to a small parking lot. Beyond it were the ruins of what appeared to be an old fort. Richard explained that it was once a prison, the Multnomah County Jail, which had closed back in the 1980s. Along the northern edge of the hill was an overlook, with a stone walkway, stone railings and stone pilasters. It overlooked a panorama of the city of Portland and the Columbia River, easing in the last red light of the day towards the immense Pacific. Off in the distance, I could see Mount St. Helens.

It occurred to me that 200 years earlier, Lewis and Clark may have stood on this same overlook, gazing west at the edge of America, the end of their journey. For us, it was the opposite: a beginning. We'd made our journey west earlier in our lives, when we were young and seeking a future. For better or for worse, that future had come to pass and now we were embarking on a different journey, a journey east, into lands we have already known, into the past, not to see how far we can go, but to see how far we have come.

Back at Richard's house, he and Meg busied themselves, packing. She ticked off mental lists and unloaded his clothes from the dryer. He smoked another bowl of hash and meticulously filled a large ice chest with food. Almonds. Dried fruit. Granola bars. A regular health nut picnic.

"That's a lot of food," I hazarded.

"We're going to be on the road for 5 days."

I had a bad feeling about where this was going.

"Don't you figure we'll stop and eat? I'm sure there's no lack of food available between here and there."

"I don't eat in restaurants. They're a rip-off. Why spend ten bucks for one meal when I can fill this whole ice chest for the same money?"

Once again, I found myself confronted. Driving cross-country in a '69 Beetle, I can handle. Richard's pot smoking I can handle. No music for a week I can probably handle. Eating dried fruits and nuts for five days straight, I cannot handle.

We all have our shoebox full of beliefs that get us through life. I'm not just talking about airy-fairy beliefs like truth and justice. I'm also talking about down-home, back-on-earth beliefs, the ones that really matter, the ones we draw upon a dozen times a day, beliefs like when and what to eat.

As a 20-something kid, I probably would have jumped aboard Richard's dietary regime just like I was jumping aboard the rest of this whole goofy trip – just to see what happened. As a 40-something, I almost wished I could, like I almost wished I could fast for a week or run a marathon. The difference was that I now had the wisdom to know what made me miserable. And living on a handful of raw almonds and dried apricots for a week would make me miserable.

And so this was the issue I chose to start rocking the until-now placid boat of Richard's highly thought-out plans. I told him I needed to eat. To stop the car, get out, go in some place, sit down and eat. Hot, cooked food. Maybe even a couple times a day.

"Fine. I'll just sit in the car."

Fine. Sit in the car. He continued packing, pulling an old, army surplus sleeping bag out the closet.

I couldn't resist. "A sleeping bag?"

"For sleeping."

"Where?"

"At night. When I get tired, I pull off the road somewhere and sleep."

"On the ground?"

"Yeah. I used to have a tent, but that's too much work."

"I was kind of thinking more along the line of a motel."

"I don't have that kind of money."

The trip hadn't even begun and we were already turning into the Odd Couple. So I decided to drop it.

The plan was to get up at 5 a.m. and be on the road just after sunrise.

"Can't do 800 miles unless you get an early start," Richard pronounced as he finished packing the cooler. Meg had unfolded the living room sofa into a sleeper bed and put on a sheet and blanket. She and Richard then spent the next hour, out in the driveway, trying to install the beaded seat covers. Evidently, they weren't quite designed for '69 VW seats. I tried to lend a hand, but there wasn't much to be done without the risk of getting ensnared in their husband-and-wife way of solving the problem.

"Do you have a piece of string?"

"What do you need a piece of string for?"

"Never mind what I need it for! Do you have a piece of string?"

I retired to the sleeper bed, where I sat with the obese cat and watched a movie on TNT. It was about a guy who was being forced against his will to assassinate a senator. A band of mysterious businessmen had his wife and child locked in a van with guns to their heads. The guy spent the entire movie searching for ways out of this unusual dilemma. He would try to escape, or he'd tell security cops what was happening, or he'd drop the gun they gave him in the toilet. But the bad guys were always one step ahead of him. No matter what he did, no matter what clever escape plan he came up with, no matter who he spilled the beans to, they always had another trick up their sleeve, and the poor guy just kept getting closer and closer to his destiny, like a modern-day Oedipus, whose fate was set not by the gods, but by some advanced form of deterministic psychology that was able to predict his every move, despite any delusions he might have about free will.

At one point near the end, he's making his nth desperate run for it, plowing through a hotel kitchen, stainless steel flying in all directions. He crashes through a swinging door, thinking that maybe, just maybe, he's escaped, when *boom*, out of nowhere, he trips over a shoeshine guy. The shoeshine guy is cryptically positioned in a service hallway with his whole shoeshine rig. I suppose he was meant to be the last person anyone would suspect of being in on an assassination plot. The one guy even a card-carrying paranoid might trust. He looks at our hero, who is in full fight-or-flight mode, gives him one of those slow, rheumy-eyed, wise-old-man smiles, points to the exit and says: "Run, you fool. Get away while you can."

I just hoped it wasn't a message someone was trying to send me.

3

# THE BAZAAR OF BELIEF

F ive in the morning came and went, unnoticed by all
concerned. I woke up just after seven, and Richard was still
asleep. I tried to take a shower, but couldn't figure out how to turn
on the faucet. So I went to the kitchen and searched for ingredi-
ents to make a pot of coffee. No luck there either.

My shuffling eventually woke up Richard, who trudged, yawning, into the kitchen. On autopilot, he pulled out a can of coffee
from the back of the refrigerator and a box of filters from a bottom
drawer.

"I tried to take a shower, but I couldn't get the faucet to go on.
I didn't want to break it."

"Yeah, it's a little tricky."

Rubbing his eyes awake, he trudged into the bathroom and
turned it on for me.

"Thanks." I took a quick shower while the coffee brewed. Richard was dressed and opening a box of instant oatmeal at the table.

"So what happened to five a.m.?"

He explained that oversleeping was part of his "going-on-a-trip" ritual. "I like to be tense the night before and relaxed in the morning. I figured we'd be out of here by nine." As I poured myself a cup of coffee, I wondered if this charade was for his benefit or mine.

"You drink coffee?"

"I'm all set, " Richard grabbed a 64-ounce plastic road mug —the kind you buy at a truck stop—and dumped half the freshly brewed pot into it. "My one remaining vice."

"What would life be without a few bad habits?"

"Here's oatmeal, and there's hot water on the stove," he said, briskly shaking two packets of instant Quaker Oats, ripping them open, dumping them both into a cereal bowl and topping them off with boiling water from a dented teapot.

I joined him at the table. "I must have passed out watching that movie last night."

"Yeah. You were fast asleep when we came inside."

"Did you ever get those seat covers on?"

"Yeah. It took a while, but yeah. I just have a few last things to pack, and then we're off. Oh, last night I found you something. Hang on."

He got up and left the room, returning a few minutes later with a small, portable CD player and a set of earphones. "Meg had these in her drawer. She said you could borrow them if you want. So you can listen to your CDs."

I hadn't even recalled mentioning my music withdrawal to Meg. "How did she know?"

"She's just like that. It's like some sixth sense thing." He scraped the last of the oatmeal from the bottom of the bowl. "I've got to finish packing." While Richard retreated to the bedroom, I walked outside to check out the day. Sunday morning. The weather was what I assumed to be more typical Portland: overcast, with ominous, dark rain clouds looming on the horizon. A red sedan drove past. The woman in the passenger seat was wearing a turquoise dress and matching hat. In the back, I could see two bouncing kids in their Sunday best, no doubt headed for church.

I tried to remember the last time I'd been to church on Sunday. When I was a kid, it was the unquestioned routine. Ten o'clock mass, then over to Grandmom's for donuts. We thank you Lord for these chocolate glazed. In the waning days of my Catholicism, my parents allowed me to stop going to Mass, so long as I attended some sort of Sunday service. I tried every church in town. And for a small town, there were quite a few. Lutheran. Presbyterian. Episcopal. Baptist. Moravian. Latter Day Saints. Greek Orthodox. A small synagogue. They all struck me as variations on the same theme. Once I ran out of new options, I stopped going altogether.

Richard came outside, giant coffee mug in one hand, ice chest of health food in the other. What little room there was in the Bug was already nearly filled. In the front trunk was crammed a spare tire, jack, gas can, extra battery, Richard's sleeping bag, and a small cardboard box of tools. Everything else had to go in the backseat: my carry-on bag, Richard's suitcase, and now the cooler of food. I noticed that the beaded seat covers were held on by an intricate spider web of string.

Meg came outside in her bathrobe to check on us just as Richard pulled a few plastic quarts of motor oil out of the trunk of the other, floorless Bug. "Just in case."

"I hope you guys make it in that thing."

"Oh, we'll make it," he pronounced, as he crammed the oil into our already overstuffed ship. "Why wouldn't we?"

"Good luck," she said in a quieter voice meant just for me.

"It'll be fun, whatever happens," I replied. "Oh, and thanks for the CD player."

"Every journey needs a muse. Even if it *is* made by Sony."

Once the car was ready, Richard went through with Meg, for what was clearly not the first time, the list of things that needed to get done while he was away: the rat's medication, the cancelled computer club meeting, the overdue phone bill.

"I'll take care of it. Don't worry. Have a good trip."

He reminded her that he'd be back in two weeks. Though he had neither a job waiting nor any deadline to meet, he'd somehow decided that two weeks was all this journey required. We'd be in Jersey by Thursday, do the reunion party on Sunday, and he'd leave to come back the following Tuesday. In and out.

She told him not to rush. "Take all the time you need."

That was our cue. Richard kissed her goodbye and grabbed his coffee mug off the roof of the Bug. I lowered myself into the newly beaded passenger seat. It didn't feel as bumpy as it looked. Before getting in, Richard crossed behind the car and pulled a brick from behind the rear tire. Tossing it off to the side, he climbed into the driver's seat, stowing his mug in a cup holder he had duct taped to the floor between his legs. Without turning on the ignition, he released the hand brake and shifted into neutral. Gravity eased the car down the driveway and back into the street, where Richard started the engine and shifted into first. Meg waved from the front lawn, and we both waved back.

We were off. As I settled into my beaded seat and watched the houses go by, the first mile of 3,000, I couldn't resist a cliché:

"Here we go." Richard seemed to share the Hardy Boys moment, "I can't believe we're actually doing this."

In contrast to our sunny mood, it still looked like it was going to start raining any minute. A heavy sky hovered over the light Sunday morning traffic as we made our way through the residential avenues to commercial boulevards, stores all shuttered except for the odd Kwik Mart and service station.

"We should get some gas."

The tank was half full, but Richard wanted to top it off anyway. So we pulled into a Texaco station.

We had never discussed who was going to pay for what on this trip. I'd assumed we'd split the costs, but as I suspected Richard didn't have a lot of money, I was more than happy to pay for whatever. So I pulled out a twenty.

He raised a refusing hand, saying he wanted to use his Texaco card. I later discovered that he'd borrowed the card from Meg as a safety net for stretching the $200 he'd brought with him. He had no credit cards of his own, partly because he didn't believe in them ("cheap capitalist bait to get you hooked on the drug of consumerism") and partly because nobody would give him one. As I began to get out of the car to at least do the pumping, Richard again raised his hand to stop me. "We don't pump in Oregon." Oregon, it turns out, is one of only two states in the country (to my knowledge at least) where the customer – the non-professional – is forbidden by law from pumping his or her own gas (New Jersey, coincidentally, is the other). So I closed my door and we waited.

A short woman, who appeared to be of Hispanic-Indian descent, eventually sauntered out from inside the station and gradually made her way to Richard's window. She didn't say anything.

She just stood there. Richard waved the credit card and said: "Fill it up. Regular."

The woman removed the nozzle from the pump and, holding it in her left hand, walked back and forth, searching for the gas tank. She stared at the left rear fender, then walked over to the right, then back again, then back to the right. I vaguely recalled that, though the engine on a Bug is in the rear, the gas tank is in the front. Richard, apparently relishing this bit of arcane knowledge, let her hunt for a good minute more before yelling out his window, "It's on the front fender. Right there. See?"

Without a word, the woman followed Richard's pointing finger until she found the gas cap. She unscrewed it with a long sigh, inserted the pump nozzle and stood by it as the gas flowed, her attention drifting off to something in the distance.

As I watched her, through the windshield, it occurred to me that she may have been part Aztec or Mayan, or maybe even American Indian, maybe even Shoshone, a distant relative of Sacagawea, the young Indian woman who traveled with Lewis and Clark, saving their white boy necks on more than one occasion. Now here she was, pumping gas for another couple of white boys on their way across America, pulling in five, maybe six bucks an hour at a job she clearly needed far more than she wanted, the current incarnation of a long cultural chain that led back through a millennium of mostly tragic history, her tired eyes gazing off to some faraway land while her weary body trudged through another Sunday shift in this one.

Five minutes later, we were on Interstate 84, heading due east along the south bank of the Columbia River. It had begun to rain lightly. On the left, the river popped in and out of view, flowing wide and gently west.

When Lewis and Clark first made their way down this river it had been considerably more treacherous. They had to leave their boats, a few pirogues and canoes, on the eastern side of the continental divide, hiking for over a month through the Bitterroot Mountains. Finally they reached a river that flowed west, which turned out to be the middle fork of the Clearwater. Figuring it was the surest path to the Pacific, they worked their way along the shoreline. But it was slow going as the forest was dense overgrowth. By then it was late October. They decided their best bet was to use the river to their advantage. Being resourceful travelers, they cut down several trees and hollowed them out to make crude canoes. The local Indians lined the shore along the first set of serious rapids, waiting for the unstable hollow log canoes to flip and the strange white men to disappear beneath the foam. But, somehow, that didn't happen. Somehow, they made it.

Today the rapids are all but gone, tamed by a series of hydro-electric dams. The Columbia moves wide and slow, like a western Mississippi, through the dense green of the Columbia Gorge. To our right, dark rock cliffs and steep hillsides, thick with redwoods and evergreens, rose up from the highway. Every so often, I could see a distant stream of water pouring from a rock face: a tiny waterfall shooting out like a spigot, then dropping hundreds of feet before disappearing behind the treetops.

The Bug held its own surprisingly well on the open road. It managed 60 miles per hour on the uphill climb. The windshield wipers left a little to be desired, but fortunately the rain had stopped. Heat seemed to ooze out of odd places, like a hole in the floor next to my right leg. The beaded seat covers were comfortable enough. Compared to Lewis and Clark, this was unimaginable luxury.

It felt strange driving without music, but I realized that the void offered an opportunity to talk. So I did, figuring now was as good a time as any to crack open a can of spirituality, a topic that until that moment I'd kept entirely in my own head.

"You know, one of the biggest reasons I decided to come on this trip was something you mentioned in one of your e-mails."

"What's that?"

"The whole idea of spiritual benefit. I wasn't quite sure what that meant, but something about it intrigued me. It got me thinking for the first time in a while about God and religion and all that stuff I left behind in high school."

"God and religion have nothing to do with spirituality," Richard declared with the assured conviction of someone whose ideas on the subject were not open for debate. "Religion is for people who are content to be manipulated."

"So I take it you're no longer a regular churchgoer?"

"Screw that. You couldn't pay me to set foot in one." It turned out that, like myself, Richard had long ago abandoned Roman Catholicism, along with all other forms of organized religion. But his mistrust didn't stop there, extending to most forms of civil authority. The essence of his case was that all these institutions existed to control, manipulate, and oppress; to intimidate people from exercising their natural born freedom so that wealth and power remained in the hands of the wealthy and powerful. "I don't care who it is: the pope, the president, the police, whoever. It's ninety percent about keeping the peons in their place."

"And the other ten percent?"

"The other ten percent is about impressing chicks who dig uniforms."

Now that he'd gotten that initial burst of venom out of his system, Richard shifted to semi-serious. "If you really take the time to look at it, most of what religion is asking you to believe just doesn't make sense. It's hard to buy into a belief system that put Galileo through the wringer. It's not a rejection so much as just processing the facts and moving on."

He was happy to leave it at that. No big deal. Like tossing out a worn piece of clothing—goodbye and good riddance. Not sure what to say, and not wanting to kick off this conversation playing devil's advocate for God and religion, I opted to let it lie for the moment, and stepped back into my own head.

Far as I could tell, Richard's rather blunt argument wasn't anything new. It has been around, in one form or another, for at least the last 500 years, ever since people discovered the value of believing what they could see with their own eyes. Science started as a reaction to superstition. Before science, most western Europeans got their truth from the Bible. The primary means of understanding how the world worked was to pry an interpretation out of scripture.

Science changed all that, making a case for getting to the truth by observing the world, coming up with your own explanation and putting that explanation to the test. This freed truth from the constraints of the scripture, from the biases and opinions of authorities, even from the biases and opinions of the person doing the explaining. Science rooted truth in the observable world, in empirical evidence. Science said, "Show me. I don't want to hear any well-argued, rhetorically brilliant opinion. I want proof. A theory that can be tested, over and over."

The beauty of science is that it has no ego. It invites people to prove it wrong, to come up with new evidence, a new theory that's even better than the existing one. It's a continuously improving brand of knowledge.

Needless to say, the Church was not exactly thrilled by this challenge to its monopoly on truth—and was even less thrilled when science started to nip at some of its most precious beliefs. Galileo was sent to prison for pushing the idea that the sun, and not the earth, was at the center of the universe. Isaac Newton theorized that all motion was caused by measurable physical forces. Finding little evidence of God's hand—but knowing what happened to Galileo—he tossed in a "Divine Mechanick," who could be credited for at least throwing out the first pitch. This kept God in the game, but retired Him from the mound to the bench, beyond the edge of the universe and before the beginning of time, far removed from daily life.

The challenges to the fundamental assumptions of the Bible just kept coming. An age of explorers opened European minds to previously unknown civilizations and rival religions that our all-powerful and all-knowing God seemed to have overlooked. Geologist Charles Lyell demonstrated that the Earth had been around for millions of years before the Church's official date for the creation. Charles Darwin made the case that design in nature arose from a slow process of natural selection, not the work of a Divine Creator. A group of German academics dug into the historical roots of the Bible, and made the case that it was a highly edited, very human creation. Sigmund Freud plumbed the inner workings of the human mind, claiming that God was merely a projection of a deep, psychological need for a father figure, a childish illusion which ought to be left behind like a childhood home. Karl Marx dismissed God as the sigh of an oppressed creature, an opiate of the masses. Nietzsche flat out declared him dead. To move forward, he claimed, we must throw off the constraints of conventionality and find the will to embrace the world honestly and make it our own.

On and on it went. Throughout the 19th and 20th centuries, philosophers, theologians and a small army of variously informed thinkers have wrestled with the question: "So what do we do now?"

So far as I can tell, in the early years of the 21st century, nobody has really nailed that one. Public opinion remains mixed. In one corner, you have a good part of the population content to overlook the arguments against God and accept religion at face value. In the other corner, there's a considerable chunk of folks who, like Richard, are content to write religion off as, at best, a quaint anachronism; at worst, a malevolent form of manipulation.

In between, there is the vast gray middle who aren't sure what they think, clinging to a half-articulated belief in some sort of creative force in the universe or some vague sense of the spiritual found in nature or in self-reflection. I suppose I count myself among them. As I've said, I sense that engaging in life requires embracing something beyond the surface of reality, a leap of faith into something that could be called spiritual. But what?

Maybe Richard had a clearer grasp of it than I did.


"OK. So I get that you have little to no tolerance for anything that smacks of organized religion. And I pretty much agree with you. But what about this idea of the spiritual? What did you mean by that?"

He considered the question, staring forward at the wet road and pursing his lips before answering. "For me, spirituality boils down to the quest for inner peace. Walking up to the top of Rocky Butte is my way of being spiritual. It quiets my mind."

"But why call that spiritual? What's so spiritual about it?"

"I don't know. It just is. It's nothing I can put easily into words." He hit the question back into my court. "What does spiritual mean to you?"

It's funny how certain concepts that we imbue with so much meaning, we also avoid defining too precisely, as if they serve their purpose best when slightly out of focus. I reminded myself that one of my goals for this journey was to stop doing that: to stop avoiding my own beliefs, to attempt to pin down those squirmy beasts. So I gave it a shot: "To me, 'spiritual' suggests something beyond one's self, beyond the surface of reality. Some force, some power, beyond the immediate."

Richard disagreed. For him, the spiritual was not something outside, it was something inside. "To me, 'spiritual' connotes something within one's self, one of the tools we use to shape our reality. I believe it has been co-opted and turned into religion, in all its many forms, for purposes of organization and control. Spirituality beyond the self is politics. What I believe is pretty much irrelevant when articulated outside of my own mind."

He had a point. If spiritually is all inside, a private matter, why bother having the conversation? Let it be. If your belief system works for you, why bother putting it under the microscope and risking somebody finding flaws? Life goes on with or without all that messy philosophical hand wringing. Whether you're an atheist or a zealot, you still have to eat, sleep, and try to get laid occasionally. Even the most clueless dolt can manage that without having to get all tied up in introspection. So what's the value of talking about it?

For Richard, spirituality was a completely private matter. What he believed was only relevant to his own self. But what exactly is this thing we call our "self"? What is it made of, if not the ideas we believe? What we do, how we act, how we steer a course through daily life, is determined, at least in part, by our beliefs, by the ideas we have about the world: customs and norms, values and principles like democracy and justice, rules and recipes about how to cross the street or live a fulfilling life.

These ideas are not genetically fixed; nor are they set in cultural stone. We pick them up as we go through life and they grow and change along with us. At any given time in our lives, the ideas we have in our head are like tools in a workshop. Some are new, like the one we picked up last week from a how-to book. Others have been passed down for generations. There are ideas that we keep around because they've always been there—or because everyone else seems to have them. Ideas about how we live, how we eat, what we wear, how we work, how we play, how to behave around other people, even who we are and what we're capable of accomplishing. Ideas like "self".

Like tools in a workshop, some ideas work better than others. Some can be relied upon without a moment's hesitation. Others require a few references to the manual, but they basically work. And then there are those ideas that tend to blow fuses, but out of habit, or pride, or the feeling that we can't afford a better one, we hang onto them. Maybe they've been in the family for generations, or we consider them an integral part of who we are. Who knows? But every time, when we open up our mental workshop and begin using that old, rusty saw to hack through the lumber of life, we are working far harder than we have to, doing far sloppier work than we might otherwise be capable of, hesitant to try anything too out of the ordinary or too complicated because we fear embarrassment or failure. Whether we admit it or not, these broken-down ideas leave us dysfunctional, unable to fully engage in some aspect of life.

Everyone has a few old saws in their workshop that they stubbornly refuse to get rid of. Perhaps there's some value in cleaning out the shop every once and awhile. Getting rid of the junk. Who knows? I might end up with better tools, a better life. But the only way to do that is to break the habit, to seek some point of reference outside your self, to talk to somebody.

"I think there's some value in articulating what you believe."

Richard had assumed we were done with this subject. He glanced over at me and wondered what I was up to. "Why is that?"

"We all have our own set of ideas that get us through life, right? The things we believe in."

"Right."

"But where do you think those beliefs come from? Do we just make them up out of thin air?"

"No. You go through life, you experience things, you see how other people live, you read books, watch TV, and in doing all that, you accumulate ideas. Some you like, some you don't. You try out the ones you like and, if they work, they become what you believe."

"Sort of like some giant cultural shopping mall. The Bazaar of Belief."

"Yeah."

"So where do you think *those* ideas came from? All the stuff in the Bazaar of Belief?"

"I don't know. People made them up."

"Exactly. The ideas that you believe didn't originate with you. They came from outside you. From somebody else who thought them up and took the trouble to articulate them."

"All right. But so what? I've made them mine. Gave them my personal touch. Just because I bought a sofa from Sears doesn't make it any less mine."

"Or a car from Volkswagen."

"I didn't buy it from Volkswagen. I bought from some guy who had it in his driveway with a *For Sale* sign."

"But you didn't create it. You bought it from somebody else."

"Fine. I bought it. And that made it mine. So what's your point?"

"My point is that the ideas we believe in are not unlike the cars we drive. They start out as one person's twist on some older model, then they get shaped and fine tuned by culture's various movers and shakers and marketing specialists. Then they have to face off against other competing ideas in the Bazaar of Belief: "What's in style this year? What can we afford? What looks good on me?" We buy into them, yes, and maybe we get this illusory sense that they are our own unique private property, like a pair of socks, but ultimately, they're not ours. They are the creation of our culture, this vast transcendent network of minds, past and present. Nobody designs and builds a car completely from scratch. At the very least, they inherited the idea of car-ness."

"But that doesn't make it any less my car. This car works for me. I went looking for it. Sought out this particular out-of-date, no-longer-manufactured car because it works for me. It's cheap, it's easy to maintain. I understand this car. I can fix it if it breaks down. I don't want some fancy twenty thousand dollar car that runs on computers and forces me to be dependent upon service technicians. I like things that are simple. Things that don't complicate my life."

"So why have a car at all? Even a simple car complicates your life."

"It gives me the freedom to go places I wouldn't be able to go otherwise."

"Just like ideas. Good ideas give you freedom. Power. The ability to go places you couldn't go otherwise."

"So what?"

For some reason, I was getting all worked up over this. I paused, thinking that maybe I should shut up before this gets out of hand. I'm not normally one to be pushing my half-baked ideas on people. But then a second thought hit me: maybe this was part of the spiritual journey twist. Rather than default back to my normal soft-spoken reticence, maybe I needed to talk more, get ideas out on the table, even if they aren't fully formed. So I risked getting this trip off to a bad start and plowed forward.

"What would you say about somebody who never leaves home, never gets involved with other people, never does much of anything, because, according to them, they prefer to keep their life simple?"

"I'd say that's their choice."

"I'd say it's also possible that they've got a head full of ideas that don't work, and they're afraid to admit it. They miss out on life because they insist on clinging to broken-down beliefs. And they're not alone. Everybody clings to some dysfunctional belief that keeps them from engaging in some aspect of life, because they don't realize that their belief isn't working. They think it's the only choice available to them. They don't know what they don't know. And they get themselves backed into a corner because they refuse to talk about it. Just like a broken-down car, the only way to fix it is to open the hood, shed some light on the situation, get some perspective, see what other people think. Talking is how we discover what's broken in our beliefs. It's how we get unstuck."

Richard wasn't biting. "What I believe is my business. What you believe is your business. There's no point getting into an argument about who's right and who isn't. We don't have to both believe the same thing."

"I'm not saying that. What I'm saying is there's value in conversation. It's like a guy who believes the only way to fish is with a spear. Every night, he heads back to his cave with maybe one pathetic little fish, maybe nothing. Sitting around the fire at night, knocking down the fermented gruel, he never talks about it because he's embarrassed. Thinks he's deficient somehow, that there's something wrong with him. One night, the gruel-tender says, 'Dude, what's bugging you?' Finally, in sheer desperation, because he's starving to death, the guy opens up. Says he's not catching any fish with this spear of his, something's wrong, but he doesn't know what it is. Maybe it's the fishing hole, maybe it's his technique, maybe it's the will of the gods.

Richard listened, his icy resistance melting into curiosity.

"Another caveman overhears him and says, 'Hey, pal. Ever try a net?' Some visiting Neanderthal chimes in, 'Ever try a rod and reel?' Maybe a third guy knows some time-tested spear fishing techniques. Suddenly, there's a whole smorgasbord of options that our poor, starving fisherman never knew were there, all because he finally opened his mouth."

Richard glanced over at me. "Where are you going with this?"

"Here's the moral of the story: why wait until you're starv-ing to death before opening up? And who knows? Maybe your beliefs stand up just fine in the light of day. Maybe you even have something valuable to contribute. By articulating them, by sharing them, by getting them out there into the Bazaar of Belief, you might be helping somebody else who is in the market for better ideas. The way to improve ourselves, our community, our country, our culture, is to put what we believe on the table, so we can work out the bugs, constantly improving the ideas that get us through life, so we can all get through life better."

"This is starting to sound like a not-so-veiled criticism of my car, not to mention my lifestyle."

"No. I apologize if it sounds that way. What I'm struggling with here is what it means, for me, to be on a spiritual journey. You and I both started from a similar background, indoctrinated in the parochial schools and Catholic families of South Jersey, with a little '60s rebellion tossed in just to make things interesting. We were brought up in a belief system that had undergone at least two thousand years of fine-tuning by some of the greatest minds in Western culture. And both of us, like millions of other people, have discarded that belief system outright, and replaced it with a bunch of ideas that we've cobbled together out of bits and pieces we've picked up along the road. Ideas that actually seem to be more or less working for us. Now here we are, for whatever reason, heading back to that homeland, that past, that tradition, that history. We have an opportunity to discover who we've become. To expose ourselves to the light. To find out how strong and courageous this self we've cobbled together really is. We have an opportunity to pit what we believe, who we are, against the monsters and villains out there that have the power to destroy us. That, to me, is the essence of a spiritual journey: putting yourself in a situation where your comfortable and unspoken beliefs are exposed and tested. Leaving the house and wandering to some place you've never been, risking potential destruction for a chance of achieving confirmation—or even transformation."

Whew. Amen brother. Where I came up with that head of steam, I'm not sure. But there it was. Richard soaked it in for a few moments, staring silently out ahead at the wet road. Then he shrugged and conceded, "Maybe you're onto something."

Maybe.

I was a bit surprised myself at where my rant had taken me. It had not consciously occurred to me until then to see this road trip as somehow heroic. In his book, "Hero with a Thousand Faces," Joseph Campbell offers up the idea of the archetypal hero. Citing tales both Eastern and Western, ancient and medieval, Campbell notes the common thread of a hero who journeys from the comfort and safety of the known world into uncharted seas in a quest to resolve some upheaval. Such heroes are of all sizes, ages, and genders: Jason and the Argonauts, Ulysses returning from Troy, Luke Skywalker taking on Darth Vader, Frodo Baggins setting off with the Ring, Dorothy getting plopped down in Oz. All trace the arc of what Campbell calls the monomyth, a tale retold in different clothing for different times and different listeners. The known world is somehow disrupted. The hero is beckoned by a call to adventure, a quest to somehow restore order and peace. At first, the hero may resist, uncertain of his own abilities, fearful of forces far more powerful than himself, confused as to why he, of all people, is being called. But eventually, inevitably, the ship sets sail, the twister lifts the house off its foundations. With the guidance of gods of one sort or another, the hero endures trials, faces temptations, passes through thresholds; he is tested to the point of releasing his grip on life itself, willing to sacrifice all, to die, in order to reach his destination. In the end, he overcomes the ultimate obstacle, unlocks the last puzzle, slays the beast, unearths the treasure, then returns home, transformed.

Why this hero tale strikes such a chord is because it parallels a journey we all make in our own lives, in times of change, times of crisis, times of transition, when our unconscious mind sends its dark vapors of doubt up into the neat little dwelling of ourselves. As Campbell puts it: "The familiar life horizon has been outgrown; the old concepts, ideals, and emotional patterns no longer fit; the time for passing of a threshold is at hand."

But to make this journey, like the hero, we must be willing to unbuckle the safety harness that straps us securely to our present selves. We must be willing to steer our ship of life into mysterious, unmapped ways of being, must be willing to face monsters and mortifications, to die on some level, in order to be reborn. The reward is discovering a newfoundland of being, where we can live a "bolder, cleaner, more spacious, and fully human life."

We are drawn to heroic myths because they "supply the symbols that carry the human spirit forward." Below the literal surface details lies a deeper truth, a "truth in symbolic clothing."

Perhaps this longing of mine for some lost land of religion, some sign of the spiritual, was also a longing for myths to guide my spirit forward, for heroes that can handle the here and now.

I also realized that this search wasn't limited to the privacy of my own mind. Until then, I would probably have agreed with Richard that spirituality was an internal affair, a tending of the garden that grew in the damp hothouse of one's soul. But the beliefs we take such pride in, our most precious ideas and values, are not our creations. They have an evolutionary past that far predates our transitory selves. They were nurtured in the inner gardens of the many living and dead before us. They are the property of our common culture. Understanding and nourishing them is not something we can do in isolation.

Religion began as a way of binding people together under the tent of common beliefs and communal mythology. God is not only the property of community; God is the essence of community. The way to revive such communal belief is not through meditation and retreat, but through conversation and connection. A spiritual journey ought to take one outside, beyond the safe harbor of oneself, out into the great potluck dinner of community and culture, sharing one's ideas the way one shares recipes. The hero's quest is enlivened by fellow travelers.

To that end, I resolved to speak up more, even if my ideas are only half baked, and to gratefully accept any suggestions for improvement.

"Thanks," I said finally.

"For what?" Richard wanted to know.

"For putting up with my semi-coherent ranting and raving."

He laughed. "Fuck. That's half the reason I invited you along."


Richard pointed across the river to the relatively treeless Washington side and told me about a museum located just beyond the mountains. Back in the 1800s, a guy named Sam Hill had built a mansion there with the intent of starting a Quaker community. Instead, he got involved with an exiled Parisian woman, who convinced him that what the area really needed was an art museum. She must have made a convincing argument, because he soon began buying art works from her friends in Paris, including the sculptor Auguste Rodin. Before old Sam Hill knew it, he had himself a world-class art museum, pretty much in the middle of nowhere. For good measure, he built a full-scale replica of Stonehenge .

"Hence the expression, "What in the Sam Hill are you doin'?"

"Not sure. But it makes sense."

Sounded intriguing to me. But getting there was a side trip Richard has no interest in taking. The Sam Hill Museum became the first of many places we didn't stop to see.

The landscape changes dramatically east of the Cascades. The Columbia Gorge reaches a pinnacle of green trees, stark rock and cascading water; then suddenly, within a few miles, becomes parched rolling hills covered by dead grass and the occasional lonely tree. The overcast and drizzle were replaced by a pale blue sky empty of all but a few lost clouds.

Welcome to the dry side, the vast expanse of the Lincoln Plateau. It felt like we were suddenly in the Midwest.

Another 100 miles down the road, we stopped for gas in Boardman, a small town with a gas station, a handful of houses and, as far as I could tell, little else. Surprised that I could get a signal on my cell phone, I called home. Esmé answered. I told her where I was, and she reminded me about the postcards. After hanging up, I fished out the one I'd bought at the airport (along with a pack of stamps) and jotted out a quick message. Looking around, I saw a mailbox a block away, walked down and mailed it.

By then, Richard had filled the tank. I offered to drive, but he said he was still good for another couple hundred miles. So off we went, across the overpass to the onramp. But as we turned down the incline to the interstate, the engine—with no warning or apparent cause—stopped running. Pulled down the ramp by gravity, Richard guided the Bug to a gentle stop in the soft dirt shoulder.

"What happened?" I asked.

"I'm not sure."

Richard turned the ignition key and the engine cranked and started, a relieving sign that this little wrinkle, this minor symptom, like a lump under your skin or a sudden dizzy spell, was in fact "nothing to be worried about."

But no. The engine coughed and sputtered, gasping for fuel. Richard pumped the accelerator pedal, eager to oblige. But to no avail. After 30 seconds of trying, it died again. Richard took a moment to review the evidence.

"It's not getting gas."

He tried to start the car again, feverishly working the accelerator. The engine again roared to life, but the moment Richard stopped pumping the gas pedal, it again choked and shuddered to a halt. He tried to start the car another half-dozen times before accepting that it wasn't going to happen.

"Hmm." Richard remained unruffled. "This has happened to me before. No big deal." I was comforted to know that we weren't in uncharted territory here. There were obvious steps to be taken. Procedures to follow. He got out of the car and opened the front hood. I followed.

He pulled out a red plastic gas can and a screw driver.

"The great thing about VW's is that everything is fixable. I know exactly what to do in this situation."

Opening the rear hatch, he unscrewed the air filter cover, a silver metal disk about the size of a dinner plate, exposing the circular air filter and the mouth of the carburetor. Lifting the gas can, he poured a splash directly down the carburetor's throat. I guessed the idea was to prime the engine like you would prime a well pump, giving it just enough gas to get things going, and hope that sheer momentum would take over.

He set down the gas can and climbed back in the driver's seat. As he turned the key, the engine gave out a great roar, the uncovered air filter bouncing like a jumping bean. He pumped the gas pedal frantically, and this time, the engine held idle for maybe a minute. It was just enough time to appreciate the beauty of a car simple enough for such homespun fixes.

Then it died again.

"Not to worry," Richard pronounced as he got out of the car again, his demeanor only slightly ruffled. Again, he tried pouring a splash of gas down the carburetor, like someone pouring water into the mouth of a dehydrated man. Again, when he turned the key, the car roared to life like a sleeping dragon, spewed smoke for a full minute, and then expired in a fit of coughing.

On the fourth try, the car turned over and roared. But this time, instead of sputtering to another halt, it settled into a constant purring idle. Richard grinned.

"That's why I love these cars."

He restowed the gas can and the screwdriver, then climbed back inside, uplifted after the brief scare, his faith in this fragile machine restored. "These things just get temperamental sometimes. Sort of like women. You just have to give them a little attention."

"Right." I was a shade more skeptical, this being only our first stop, but I kept it to myself. Richard threw the car into gear and headed east.

Here we were, not 100 miles into a 3,000-mile journey, and already the car was getting moody. Though he solved the problem, I could see Richard still pondering the causes, weighing the evidence, trying to figure out just what this girl needed to make her happy.

His mechanic, Mike, had given the car his blessing. Richard had personally taken it on a test drive to the coast, where it performed flawlessly. What new variable had been thrown into the mix?

Then it hit him.

Heat! We had been driving the car full out, at 65 miles an hour, for two hours now. The engine had never been run this full out for this long. It had never run this hot.

"Vapor lock." He spoke like a Zen master, delivering his wisdom as tersely and cryptically as possible.

"Huh?"

"Vapor lock. The problem is vapor lock."

"What's vapor lock?"

"It's when the gas in the fuel line gets so hot that it evaporates before it reaches the carburetor. The car is just getting too hot."

That didn't sound good. And it also didn't make sense to an admitted car novice like myself. If it was vapor lock, then why did it only manifest itself when we stopped and tried to start up again? Wouldn't it be worse when we were moving and the car was even hotter?

"We just need to let it cool down when we stop."

As far as Richard was concerned, the problem was solved. A calm settled over his face as he and reality clicked back into sync.

My reaction was somewhat different. I knew almost nothing about engines and even less about Volkswagens. If I'd had access to a manual, I'd no doubt be boning up right now. But I didn't. And I didn't want to. My goal on this trip was to go on a spiritual journey, to surrender to the experience. That meant ignoring my standard responses and simply letting reality happen. It was not my goal to keep the car running. It was not my goal even to get across the country. It was my goal to let this trip take me wherever it was going to take me, to exist in this interface between Richard's brain and reality, and to learn from it what I could.

With that thought, any anxiety I felt went away. I was more than willing to let Richard be my guide. I was, to my own surprise, happy. If nothing else, this little wrinkle might make the trip more interesting. We'd encountered our first monster.

A faint smile appeared on my face.

"Vapor lock it is."

A few miles east of Boardman, we turned onto Route 730, a shortcut up to Umatilla and the bridge across the Columbia into Washington.

4

# THE STRAITS OF GOOD AND EVIL

A s we crossed the Columbia, we could see the McNary Dam, its stolid face basking in the sun as it effortlessly squeezed the energy out of this once wild river, which flowed broad and tame below us. On the far side, southeastern Washington was an undulation of barren hills that were even more desolate than northeastern Oregon. Few houses, the occasional irrigated patch of farmland, mostly just desert. Richard pointed out, off to the left, the Umatilla National Range, a vast military testing ground for weapons of mass destruction. I could see no visible sign of it, but took his word that it was out there somewhere.

Shortly after noon, we reached the tri-cities of Richland, Kennewick, and Pasco. It struck me as odd that even one city would flourish in such a stark landscape, much less three, but a glance at the map offered an explanation. The Tri-cities were at the confluence of three major rivers: the Columbia, which had made an about-face to the north; the Snake, coming in from the

east; and the Yakima, flowing northwest towards Seattle. Each city occupied a pie slice of this geographic peace symbol.

"You have to be careful," Richard warned, "I got lost last time I came through here." The Tri-cities were also the confluence of several dozen interstates, highways, and county roads, descending from every direction to join into an indecipherable knot on the map page. We were on 82 North, and had to re-cross the Columbia to get on 395 headed towards Spokane. As Richard seemed to have a handle on it, I didn't bother trying to help navigate.

In passing, the Tri-cities seemed non-descript and uninviting: sun-beaten buildings, empty lots, farm equipment, car dealerships and sundry franchises. As it was midday Sunday, there wasn't a lot going on. Still, I felt a faint pulse of curiosity. Plus, it was lunchtime.

"You want to stop for lunch? Maybe take a look around?"

"There's nothing to see here. We should just keep going."

I recalled that Richard had done a stint as a truck driver, and even though we were in the antithesis of a big rig, I was getting the sense that he still drove like one. Success is measured by the odometer. The only excuse for stopping was to exchange liquids — fill the tank and empty the bladder. If you're hungry, eat nuts.

I, on the other hand, was in no big rush. I am one of those drivers who impulsively divert onto back roads, pull over in the shoulder just to breathe the air and look around, even if there's not much to see. As I'd come all this way, I wanted to at least feel that I'd been here. Put my feet on the ground. But I was not in the driver's seat, and not inclined to press the issue.

So the Tri-cities went by in a blur. On our way out of town, we did come upon one unusual, if not exactly tourist-friendly, attraction: a nuclear power plant along one of the rivers. Stark white buildings set back a secure distance from the road, cryptic round storage tanks, tall smokestacks emitting only the faintest whiff of vapor. The utility companies were clearly milking this river for all it was worth.

"This isn't right," Richard commented, glancing from side to side. I figured he was making a political statement.

"What isn't right?"

"I don't remember passing this power plant last time."

He'd made a wrong turn. Not the same one he'd made the last time he got lost in the Tri-cities. A different wrong turn. I pulled out the atlas and I tried to pinpoint our location in the spaghetti of roads, looking for some sign of a power plant in the Tri-Cities tangle. There were a lot of rivers, but no nuclear power plants. I looked out the window for a road marker. Nothing. Best guess, we were heading east along the Snake on a gray line that didn't have a number.

"We have to go back." Richard was immediately irritable. His internal map had once again let him down. At the first opportunity, he pulled a U-turn, barely slowing down. "I can't believe I went this far without noticing. We're supposed to be on 395. I should know that."

"Hey, what's a road trip without a few wrong turns?"

"I know these roads. I shouldn't be making this kind of mistake." It was one of the few ripples I'd seen in his calm self-confidence. Richard had this "trust-me-I-know-what-I'm-doing" air about him that made it easy for me to defer to his judgment. But when the car broke down earlier, and now again when he'd steered us briefly off course, I noticed this ever-so slight hint of panic, like a fugitive sensing his predator.

After backtracking five miles, we saw a sign for 395 North.

"Here's where I screwed up," Richard pronounced as he navigated the Bug towards the entrance ramp, his confidence once again restored, his doubts safely tucked away from view.

And with that, we were back on course.

As Richard drove, my mind, lulled by the persistent putter of the VW engine, wandered back to our conversation about the Bazaar of Belief. Here I was with my cafeteria tray full of ideas about how to get through life, sitting at my table off in the back corner, relatively content with my meal, getting enough spiritual nutrition to survive, but also relatively disconnected from the many others sitting around me in the vast lunchroom of humanity. I wanted to know what they were eating. I wanted to know if there were other foods I might enjoy. But more than anything, I wanted to join the conversation, to connect, to share this experience of being human. Maybe I knew something that they didn't. Maybe they knew something that I didn't.

Maybe that is the hero's journey of our time. So many of us sit alone in our semi-comfortable folding chairs eating our semi-edible meals, keeping to ourselves, warily watching the many who inhabit this vast cafeteria of our culture. Maybe the hero's journey is to leave the security of our seats and navigate the treacherous seas to someone else's table; to attempt conversation with total strangers about things that matter, to risk ridicule and rejection. Not to sell them our ideas, not to steal theirs, but through connection and conversation to create a comunity that would never otherwise have existed. Maybe that is the process by which we recreate religion.

---

But where to begin?

From the list of things that once, for me, belonged to the realm of religion, I randomly selected morality, the question of distinguishing good from evil, the quandary of sorting out what we should do from what we shouldn't.

My first thought was of another old friend, a guy I considered to be well educated, well read, very worldly, very open to anything. He was also a practicing Catholic. We'd once had a conversation about why he'd stuck with religion in the face of so many arguments against it. He told me that the big reason he hung in there was his kids. He felt it was important to raise his kids Catholic in order to give them a solid ethical foundation. Without a belief in God, specifically a belief in a higher power that has imposed a set of moral rules on all of humanity, ethics has no solid ground to stand on. Without God, who or what gives anyone the authority to say what's right or wrong? Without God, we're on our own. The social fabric shreds into moral relativism.

I was raised to believe in sin, the idea that my every transgression was recorded as a black mark on my soul and that after I died, barring confession and forgiveness, I'd have to burn those sins off in the painful fires of purgatory (if I was lucky), or hell (if I was not). Now, I'm the first to admit that this is a brilliantly effective story, especially for the young and naïve. It gets people to police themselves: self-regulation motivated by the fear of eternal punishment—with a bonus shot of guilt over disappointing God. It takes morality out of human hands and puts it on a level that is absolute and unquestionable. You don't debate with God. You don't hire a lawyer in hell. It's a carved-in-stone set of ethics that gives people a clear moral compass—plus the reassurance of eternal justice: "That asshole who ripped me off may win out in the short run, but just wait until he has to look God in the eye. God will make him pay. While I'm kicking back on a cloud in heaven, he'll be on the seventh circle of hell frying like a burnt hotdog. Judge God doesn't miss anything. He'll get his."

I'll admit, all that fire and brimstone and Ten Commandments stuff kept me in line as a kid. I carried my transgressions around like a ball and chain until I could unload them in the confessional, sweating bullets that I wouldn't die in the meantime. Hail Mary. Whew.

But gradually, the wheels started to come off the whole heaven/hell, judgment-in-the-afterlife scenario. On top of suspecting it was a fabricated fantasy intended to herd the masses, it didn't make internal sense. What kind of a warped God would come up with a system of justice that most earthly societies would condemn as brutal and inhumane? Eternal agony? C'mon. The A.C.L.U. would be all over that. Not to mention that this was same God who created such flawed and easily tempted creatures in the first place. I mean, consider the liability exposure alone. If God were a major corporation, He'd have lawsuits out the kazoo.

Then there's the question of who would want to spend all of time and eternity with the kind of people who qualify for heaven? Who do you know who makes it through life unblemished by human frailty? They're not exactly a fun crowd here on earth.

Picture a typical day of eternal bliss. What exactly is on the schedule? Praying? Why pray? You're already in heaven. A hike? Watercolor class? Another party? Sitting on a cloud with a big smile on your face? Is heaven like an opium den? All bliss and no action?

Then there's the question: Once you leave your body behind, what's left? Pain receptors? Flesh to burn? Memory? Hunger? Sex?

Take those away, and what's left to generate all that pain and suffering? Or for that matter, all that joy and bliss?

Initially, after I'd stopped buying into the divine comedy of heaven/hell, moral behavior took on the patina of a con game played on the gullible by the powers that be. Being good was for suckers. I'd been tricked into being good when I could have been lying, cheating and stealing to my heart's content—and gotten away with it! I should be going wild in the candy store of guilt-free sin. What's to stop me?

But that's not what I did. With the exception of religion-specific rules (go to church, don't eat meat on Friday), I behaved almost exactly as I had before. My moral compass didn't waver. I was neither sent spiraling into hedonism nor careening adrift on the shifting tides of choice.

So what kept me from going haywire? Force of habit? The reactions and expectations of the people around me? Some hard-wired neural equivalent of conscience? I don't know. All I can say for sure was that it wasn't faith in God or belief in any other absolute moral order.

My daughter, who my wife and I have raised without any religion at all, seemed to be, if anything, more morally grounded than I was at her age. At 11, she clearly got that lying, cheating and stealing were wrong. She recoiled from meanness and steered clear of conniving peers. She was, as far as I could tell, a good-hearted, decent human being, with no notion of sin, no fear of God's wrath, no concept of commandments sent down from on high. So where did she get her moral compass?

It was time to wander over to Richard's table and get his take on the question.

"Did you and Meg raise Kevin to believe in any kind of religion?"

"Are you kidding? No. Why?"

"Just curious. I was just thinking about what makes people behave the way they do, and the whole idea that you need religion to be moral; to teach your kids right from wrong."

"That's a load of crap. That kind of by-the-book morality bullshit is just a way for the high priests to manipulate the ignorant masses. To keep check on their economic interests."

No waffling there. "OK, fine. But if you take away religion, how do you teach your kid right from wrong?"

"It never seemed like it was that much of a problem. I don't need some priest to tell me that cheating on a test or stealing some kid's bike is wrong. Wrong is wrong."

"But why? Who gets to decide what's right and what's wrong?"

"I do. I decide what's right and what's wrong for me. And frankly, I don't think it's anybody else's business."

"Then who decides what's right and wrong for your kid?"

"When he was still a kid, Meg and I did. Now that he's getting older, to a large extent, I think it's up to him. He's got to make his own moral choices."

It made sense, but there was something about this brand of ethical relativism I didn't get. We can't all be completely independent entities. But what else is there? Not sure, I rebutted Richard's argument.

"I don't believe everybody gets to make up his or her own morality."

"Then who do you think does?"

Good question. Who else is there but you? All the other people in your life? Isn't morality ultimately about your relationship with them?

"To me, morality starts with people trying to live together, be it as a family or a country or whatever. To function as a group, there has to be some common-ground acknowledgment of what's acceptable behavior and what isn't. Everybody sticking to the same set of rules makes everybody's behavior predictable. It creates a sense of trust. I don't have to be watching my hoard of food all the time. I trust you won't steal it because there's a tribal rule against stealing. There are consequences. If you steal my stuff, it's not me who is going to come after you, it's the whole tribe. So now I can relax and my energy can be freed up for the common good. I feel secure enough to go out to hunt and gather more food. And that means more for everybody. So everybody wins. But take away the rules, and it's every man for himself. Nobody wants to play together, because now they've got to spend all day guarding their stuff, watching their backs. Nobody can trust anybody else. The community crumbles. Game over."

Richard took all this in, but I could tell he wasn't buying it. "Maybe so. But I think each individual still decides what rules they want to play by and what rules they don't."

"Sure. You can decide not to play by the rules. But you don't get to decide what the rules are. You can do whatever you want, but you don't get to decide what's right or wrong."

"Then who does?"

"The group. The community."

"Well then, how does group come up with these rules in the first place?"

"I think rules evolve over time. From general consensus, from tradition, from the leaders of the group coming up with new rules. Think of a made-up game you played as a kid. You started off agreeing to a few ground rules: what's out of bounds; what's a foul. But as you played, you found that you had to continually refine the rules. When something came up that wasn't covered, you made up a new rule. How those rules got made up depended on the group. Maybe it was your ball, so you got to be the dictator. Or maybe the guy who shouted the loudest got to make the rules. Or maybe everybody decided: democracy. But for the game to go on, for the community to continue, all the players needed to accept that, like it or not, they've got to play by the rules. They didn't get to individually pick and chose which rules they wanted to obey."

"But life isn't as simple as a stickball game. What I would call my 'rules to live by' aren't written down. They're embodiments of my personal values: 'Say thank you, don't rip people off, don't rape and pillage the earth.' Those are my rules."

We were drifting into deeper water. Entire libraries have been written about this stuff. Philosophers have made careers parsing the finer points of ethics. But just because morality is complex, doesn't negate the value of trying to get a grasp on the basics.

I waded out a little further: "I agree with you that a lot of the rules we live by are not written in stone or codified in law books. But I disagree that they are personal. They don't originate anew with each individual. Even unspoken, unconscious rules ultimately come from the people around us."

"How? How do the people around me communicate an unspoken rule?"

"By the way we interact with each other, by the stories we tell, by the TV shows we watch, by the look a mother gives her kid. Whatever culture you grow up in, I think that culture has all sorts of unspoken ways of letting you know its rules and values, from how your parents react to you as an infant to how the kids in school treat you on the playground. They smile when you do good, they frown when you don't. And we soak all that in. It's cultural conditioning. As you grow up and join larger, more sophisticated groups of people, the rules become more overt, posted on the blackboard, written in the driver's ed manual. Every little group within that wider culture has its own subset of rules, and its own way of letting you know what they are."

"That assumes we're all just robots. That we have no choice. That we just do whatever society tells us."

"No. You do have a choice. You can obey the rules or not. You can choose to be part of a group or not. That part is up to you. All I'm saying is that you don't get to make up your own rules."

"So what happens if I don't play along? If I refuse to obey one these rules? Do I suffer the stain of sin and go to hell?"

"No. I think you suffer the consequence in *this* life. I think communities have come up with all kinds of clever ways of letting you know you're wrong, from a dirty look to sending you to prison."

"But people get away with breaking the rules all the time. If you think you can get away with something, like stealing this box of felt tip pens from the office supply closest or defrauding your stockholders or dumping toxic waste on the Jersey Turnpike, what's to stop you?"

"For a lot of people, nothing. People see that they can get away with something, so they figure 'Why not?' Sometimes they get caught, sometimes they don't. For me personally, I chose not to operate that way. Even when I think I can get away with stealing that box of felt tip pens, I don't. I see myself as a member of a lot of different communities: at home, at work, as a citizen of various governmental entities. I make the choice, as a member of those communities, to abide by the rules. And I expect my kid to abide by the rules. I tell her that's the price of living with other people.

---

And she seems to comprehend that, without heaven or hell entering into the picture."

"O.K. I'll buy that you make the choice to be a good citizen of wherever." By now, Richard's tone of voice had shifted from dismissive declarations to calm consideration. "But what I'm still not buying is what happens when, let's say, you disagree with those rules? Are you saying that you just have to suck it up and submit?"

"That's one option. Or you can try to change the rules from within. Or you can break the rules and take your chances of getting caught. Or you can move to Canada."

"If they'll have you."

"But you're right. I don't consider myself an automaton, a blind follower, or a mindless model citizen. The point is that you *can* disagree. You *should* disagree. Disagreement is what keeps the rules fair and society healthy. It's what keeps the rules in sync with an ever-changing world. That's the problem I have with an absolute morality dictated by God and written down in the Bible. There's no room for disagreement, for evolving with the times, for adapting to changing circumstances. The rules that worked in ancient Judea are supposed to work in 21st century U.S.A. And in a lot of cases, they don't."

Richard soaked all this in, nodding his head slightly as he looked out at the road ahead. He reached into the glove compartment and pulled out his hash pouch. "So what's the verdict on me smoking pot?"

"Illegal. Immoral. No question."

"Good," he said, unzipping the pouch and filling the bowl with his one free hand. "I prefer being an outlaw."

\* \* \*

About two o'clock in the afternoon we passed a sign: *Gas Food Next Exit.* As we were again running low on gas, Richard conceded to stop for refueling and lunch. A mile down the road, we took the exit to find a gleaming, unnaturally white Kwiky Mart plopped down on the otherwise unpopulated terrain.

Richard parked the car beside a row of gas pumps and got out. In accordance with his vapor lock theory, he decided that we should let the car cool down for at least 20 minutes. I went inside to pay and find something to eat.

Inside, the store was divided in half. To the left were shelves of tourist impulse buys: hats with goofy sayings, *Welcome to Washington* coffee mugs. A sign hanging from the ceiling read *Traveler's Necessities.* Below it was half an aisle of auto supplies, half an aisle of toiletries, half an aisle of groceries in junior-sized boxes, and two full aisles of nothing but candy, in a mind-boggling variety of shapes, colors and goofy names. Resisting temptation, I wandered over to a near-empty post-card rack and found a picture of a combine harvesting a field of wheat above which red block letters read: *The Other Washington.*

On the opposite side of the store was an eating area: four wood-veneer tables surrounded by folding chairs. Three women, wearing generic uniform blouses, sat at one of the tables, drinking sodas. Beyond them was a counter where you could order food from a glass case. Inside the case were several stainless steel serving trays filled with fried chicken and large slices of fried potatoes. That was about it. There was no menu and no one behind the counter. I waited for a minute, a customer in need of attention, but none of the three women seemed to notice, carrying on their conversation as if I wasn't there. Maybe they didn't work here.

"Excuse me? Do you folks work here?"

The eldest woman slowly turned her head and looked me up and down before responding: "Yeah. What can I do for you?"

"Can I get some food?"

"Sure. I guess." She nodded to the youngest of the three, who rolled her eyes, took a sip from her soda, pulled herself to her feet and trudged over behind the food counter. Her lack of enthusiasm bordered on comedy. "What do you want?"

"What do you have?"

She looked down at the serving trays, annoyed at having to state the obvious.

"Chicken and potatoes."

"That's it?"

"That's it."

"OK. I'll have a piece of chicken."

"You can't buy just one piece of chicken. You either have to buy the chicken meal or the chicken dinner."

"What's the difference?"

"One has three pieces, one has four pieces."

"I can't just buy one piece?"

She called over to the older woman, seated at the table. "Can he just buy one piece of chicken?"

The older woman, like an irritable mom tired of having this conversation, didn't hesitate a beat: "No. Either a Chicken Meal or a Chicken Dinner." The girl who was serving me simply shrugged. The law had come down from on high. It was out of her hands.

It didn't even occur to me to argue. "Fine then. Whichever one is the three piece."

In slow motion, she picked up a cardboard box and a pair of tongs. "You get two sides with that."

"What are the sides?"

"Potatoes, coleslaw, baked beans, corn bread. I forget what else."

"O.K. Cole slaw and corn bread."

"All we have is potatoes."

I was beginning to suspect a hidden camera.

"Well then, I guess potatoes it is."

What this establishment lacked in variety, it made up for in quantity. No pawning off scrawny legs and wings as chicken pieces here. No sir. My "meal" consisted of three plump chicken breasts, two full orders of fried potatoes and a 48-ounce drink to wash it down. All for only $6.95.

Outside, Richard had moved the car into a small patch of shade cast by the station's towering sign. He was sitting in the open driver's side door with his bag of almonds. I opened the passenger side and sat down next to him, juggling my big box of chicken, sack o' taters and sloshing bucket of Coke, feeling like a poster boy for obesity. As I pulled out a chicken breast the size of the average chicken, Richard watched in calm disbelief.

"Believe it or not, this is the smallest amount you can buy. Want some?"

"No thanks. I don't eat fried food. And I don't eat chicken."

Whatever. I settled into the passenger seat with the door open, balancing all this food on my lap, my legs hanging out of the car. As I began picking away at the chicken and slurping down the Coke, Richard patiently nibbled on his almonds.

"So you just eat almonds? Is that it?"

"No. I have other things in here. Some dried fruit. Some oatmeal."

As I mentioned earlier, back in high school, Richard was the fat kid, always overweight, always feeding his face, never one for exercise. I wondered what had caused the transformation.

"When did you get so food-conscious?"

He held up an almond, pondering a second, weighing how much he wanted to tell me. "It's been kind of a lifelong battle. The short answer is that a few years ago I bent over in a chair to tie my shoes and got so disgusted with myself, I decided it was do-or-die time."

"So what did you do?"

"Started to exercise. Took walks everyday. Stopped eating fast food. I gave up fried food, pastry, candy, all the usual suspects. Basically stopped being a pawn to the Junk Food Industrial Complex. Now I tend to graze versus the traditional breakfast lunch dinner drill. The reality is that you need a lot less food than you think."

I couldn't agree more, but..."Easier said than done." Eating was one of the aspects of my life I wished I had more control over. But, driven by force of habit or laziness or whatever, here I was again, eating some slab of fried chicken that would no doubt leave me feeling sick to my stomach in an hour. What was Richard's secret? "Don't you ever just yearn for a cheese steak or a chocolate glazed donut?"

"For me it was not so much about specific cravings. It was about eating when I wasn't hungry. That has always been the nut of the issue for me. Eating to satisfy some other hunger than just a physical one."

"So what did you do?"

"It wasn't easy. Basically, I had to confront all the other psychological crap I was carrying around. Take a long hard look at how I was using food to bury some other unmet need."

"Like what?"

"In my case, you name it: money, sex, love, security. Pick one. Whenever I couldn't get what I wanted on one of those fronts, I would eat. Because eating was easy. It usually didn't involve having to interact with other human beings. But it also didn't satisfy what I was really craving."

"So how did you break that habit?"

"Determination and persistence. Just like any other addiction. I just kept reminding myself how sick I was of being overweight and out of shape. And gradually, I'm talking years here, I managed to unplug from all the previous conditioning, the lifetime of bad habits, and replace it with a life of my own design."

I'd looked down at my half-chewed chicken. It had never occurred to me how much a simple meal could reveal about the ongoing drama of one's life. Richard ate a final almond. "For me, it became a matter of whether I wanted to spend the rest of my life wallowing in the muck, or whether I was ready to stand up and move on. The toughest part is that you've got to confront all these other areas of your life where you're not satisfied, not happy. You've got to look at what a mess you are on all these other fronts. You've got to set aside the Big Mac, turn away from the Super Gulp, and start dealing with all that shit that you've been avoiding dealing with for so long. All those other things that you're starved for."

"Not an easy task."

"No. Frankly, it sucked. I was miserable. But I was also determined, because there was no way I was going back. It's all about trying and failing, trying and failing, having some success, failing and falling back, trying and failing. One bite at a time. Eventually, a little success builds on the last little success. One day, you look down and you see you've made it a hundred feet up the cliff. You drive by Burger King and you realize the thought of picking up a quick Whopper never even crossed your mind. And that, my friend, is sweet victory."

Richard's revelation reinforced my suspicion that, even in this myth-less world of ours, the hero's quest is still alive. The only thing that's changed is the face of the beast.

Richard got out to pack away his almonds. The sun had come around the sign and our little patch of shade had moved on. I was about halfway through the first chicken breast and feeling more than full. Suddenly spooked by whatever demons were urging me to finish it, I tossed the half eaten breast and quarter full vat of Coke in a nearby trashcan and stowed the rest in the back.

Across the parking lot, a wiry man climbed out of the cab of a semi, parked in a far corner of the lot, which had been there since we'd arrived. The guy looked like he'd just woken up. His half-buttoned shirt was half-tucked into his blue jeans. He hadn't shaved in a few days. As he crossed over to the store with long slow cowboy strides, he ran his hand through his thin hair to smooth it down, then put on a brimmed cap. He gave us a wordless nod as he passed.

"Ahh, the good life," Richard commented, "Nothing quite like waking up in a truck stop in the middle of the afternoon."

"I thought the idea was drive all day and sleep at night?"

"There's no night and day in trucking. It's all a game of timing your arrival. My guess is that he wants to hit Seattle after rush hour." He looked at his watch. "Time to hit the road. Your turn to drive."

From the perspective of the driver's seat, the Bug seemed even smaller, like driving a bumper car. I fastened the lap belt, put it in neutral, pumped the accelerator and turned the ignition.

Nothing. Great.

"You have to pump it seven times, keep your foot on the gas, then turn it over, and pump a couple more times."

So I pumped seven times, held the gas down, and hit the ignition. Sure enough, the engine turned over. I coaxed it to a full heartbeat with a few more pumps of the gas. To my relief, it held idle.

"See that? It just had to cool down. Vapor lock."

Works for me. I shifted into first and steered toward the access road. Driving the Bug was a little trickier than I'd expected. The manual steering was a few notches shy of precision. You had to wrestle it into each turn, like steering a power mower. The brakes sounded and felt like metal grinding against metal, suggesting that Richard considered brake pads to be another unnecessary luxury item.

But at least we were moving... though not for long.

Midway across the overpass, the accelerator stopped responding. I pumped the pedal as instructed, but it was no use. Lacking gas, the engine sputtered, coughed and died. The Bug coasted to a stop.

Richard remained unflustered. "We fixed it once, we can fix it again."

He got out and lifted the rear lid. I followed. By the time I got there, he already had the top off the carburetor.

"Aha. Here's the problem."

I glanced down over his shoulder.

"What?"

"Check out this fuel line." He pointed to a rubber hose held up by a...wait a minute...is that a coat hanger?

Richard explained. In a VW Bug, the gas tank is in the front (after all, what would a head-on collision be without a nice explosion?). The fuel pump, located beside the engine, sucks the gas backward via a rubber hose. Mike, Richard's mechanic, had replaced this rubber hose, but apparently with one that was not quite long enough. Instead of running it up and safely over the red-hot exhaust manifold, as the German designers had apparently intended, he was forced to take a more direct route, which left the hose sitting on top of the manifold. Having the foresight that this might lead to a problem (like igniting the fuel line), he cleverly used a bent piece of coat hanger to give the hose maybe an inch of clearance. I'm sure it seemed ingenious at the time. But (surprise, surprise!) after 300 miles of driving, the coat hanger had begun to sag, lowering the fuel line closer and closer to the hot plate of the manifold and, at least in Richard's mind, causing our vapor lock problem.

Richard bent the coat hanger up and wiped his hands.

"That was easy."

He then proceeded with unflagging faith to perform his gas-down-the-carburetor ritual while I sat behind the wheel turning the ignition on command.

"Now."

Pump seven times. Turn the key. ROAR!!!! Ease down on the gas. Cough, cough. Die.

After a half dozen failed attempts, I suggested maybe he should try to start it himself. After all, he knew the car better than I did. He agreed. I got out and after a few more attempts, the engine turned over and held.

"There you go." He put it in neutral, pulled up the hand brake and crossed back to the passenger seat. "All set."

I climbed back in, and off we went.

The conversation turned to a game of "Remember the time?" Remember the time we did this? Remember the time we did that? Remember the time we drove to the Jersey shore? Remember the time we cut our school ties in half with scissors? Remember the tree we used to sit underneath during lunch? Remember the giant spider web?

"What giant spider web?" Richard asked.

"Don't you remember? Senior year we made a spider web for art class that went from the ground all the way to the second story. In the courtyard. I thought you'd worked on it?"

"No," he replied, "That was after my time."

At first I wasn't sure what he meant, then it hit me: As I'd mentioned earlier, Richard had been expelled from high school. The exact details were obscured by rumor and legend. I'd heard he'd gotten into a fistfight with the principal. Then I'd heard he'd gotten caught with pot in his locker. In all these years, I'd never directly asked him for his side of the story.

"When was it exactly that you were expelled?"

"Two weeks into senior year." I'd forgotten that it had been that early on.

"You know, I don't think you ever told me what happened."

Richard smiled. "That's because I preferred not to talk about it." He paused, considering whether or not he wanted to talk about it now. "It all went down during lunch period..." The entire senior class, roughly 350 kids, ate together in a large cafeteria with two dozen long rows of tables. Along one wall stood a row of vending machines: soda, candy, chips. Most of us brought a bag lunch and bought a drink and a snack.

"I was standing in line to buy a soda. There's like four or five people in front of me. So I'm patiently waiting my turn. Just as I get to the front of the line, this vending machine guy steps in and opens the machine to refill it. I say, 'Excuse me. Can I buy a soda first?' He tells me to try another line. But the other lines are now ten people long. So, pissed, I mumble to myself 'Fuck this' and walk away. I go back to the table to eat lunch with no soda."

"A minute later, I feel this presence hovering over my shoulder. I look around and the guy's standing behind me. He says to me: 'What's your name, young man?' I look up, wondering what this is all about, and say, 'Why do you want to know?' He says: 'Did I just hear you use vulgar language?' I said, 'I don't know. Did you?' The guy just stares at me for a second, not saying a word. So I go back to eating my sandwich. He takes off and I figure that's the end of it. Two minutes later, he comes back with Mc-Smithy."

Father McSmithy was our new principal. He had a portly, Santa Claus body, thin middle-aged hair, and military-issue glasses. Most of the time (at least when he was around students) his face was scrunched into a bulldog scowl that gave him the look of a meek bureaucrat trying to act tough. Mort Mussolini. Wandering the halls with his hands behind his back, grimacing like a bad actor, occasionally giving somebody grief over a crooked tie, he seemed harmless enough, all bark.

Richard went on with his story: "McSmithy makes this little gesture with his index finger and says, 'Follow me.' So the three of us go to the main office. He tells me to sit in the waiting area while he and the vending machine guy go into his back office. A couple minutes later, they come out. The vending guy's got a gloating look on his face. He splits, and McSmithy again motions with his index finger for me to follow him. So I do. He holds open the door to his inner sanctum and I step up to his desk, my back to him, waiting for the door to close and him to walk around, sit down in his big leather chair and ask me for an explanation. But that's not what happened. 'Turn around,' he says. So I start to turn around and before I'm even facing him, BAM! He smacks me in the face."

"He punched you?"

"Yeah. And as I didn't expect it, he caught me off balance and I fell down. He's standing there, looming over me, and he says, 'Get up.' All very calm and in control. So I got up. I didn't say anything. I just look him in the eye. He looks right back at me and then, BAM, he hits me again. Only this time I was ready. I didn't fall down."

I sensed he wasn't making any of this up. "Then what did he do?"

"He says, 'Go to your locker and get your books. I want you out of my school. I'll call your parents to come pick you up.' That was it. I didn't say word one. I went to my locker, cleaned it out and came back to the main office. The secretary tells me that my mom is on her way. So I just sit there with all my stuff. Everybody else in the office carries on like nothing happened. About an hour later, my mom shows up. She has no idea what's going on. Before I get the chance to explain anything, McSmithy appears and takes her back in his office. They're in there maybe five, ten minutes when she comes out, looks at me, and says, 'Let's go.' Very resigned. And so we just went."

"What did you tell her?"

"I told her exactly what happened."

"And what did she say?"

"Not much. At that time, she was pretty overwhelmed. She had my four younger brothers and sisters to worry about. I think she was browbeaten into accepting this as a *fait accompli*."

"Did you tell her that he punched you in the face?"

"Yeah."

"And she didn't have a problem with that?"

"I think we both knew that it was wrong, but she had no ability to confront the situation properly, and I was so buried in my own bullshit that I was pretty much ready to give up by that point anyway."

"It didn't bother you?" I know it bothered me.

"Not really. I was kind of used to it."

Kind of used to it? What did that mean? It was one of those comments that's like a door, opening to a back room of someone else's life. What do you do? Do you ignore it? Do you step inside?

"What do you mean, 'I was kind of used to it'?"

He stared ahead, weighing whether or not he really wanted to go down this road. "I had received far more physical abuse at the hands of my father, may he rest in peace. A couple of slaps from a fat priest didn't really faze me all that much. I just figured that this was the way it was."

I had never met Richard's father. He had died the spring before Richard was expelled. Sudden heart attack. I knew about it only because Richard had missed a few days of school and my mother saw an obituary in the paper. He came to school the day after the funeral like nothing had happened. He never talked about it, and I don't recall him showing any sign of grief. He seemed to prefer keeping it to himself. And so the subject went away.

"I was pissed that I was kicked out on such a lame excuse, and made a lot of noise for a few weeks. But I was far too timid to do anything concrete. The whole experience just felt like a huge confirmation that I was somehow 'less than.'"

"Less than what?"

"Less than what I was expected to be. Academically. Socially. Physically. Less than *I* expected myself to be. I was like the living embodiment of disappointment. I'd gone into high school with all this promise: grade A student, the son who's going to grow up and make everybody proud. And I end up getting thrown out of high school for some stupid nothing bullshit."

All this was news to me. I flashed back on my conversation with his wife Meg about his barely speaking to anyone in his family for the last 14 years. And that made me wonder what this trip was really all about.

But we had many days and miles for all that. And Richard seemed to have said all he wanted to say for now. I decided that the occasion called for opening a few doors of my own. It seemed only fair. It turned out I had a Father McSmithy story I'd never told anybody outside my family.

"You know, McSmithy tried to throw me out too."

"Really? When?" Richard replied, happy to change the subject.

"Spring of senior year, I think it was. I never told you this?"

"No."

I had been the editor of the school newspaper. The newspaper was a harmless enough affair: four mimeographed pages of news people already knew and sophomoric stabs at humor. Despite its utter innocuousness, before it could be printed, I had to submit it to the principal for approval.

In the April issue, I decided to hazard an attempt at some satire. I wrote a piece about a school where magically, overnight, all the students had been transformed into washrags. Rather than be upset by this turn of events, the teachers and the principal felt no cause for alarm. In fact, they saw a definite upside. As washrags, the students would be easier to keep in line. And they'd be cleaner.

I submitted the four-page newspaper with the washrag piece to Father McSmithy for approval. In retrospect, I can't imagine what I was thinking. I guess I just wanted to see how far I could push the envelope. Turned out, not this far.

I was called out of class to the principal's office. I got the same "clear out your locker and go home" order, minus the beating. I was told that I would not be allowed back in "his school" until my parents and I came in for a meeting. This was two months shy of graduation.

I remember walking home midday in a state of shock. My parents were half furious, half baffled. I couldn't begin to explain to them what I had done wrong, because I wasn't sure myself. Calls were made to the parish priest to intercede on my behalf.

Later that afternoon, my parents and I went to see Father McSmithy in his office. Sitting behind his desk, holding the only existing copy of the newspaper as if he were reading from it directly, he accused me of writing an article about three girls who had gotten pregnant. As if that weren't bad enough, he added that I mentioned them by name, mentioned their boyfriends by name. Scandalous. Outrageous. Was it my intention to bring down this entire school? Was that my nefarious plan? Well, he wasn't going to allow it. As long as he was in charge, he wasn't going to allow a wiseass like me to defile his precious institution. I deserved no mercy. After all, what mercy had I shown these poor unfortunate Christian children? I deserved to be expelled.

"But…"

"I think we've heard quite enough out of you, young man."

My parents sat in slack-jawed disbelief. After 15 minutes of this hellfire, the good father revealed that in his mercy, he would open a path to salvation, give me a single shot at redeeming myself: if I were in his office first thing tomorrow morning, with a rewritten newspaper and a sincere apology, he would consider letting me back in.

On the ride home, my parents were furious. How could I do such a thing? Only then did I have an opportunity to defend myself, to say that the offending article had nothing to do with pregnant girls. It was about a school where kids turned into washrags.

They didn't believe me. When we got home, I showed them my rough draft. They were stunned. But they were also pragmatic enough to insist that I rewrite the thing and do as I was commanded. And so I did.

The next morning, contrite, washrag-free newspaper in hand, I arrived at school and went directly to the main office, where I sat and waited through homeroom and well into the first period. Finally, one of the secretaries told me Father McSmithy was ready to see me.

I walked back to his office and knocked on the door before entering.

"Come in."

I went in, closing the door behind me. He sat at his desk, apparently absorbed in some paperwork, my fate a minor distraction in his routine. Finally, he mumbled: "What do you have to say to me?"

It was like forcing down a tablespoon of foul medicine.

"I'm sorry."

"Did you take that crap you wrote out of the newspaper?"

"Yes." I handed him the rewrite. He read it over and set it aside without comment. Then he pulled something out of his desk. A satiric, homemade comic book that had been put out a few months earlier by two wannabe comedians. I had read it. It was less offensive than my washrag piece.

"Before you can return to my school, I want you to tell me who did this."

This prick had not only lied to my parents and forced me to apologize for something we both knew I never did, he now wanted me to rat on two equally innocent friends so he could subject them to the same sadistic treatment.

And the worse part was, he knew he had me. I tried to squirm out of it, saying I didn't know their names. He pulled out a year-book and laid it open in front of me.

"Then find their pictures."

He was determined to rob me of my dignity, to drag me down to his level of loathsomeness. And to my shame, I did it. I lacked the intestinal fortitude to do what I should have done: tell him to go fuck himself.

I got to graduate and stay in the mainstream. The two guys behind the comic book were put through the grinder. They weren't expelled, though I never asked what did happen to them. And I never told them I was the one who turned them in, though I don't doubt McSmithy did.

So much for a good, upstanding Catholic education.

"What a pig," was Richard's reaction. Oddly enough, he found my McSmithy encounter far more egregious than his. "That's why I hate religion. They pick a sadistic nutcase like that to tell *us* how to behave." I had to agree. At the time, McSmithy certainly seemed to be a gold standard for evil.


Evil. There's an idea for you. There's an adage among actors that "you can't play evil." To portray a credible villain, you have to find some positive motivation for that character's actions, because in reality, most bad guys aren't being bad for the sheer hell of it. They are driven by some positive agenda, defending some way of life they feel is being threatened, seeking justice for some perceived wrong. They see themselves as good guys from a different army.

In hindsight, I don't doubt that from his perspective, Father McSmithy's motives were entirely justified. Perhaps he felt he was entrusted with the moral upbringing of a whole school full of impressionable teenagers. Perhaps he saw it as his duty to get rid of the bad apples, to squash any questioning of his authority or judgment. In stormy seas, a ship needs a strong captain.

I'm not sure that I'd call him evil now, not because I think he's any less of a prick, but because I'm not sure I still believe in evil. The idea of evil leads back to the idea that morality is somehow absolute, that it comes from outside humanity, that the same rules apply to all people everywhere, laid down in the holy scriptures, created by God. The idea of evil presupposes a world of black and white, lacking shades of gray, all seen from one perspective only.

Granted, evil is a very tempting idea. Believing in it lifts an ethical burden from our shoulders. It frees us to react with an unfettered conscience, a clear-eyed sense of certainty; it gives us the ability to go through life without all that moral hand wringing. To attack without hesitation. To fire at will. Amen.

But that idea of evil is also what empowers people like McSmithy to behave so badly, to justify their actions, to impose their will because they're "doing God's work". They're stamping out the devil, fighting evil. How can you argue with that? The most despicable deeds of terrorists and tyrants are motivated not by the desire to create good, but by the desire to destroy what they perceive as evil. This idea of evil is a luxury today's world can scarcely afford.

And so what do you do? How do you respond to that kind of misbehavior? Do you just let him get away with it? Do you just accept that even psychos have their own perspective? Live and let live? That doesn't seem right either.

I think this bind is what so infuriates the religious right about moral relativists: they can't make up their minds. They're too chicken shit to see the devil for who he is. While they're busy wringing their hands and trying not to offend anybody, the forces of evil are infecting the souls of humanity like so much dank, polluted air.

And they have a point. I think we need to be able to look at the Father McSmithys of the world and declare, flat out, "You are wrong." Not because *we* say they're wrong, but because they *are* wrong, as measured by some standard that transcends us all.

Here's what I believe: morality is neither absolute nor subjective. It is objective. Ethics comes from a community, from a group of people trying to work out acceptable rules for coexistence so they can reap the benefits of cooperation and cohabit the same space with a tolerable sense of security. As members of a community, we give something (freedom, time, money, energy) in exchange for something else (food, shelter, security, assistance, organization, companionship). We agree, overtly or implicitly, to abide by the ethical standards of that community. Our fellow citizens have the right to expect us to behave according to those standards. If we don't, they have the right to do something about it: to complain, to refuse to deal with us, or to call the cops. A community has the moral authority to enforce its rules upon its members, to judge someone's actions as wrong, to provide justice.

Which isn't to say these objective communal laws are set in stone, because communities are not set in stone. They need to change as the world changes, incorporating new people, new ideas, new technologies, new economic circumstances, new threats, and new opportunities. They have to coexist in a world that contains hundreds of other communities. For that to happen, the rules need to have some flexibility. To adapt to an ever-changing world, the rules need to change as well. For a community to thrive, it needs to allow dissent. Citizens must have the right to object. There needs to be some mechanism for weighing complaints and bringing about change. Not for the benefit of the individuals, but for the benefit of the community. A community that refuses to listen, a tyranny that insists on absolute control, ultimately suffocates itself. Morality is born from community and, like a living thing, it must be allowed to grow and adapt to the world around it.

The key to a successful community is in how its members perceive themselves. In the context of a community, we become more than self; we become parent, teacher, worker, leader. We take on roles that demand that we set aside our individual priorities and accept those of the community, to become something greater than an isolated individual. Community demands transcendence.

And that's where it interfaces with the spiritual. One of the recurrent themes of religion is transcendence—acknowledging some power greater than self. Most religions emphasize the virtues of sacrifice, charity, forgiveness, love—virtues contrary to self-interest, virtues that benefit community.

But what is a community? Isn't it just a product of the imagination, a story whose existence depends on the people who believe in it? In that sense, a community is not unlike an unseen god or spiritual realm. Both Zeus and Valhalla are now considered mythical, not because anything physically disappeared, but because people stopped believing in their existence. But what about Babylon? What about America?

Are we so different now, in the 21$^{st}$ century? Cross the border of any state line and see what really changes: the land is continuous. The border exists only because we believe it does. Or, more accurately, it exists because a group of people share the belief in its existence, behave as if it exists, and enforce laws that presume it exists. This belief is the key to transcendence. It brings this thing called community into existence, creating an entity that allows the individual to overcome the gravitational pull of the self. But it's a belief that ultimately requires a leap of faith, faith that this community we belong to is real.

We passed a road sign indicating the exit for Washington's capital, and it occurred to me that Olympia was no less mythical than Olympus.

# 5

## THE CHASM OF DISAPPOINTMENT

D riving was better than being a passenger, if only because it gave me something to focus on—and there wasn't a jet of hot air blasting my leg. Getting a little breeze going was a tad tricky. The crank that controlled the driver's side window was so stiff that it took both hands to turn. Fine tuning the airflow meant waiting for a straight stretch of road where it was relatively safe to briefly steer with my knees while using both hands to lower or raise the window. There was a small, triangular vent window, but it was held in a fixed position by a jerry-rigged clamp Richard had bought at Pep Boys.

"Don't touch it. The clamp tends to fall off when you mess with it." Richard also warned me to keep the car below 65 mph, given our vapor lock issues. Just to keep things interesting, a VW Bug has no heat gauge or warning light, because it's one of the few cars with an air-cooled engine. There's no radiator, thus no radiator fluid that can overheat. This was allegedly a design spec requested by Hitler himself. With world conquest in mind, he wanted a car that could be relied on in both the North African desert and the frigid wastes of Siberia. Evidently, nobody told him about vapor lock.

Route 395 headed northeast, joining up with Interstate 90 about halfway to Spokane. The landscape remained barren, broken only by optimistic stabs at farming. Every four or fives miles, patches of green flourished under immense, self-propelled irrigation systems: a quarter-mile line of pipe, held twenty feet in the air by triangular towers, spaced every 100 feet or so, with wheels on their base. There was no driver, no control room (or at least none that I could see). Somehow this whole contraption drove itself back and forth across the field, like a robot overseer with a watering can, delivering controlled, manmade rain showers to the parched earth.

"Do you know what those things are called?" I asked Richard.

"What things?"

"These irrigation towers we keep seeing."

"I think they're called pivots. There's usually a water pump in the middle and they rotate around it in a circle." I flashed back on all those mysterious green circles I'd seen from airplane windows while flying over the Midwest.

"These fields don't look like circles."

"Maybe they've figured out some way to make pivots go in straight line. Or maybe it's just an optical illusion."

We fell back to talking about the past. I realized how little I knew of Richard's life after he left Jersey.

"When was it that you moved to Tulsa?"

"Let me think. A couple years after high school."

"What prompted you to move there, of all places?"

"You remember my roommate, Bob?"

Bob was a high school dropout who lived briefly with Richard in his garden apartment in Jersey. "Yeah."

"His parents moved to Tulsa for work. His father got transferred, I think. So he followed them, and I went with him."

"Why?"

"Why not? Adventure. Getting away from Jersey. I figured, what have I got to lose? We lived with his parents for a while, then we rented this little one room apartment over a garage."

"What did you do for work?"

"I got a job for an oilfield-supply outfit, hauling pipe around northeastern Oklahoma, which is how I got my first taste of truck driving. That's where I met John—Big John, everybody called him. He was huge: six-four, 300-plus. One of the seminal characters in my life. He could handle a semi like he was tying his shoes. He and I worked side-by-side for about a year, unloading railroad cars. Crate after crate of these forged steel flanges and fittings, load after load of pressure tubing. They had me driving a short truck called a bobtail and a 20-foot flatbed. Straight rigs, because I didn't have experience driving the 'float': a Ford tractor hooked to a 40-foot trailer. Now John, he could poke that thing in a hole barely wide enough to hold it. It was pretty amazing to watch." The memory lit up Richard's face.

"How long did you do that?"

"A year, maybe. John eventually left to drive for J.B. Hunt, cross-country hauling. I stayed in Tulsa, and went to work moving office furniture and such, until one day my back gave out. I got carted off to the hospital where they did a spinal tap. Turned out I had a partially ruptured disc between vertebrae 14 and 15, which pretty much spelled the end of my heavy lifting career."

"So what did you do for a living?"

"I drove a cab for about 4 months. At that time, Bob was working at a place that processed microfilm. I figured, what could be easier to lift than microfilm? So I kept calling the guy who did the hiring, until they had a job opening. And that's where I learned to operate this thing called a COM machine: Computer Output Microfilm. Documents in, microfiche out. It took the picture, did the processing, all in one. They had me doing the four-to-midnight shift, squeezing 200 sheets of paper onto a little tiny photograph. It was Kafka material."

"Were you still living with Bob?"

"No. Shortly after that, Bob moved to Salt Lake City. I was living in a little one-room apartment in a run-down brick building, right on the edge of downtown Tulsa. I could walk to work."

"What was that like?"

"It was a fairly solitary existence. There were a few people I hung out with. Actually, there's a funny story about one of them: Bobby D. He was a little surly guy. Basically, a small time criminal. He was a bad check writer, originally from Connecticut. How I hooked up with him, I don't even remember. But there was something about him that didn't bother me, and he and I, we could talk, you know?"

I tried to imagine a 20-year-old Richard hanging out with the Tulsa underworld.

"Anyway, about a block away from where I lived, there was this restaurant, Jerry's Restaurant. I'd go in there every day. I'd get up at nine after working until midnight, walk down to Jerry's and order a BLT. I'd sit there and eat it with my coffee. It was like that every single day. The same thing. So they knew me. The waitresses knew me. Jerry, the owner, knew me. I was a regular."

"One morning I'm in Jerry's with Bobby. D. We were just sitting there chatting, whatever. All of a sudden, Jerry comes over, swipes up Bobby's coffee cup and orders him out of the restaurant. Which was not like Jerry. He was an older guy, in his sixties, and pretty mellow 95 percent of the time."

"I was like, what the hell is this? I looked at Jerry and I said, 'What are you doing? He's just sitting here talking to me. There's no reason to be acting like this.' Jerry's all wound up, and he explains that Bobby D. had been bothering one of the waitresses, and he doesn't tolerate that kind of behavior in his place, and so on. I figured there had to be something else going on, but he wasn't telling me. Clearly, he was not going to relent. He was going to kick this guy out."

"So I said to him, 'Jerry, look, you know who I am. You see me come in here every day, sometimes twice a day. Now, if you don't put his coffee right back, in fact, give him a fresh cup, I'm gonna walk out of here and you're never gonna see me again.' And there was, like, this moment of silence. It lasted about ten seconds. I can see Jerry thinking, giving Bobby D. the eye, glancing at me, thinking. I was totally prepared to walk out of his restaurant, never to return. I didn't care. I'm staring at Jerry, not backing down. It's like a showdown in some cowboy movie. Who's going to make the first move?"

"After about half a minute, Jerry shakes his head. He doesn't say a word. He just turns, picks up the coffee pot, pours us two fresh cups of coffee, puts them in front of us, and walks back to the cash register. I was shocked. Here this guy, in his own place, decided that keeping me around was more valuable to him than getting rid of this lowlife. A rare moment of glory in an otherwise dark and dreary existence."

Richard smiled to himself. His expression made me reconsider the value of small victories. We have this tendency to think that life's milestones are always big events. Graduations and weddings. But that's not always the case. Sometimes, our biggest breakthroughs in life hardly seem all that significant at the time. But often, it's the baby steps—the showdown with a guy in a restaurant, the laughter at a one-act play, the sentence uttered on a car trip cross-country—that can have the greatest impact, and that can change forever who we are and who we become.

The Bug drove flawlessly for the next several hours. By late afternoon, the dry, rolling hills became lush, evergreen mountains. We passed through Spokane and headed due east again, into Idaho.

For my money, Idaho is the most beautiful state in the country. I'd been through here before, on a family vacation a few years back when we drove from Boise up to Glacier National Park in Montana. The landscape is thickly wooded and largely undeveloped. What towns there are seem refreshingly free of the franchise sameness that has turned so many other American towns into clones. As the interstate began to weave its way around ever higher mountains, the late-day vistas unfolded like an IMAX movie.

I wanted to stop in Coeur d'Alene, partly to get gas, partly to just briefly *be* somewhere. As we came up to the first of its half dozen exits, I floated the idea of stopping for dinner or even the night, but Richard refused to even consider it. His rule was that we had to keep driving as long as there was daylight (and thus our moral code began to take shape). I wasn't hungry enough after my chicken extravaganza to argue. So we passed the last Coeur d'Alene exit and kept going.

Until now, Richard's truck driver style of plowing ahead hadn't bothered me all that much. But as Coeur d'Alene slipped away, I began to realize that I might pass through the great state of Idaho without so much as touching the ground. A cloud of disappointment settled over my spirit like a slow fog. My inner defense attorney began stirring up my conscious mind: what was the point of this manic effort to log miles? At this rate, we'd be in Fargo by Tuesday morning, with nothing to do but hang out until Mars got off work. We'd be in Jersey by Thursday. I hadn't signed up for an endurance contest. I was actually hoping to see a little bit of America here, have some adventure, at least step away from the car once a state. This nonstop driving crap sucked.

Ten miles later, this interior monologue percolated up into actual conversation. "So what's the plan here, Richard? Are we just going to drive until we drop or what?"

"We still have some good daylight left. We can get a solid way into Montana tonight. Last time I did this drive we made it to Butte the first day."

Objection! Your honor, I'd like to point out to the court that it's 5:15 p.m. and Butte is another six hours away.

But let's not get hysterical here. Stay calm.

"Don't you ever like to stop somewhere? Just to check things out? Walk around, see what there is to be seen?"

"Not usually, no."

It's funny how expectations go unnoticed until they go unmet. As we blazed through Idaho, my disappointment morphed into resentment as the experience that I'd expected seemed to be slipping away. My road trip fantasy was turning into a vision of dreary 15-hour days of nonstop driving.

The soothing voice of my inner guru was trying to calm my ranting attorney: "Remember, grasshopper, this is not a vacation. This is a spiritual journey. The whole point is to challenge expectations. Do what I wouldn't normally do. Surrender to the experience. Go with the flow. Blah, blah, blah.

"How about we just shoot for the Montana border?"

To Richard's credit, he sensed that he was pushing me too far. "Fine."

With our goal for the night resolved, I noticed a more pressing problem. We were running out of gas. One of the great things about Idaho is that there isn't a franchised gas/convenience store/ fast food multiplex every 20 miles. But there's a down side. Fifty miles east of Coeur d'Alene, we'd yet to pass our first gas station, and the dial had dipped below "E" big time. With all Richard's carburetor priming, even the gas can had to be near empty.

For the next 20 miles, we passed nothing but towering evergreen cliffs, crystalline streams and the occasional log cabin. Running out of gas is, of course, a sure recipe for adventure. There's that silence when the engine takes its last gasp; that "where are we?" feeling when you first get out of the car; the hitchhike trek along the shoulder as its gets colder and darker by the minute; the grateful ride in the back of some pickup truck to a gas station 10 miles up the road; the trip back in a tow truck, making lame excuses to the toothy mechanic who's heard it all. "We'd thought for sure there would be some place to buy gas east of Coeur d'Alene…"

Been there, done that, and frankly, it wasn't the kind of adventure I was in the mood for. It was an adventure for knuckleheads. An odyssey for the obtuse. I had hoped that between us, we'd be a little more seasoned than that. At least on the first day.

Fortunately, we were spared that experience. Riding on fumes, we turned a bend in the road and I saw a *Gas Next Exit* sign. A beacon in the storm. I took the off ramp without a word, and half a mile up a two-lane road, came upon the solace of an unassuming mom-and-pop gas station/food market.

I eased the Bug up to the single pump and got out. Pulling out my ATM card, I discovered another pleasant surprise. You could fill up your tank *before* paying. "Check this out." I hadn't been to a gas station in years where they actually trusted customers not to rip them off. As I began to fill the tank, Richard wandered into the store to find a restroom.

When I went inside to pay, he was talking to a middle-aged woman behind the counter, telling our story: that we hadn't seen each other in 30 years, that we were driving all the way to Jersey in his old Bug, that we'd been having 'vapor lock issues.'

I remembered that I needed to buy an Idaho postcard. There was a small rack of them in the back corner. I bought one that featured a photo of the Bitterroot Range, because it reminded me of Lewis and Clark. When the Missouri River had taken them as far west as it went, they set off on foot, hoping to find an Indian guide to lead them across the mountains just south of here. After wandering the woods for a few days, they came upon a group of Shoshones on horseback. They followed them back to their village and bartered supplies for a few of the older horses. But no Shoshone wanted to lead them across the Bitterroot Range. Few of them had ever been across it themselves. Though it was only September, it was already snowing. Finally, an old man, whom they dubbed Old Toby, agreed to be their guide. He led them along a dubious, winding route across the Continental Divide.

They traveled by foot, in the snow, using the horses to haul supplies. It took them over a month. It struck me as quite an act of faith to follow this old guy through the mountains, clinging to the hope that this crazy journey was going to lead somewhere other than disaster.

I paid the woman behind the counter for the postcard and the gas. Richard filled his coffee mug and pulled out his money clip to pay for the coffee, but she waved it away. "Free coffee with a fill-up."

That made Richard's day. "Pump your own gas. Free coffee. I love this state."

Every journey has its ups and downs. Moments when everything seems to go wrong get offset by moments when everything seems to go right. One minute, you're riding on fumes, the next you're drinking free coffee.

I stepped outside and looked off at the mountains and tried to imagine slogging through them in the snow, following an old Indian guide whose language I didn't speak. Where does faith that strong come from? What hope allows you to put yourself that far out on a limb? What kept Lewis and Clark's ragtag army from turning back, from deciding that the whole idea was delusional, crazy?

Richard took over driving. He set down his coffee and turned the key. This time, the Bug didn't wait until we got back on the road before stalling out. This time, it refused to start right there, at the gas station.

Richard didn't flinch. Without a hint of irritation, he got out, pulled the gas can from the front, opened the back hatch, popped off the air filter cover, and started pouring shots down the Bug's carburetor throat. I stood there watching him without saying a word. He got back in and turned the key. After only two attempts, the Bug was purring like a kitten.

"It's getting colder. So the engine is cooling down faster."

Works for me. I got in the passenger seat and we headed for Montana.

It was June, the month of longest days, especially in these more northern latitudes. By seven o'clock, the sun was still hours from setting. We had crossed into Montana and the conversation had faded. I dug out the CD player and earphones that Meg had loaned me and tried listening to Beethoven's First. Unfortunately, the roar of the car overwhelmed the CD player's meager wattage. I tried to mentally tune out the background noise, but that only made it louder. Halfway through the first movement, the noise had become foreground. Against my will, my mind began to pick apart the cacophony, distinguishing between the sound of the fan belt, the engine cylinders, the tires on the road surface, the various whistles and roars of wind leaking into the car. A dissonant symphony. Without hope of resolution.

"Can we please stop and eat somewhere?"

"Just say when."

As in Idaho, road stops remained few and far between. I sighed and gazed out the windshield, waiting for a sign. Ten minutes. Nothing. Twenty minutes. Nothing. Finally, after forty-five minutes, we passed a handmade, wooden sign: *Katy's Kitchen Just Ahead*. Two miles east, there was a larger sign, the size of a billboard, all lit up. A stark red arrow pointing to the right. Above it was a cartoon of a bucking bull, its eyes bugged out and bloodshot red to suggest intoxication, and the words: *Welcome to*

*Katy's Kitchen, Home of the Rocky Mountain Oyster.*

For the uninitiated, Rocky Mountain Oysters are bull testicles, a delicacy that until then I'd assumed was urban legend. We pulled off the interstate onto an unlit dirt road that led to a large, near-empty parking lot. Behind it was a long, two-story building, decorated with a patchwork of flickering neon and rusty metal road signs that advertised a multitude of beers, hard liquors, and chewing tobaccos. A wooden porch ran along the front, with arrows pointing to the restaurant, to the sports bar, and to *Rooms for Rent*. A large mural, painted on two sheets of plywood, portrayed a bacchanal of whooping cowboys and drunken steers celebrating *The Testicle Festival!* Above the door, a metal plaque read *No Assholes Allowed.*

It all seemed a little contrived, meant to appeal to the car-bound, cross-country vacationer itching for a little eccentricity to justify all this driving, but I wasn't complaining. Here, finally, was something promising, an experience we were likely to find nowhere else.

Unfortunately, once inside, the contents didn't quite match the packaging. Sunday was an off-night for the Testicle Festival. The guy behind the counter informed us that not only were Rocky Mountain Oysters out of season, but the cook had just shut down the fryers. As everything on the menu involved frying, that meant no dinner.

The sports bar was only slightly more promising. Several hundred caps, from every imaginable sports team, covered just about every inch of wall space. A quiet handful of unenthusiastic locals were half watching the final quarter of the NBA Finals—L.A. Lakers versus New Jersey Nets—on several wall-mounted TVs, all with the sound inexplicably turned off. There was no music.

Nobody was talking. A sleepy woman behind the bar informed me that it was just about closing time.

I looked at my watch. "It's only eight o'clock."

"That's closing time."

"Can I at least get a beer?"

"As long as you buy it in the next thirty seconds."

So I bought a beer. Richard asked for a glass of water. We sat at a small bar table and stared at the TV.

"So much for the Testicle Festival."

"Well," Richard noted wisely, "that may be a loss we should be thankful for."

Determined to make something of the moment, I went back to the car and dug out my bag of leftover chicken and fried potatoes. I returned to the bar table, watched the silent game, and tried hard to enjoy the beer and cold chicken. That lasted maybe 10 minutes. By then we were both happy to get out of there.

Outside, dusk had finally turned to dark. The sky was overflowing with stars. The aforementioned rooms for rent, which loomed darkly at the top of a rickety outside staircase, held zero appeal. So it was back on the road.

This time, the Bug started on the first try, a result Richard, still preaching the gospel of vapor lock, attributed to the cold night air. We pulled away from Katy's and drove back up the dirt road to I-90. We got maybe 100 yards down the interstate, when the engine once again, for no discernable reason, stalled and died. Richard coasted to a stop on the pitch black shoulder.

Without saying a word, he fished for a flashlight he had stuffed under the driver's seat and began the ritual anointing of the carburetor. Figuring I should at least do something, I got out and stood at the back of the car, picking up the flashlight he had resting on the engine while he poured gas, and silently tracked his hands with the beam.

"You still thinking vapor lock?"

"What else could it be? We just didn't let it cool down long enough."

He set down the gas can and crossed to the driver's seat to crank the ignition. It roared to life and died. A passing car zipped by without so much as slowing down. Richard got out and tried again. And again. I held the flashlight and shut my mouth, listening to the distant croaking of pond frogs.

The Bug turned over and held idle on the third try. Richard screwed the cover back on the air filter, replaced the gas can in the front, and got back in the car.

"Let's go."


By now, my fog of disappointment was morphing into a downpour of despair. We drove in silence, reaching Missoula about half past nine. I was beginning to feel like a kidnap victim. The incessant blast of hot air was scalding my right calf. The sensory deprivation of the big sky darkness wasn't helping. Not only could we not stop, now we could not even see where we were.

"Can we stop soon and get some rest?"

"Sure. I just wanted to get past Missoula. Next town."

The next town turned out to be another 50 miles away, an oasis of fluorescent light called Deer Lodge. Two franchise motels, two service stations and not much else, at least in the near distance. We pulled into the parking lot of the Deer Lodge Super 8, and settled our overworked steed into a parking space.

The Deer Lodge Super 8 was a standard issue, stucco highway

motel. I went inside the front lobby where a desk clerk, a kid in his mid-twenties, was sitting behind an orange Formica counter, flipping through the pages of Maxim magazine.

"You got any rooms for the night?"

He looked up at me, then clicked a few keys on a computer that was on the counter below. "Single or double?"

Richard came through the door holding his duffel bag of clothes. I assumed he had lost his desire to sleep outside next to the car. "A double," I said, pulling out a credit card. Now that we were finally stopped, I felt a restless energy. We'd driven close to 600 miles and it felt like I'd been nowhere and done nothing. Even the Testicle Festival turned out to be a tease.

When I went back out to the car to get my bag, I noticed that adjoining the Super 8 was something called the Lucky Five Casino. I couldn't hear any sound coming from inside, but it appeared to be open for business. I asked the desk clerk as I headed up to the room, "Is the place next door open at this hour?"

"The casino. Yeah. Open until 11."

Richard was already in the room, unpacking his bag and getting ready to take a shower. As I set my carry-on down on the far bed, I told him about the casino and asked if he wanted to check it out. He was content to take a shower and go to bed. So I went on my own.

From the outside, the Lucky Five seemed unusually low-key for a casino. No flashing neon, just a small sign with lively lettering and a nondescript front door, a place slightly embarrassed to be in the business of catering to mankind's baser appetites.

Inside, it looked like a standard small town bar. Dim lighting that favored reds and golden yellows. My first reaction was: Where's the casino? There were no slot machines, no electronic blackjack games, no nothing. No sign of gambling whatsoever. Two elderly couples sat at the bar. All four of them were easily over 70 and dressed for line dancing, the men in brand new, tight-fitting jeans and bright, sky blue cowboy shirts with pearl snap buttons; the gals in billowy skirts, puffy blouses, and big hair. But the line dancing, if it had happened at all, was long over. Even the jukebox was silent.

As I got closer, they all turned to look. All four had deeply weathered faces, with long crevasses running like mountain ranges down dark leathered cheeks. They were all blearily, hardcore drunk. Their eyes were bloodshot and yellowed. Their boney hands clung trembling to their drinks. Their heads bobbed as if the fear of falling over absorbed their full attention. Through the veil of my sour and foreboding mood, they seemed a bad omen, a dark vision warning me away from the rocks.

"Can I get you something, hon?" the woman behind the bar asked.

I nodded towards the couples and one of the men nodded back. Then they all turned to face the bar, heads still bobbing, gazing at their reflections in the mirror.

"A beer. Please."

The bartender drew me a draft. I paid her and walked away from the quartet, into an adjoining room that had a pool table. A television mounted on the wall played QVC in silence. What was it with TVs around here? Did nobody turn up the sound? Back in the bar, the two couples continued drinking in equally eerie silence.

I shot a rack of pool and drank the beer, resigning myself to the fact that, despite my efforts, this day was determined to be what it was. When the last ball had fallen and the beer was gone, I put my cue back on the rack and surrendered my empty glass.

"Another?"

"Not tonight."

Back in the room, Richard was already sound asleep. But I was still wired. So I lay in bed, gazed up at the ceiling, and wondered what the hell I was doing here. At that point, the idea of a spiritual journey seemed pure poppycock. What was I thinking? This isn't a spiritual journey. This is bullshit.

It was hardly the first time I had encountered such flat-out disappointment. In my experience, disappointment is one of few things you can always count on in life. As kids, we're disappointed by what mom packed in our lunch bag, by the gifts we got for Christmas, by kids at school laughing at our new shoes that seemed so stylish in the store. Rather than outgrowing disappointment, it seems to grow with us. We're disappointed that we didn't get into the college of our choice, disappointed that the date we had such high hopes for turned out to be a dud, disappointed that the job we worked so hard to get turned out to be a thankless dead end, disappointed in where we live, disappointed by those we love, disappointed by who we've become.

Disappointment happens whenever the story we have in our head doesn't sync up with the reality in front of our face. We imagine a turkey sandwich and end up getting peanut butter. We picture becoming the next Spielberg and end up fetching coffee. We want Walden Pond and we get the Lucky Five Casino. We tell ourselves all these stories about the way life is supposed to be, and more often than not, it doesn't turn out that way. There's a gap. A chasm. And through that chasm flows disappointment, a cold river that stops us in our tracks.

What's that next step: Turn back? Morph that disappointment

into resignation? Eat the crappy sandwich with a sigh and blank stare? Dial your expectations down to zero? Get all cynical and withdrawn? Or maybe get dramatic? Stomp off the field, toss your lunch into the trash, complain loudly, point the finger, play the blame game and hope some sympathetic sop comes to your rescue? "Don't cry, baby. Everything's gonna be all right. Your story is true. It's reality that's wrong."

Maybe. Or maybe you forge ahead. Try to figure out how to ford the chasm of disappointment, maybe build a bridge or find an alternate route between the world in your head and the world at your feet. Get back in the ring, chin up, and pound away at reality until it either gives in or beats you silly.

Perhaps different disappointments call for different responses. You have to assess: How much do I want this? What do I need to overcome to get it? At what price? What went wrong this time? What should I do differently? What are my chances?

I remembered a prayer card my mother used to have on a refrigerator magnet: God grant me the serenity to accept the things I cannot change, the courage to change the things I can, and the wisdom to know the difference.

But what if God isn't there to grant you anything? What if you're standing at the edge of the chasm, the object of your desire on the distant shore, blurred by the heavy mist rising from the cold river of despair, and you pray, "Please God, tell me what to do. Should I turn back? Or should I dive into this river and hope I have the strength to make it to the other side?" and nothing happens.

Are there people who have that relationship to God? People who God actually whispers to and says, "Go for it" or "At least you tried"? If so, I envy them. Whenever I reach that chasm, I reach it alone. It's never obvious what to do. Inside my head, a debate rages like so many congressmen arguing over a piece of legislation. But somehow, that debate rarely results in a definitive answer. In the end, voting yea or nay always seems to come down to gut instinct. A gamble. An act of faith.

More often than not, in that situation, I back away from the edge of the chasm, either out of fear, doubt, or exhaustion. I decide the fight is not worth it, the risk too great, the dream too unrealistic. But occasionally, I find the courage to take the plunge. And when I do, more often than not, I make it to the far shore. Once I get there, sometimes what I find isn't what I had expected to find. Sometimes the effort only leads to more disappointment. But more often, it opens me up to a new and larger reality, the frontier of another side of life that I had suspected was there, but had never set foot on, had never seen with my own eyes.

So much of the world is closed off to us because when we reach that chasm of disappointment, we turn back. We choose to live out our lives on the same little piece of reality where we were born, preferring to believe the stories about all the dangers and demons that lurk on the dark far shore. But if we would just, every so often, set aside our stories and open our eyes, we might cross those boundaries we've made for ourselves, and discover that there's a vast Louisiana Purchase of life out there, a Promised Land that's ours for the risk of venturing.

Lying there in a motel bed, gazing down on the river, I realized that the Lucky Five Casino was indeed a place for gamblers.

# 6

# ACROSS THE MANY STORIED LAND

I woke up just before seven the next morning, bright light blaring through the window of the motel. Richard was already awake and packing to leave as I crawled out of bed and headed for the shower.

"Morning."

"Morning."

"How was the casino?"

"Not to be missed."

By the time I got out of the shower, he was gone, apparently to get an early reading on how the Bug was going to behave today. I was a little less eager to strap in for another 12-plus hours of non-stop driving. So I decided to make yet another attempt at eating.

There was a small breakfast room at the Deer Lodge Super 8 where they had set out coffee, orange juice, and a plate of cold and stiff mini-muffins. I grabbed some of each and took a seat at one of the three pink Formica tables. With no newspaper to read, a rack of brochures caught my attention. It stood three feet away, the brochures beckoning customers to visit a variety of tourist attractions. These racks are a fixture at most interstate motels. The attractions they advertise seem to be the same no matter what part of the country you're in. Hot air balloons. Ride the rapids. Petting zoos. Wine tastings. Car museums. Most of them also seem to be several hundred miles away, their ads placed here just to fill some quota ("Your brochure will be seen in over 500 motels!"). Canned adventures for those without the time or inclination to search out real ones.

One brochure, however, did catch my eye. It was for Yellowstone National Park. The crown jewel of the National Park system. A place I had never been. I reached over and pulled it out.

Yellowstone National Park, with its towering snow-capped mountains and Old Faithful geyser, has to be one of the most visited—and overrun—tourist spots in the country. But it is also spectacularly beautiful. And today was the first Monday in June, a Monday before school let out and the summer season officially began. And according to the map in the brochure, it was an easy side trip off our planned route. We could take Route 89 at Livingston, enter the park at the Wyoming border, head down to Yellowstone Lake, then take Route 212 northeast, connecting back to Interstate 90 near Billings. It added an extra two hours driving, three tops. Feeling a bit Chevy Chase, I decided there and then: "That's it. Come hell or high water, today, the Griswolds are going to Yellowstone."

Stepping out of the motel into the clear, chill morning, Deer Lodge looked entirely unlike the neon oasis of last night. There was still no sign of a town. Just this 21st-century stagecoach stop, a place intended only for travelers, with a few recently constructed chain motels and gas stations, hosed-down parking lots glistening in the morning light, and brilliant red and yellow signs as welcoming as a false smile. The road that came off the interstate ran only another a quarter mile before turning to gravel. No town. No deer. No lodge.

To the south, a distant blue-green mountain range held back ominously dark clouds. But in every other direction, the sky was bright and clear. Looking around, I could see immediately why they called this Big Sky country. The heavens were a Sistine Chapel of cumulus and cirrus: pink puffy cotton balls to the northeast, wispy vapors drifting in languorous slow motion to the west.

Richard was sitting in the Bug, driver's door open, listening to it idle like a proud parent listening to his kid's piano recital.

"Started up first time I turned it over. My Old Faithful."

"Speaking of which…" I showed him the Yellowstone brochure. "Check this out. It's on the way. Maybe take us an extra hour or two. Supposed to be spectacular. And I've never been there."

Unlike women and children, most men, certainly me at least, have a difficult time attaching emotion to our requests. We tend to keep a certain distance between ourselves and our desires.

Richard took the brochure, quickly flipped through it, then dismissively handed it back.

"I drove through it once. Just the top part."

I continued to press my case. Never been there. Monday in June. What's the big hurry? "At the rate we're going, we'll be spending a day hanging out in Fargo anyway."

I could see him factoring in the additional benefit of shutting me up.

"Sure. Why not?"

Hallelujah.

---

\* \* \*

Richard loaded the car while I checked out of the motel. Though we were again near empty, he opted not to get gas on the chance we'd find a Texaco station. The morning shift desk clerk had told him that there might be one in town. It turned out the town of Deer Lodge proper was one exit east.

So off we went. Day two. The Old Bug was running without complaint. The weather couldn't have been better. Both of us were in good spirits as we pulled back onto I-90. Like many of life's problems, our car troubles appeared to have simply gone away, like a bad headache or a foul mood.

Ten minutes later, we were one exit up the road, in the real Deer Lodge, a small town with actual hints of a history: a Western façade, an old fire station. Even a Texaco. And once again, Richard got free coffee with his fill-up.

"I'm starting to like this part of the country."

I bought a pack of peanut butter crackers to supplement my cold muffin breakfast and a Montana postcard for Esmé, a montage of scenic vistas with the words: *Big Sky Country*. Two hundreds years ago, when Lewis and Clark passed just north of here on the upper reaches of the Missouri, they came upon herds of buffalo as far as the eye could see, the occasional grizzly, clear water riddled with trout, a landscape brimming with possibility.

Back outside, the pale blue Bug shone like a puppy eager to play. It again started up with the first turn of the key. Richard took a long, satisfying sip out of his mug and then, shifting it to his right hand and raising up his right leg, he carefully maneuvered the mug down into the plastic cup holder he kept on the floor. It was a curious little juggling act he performed every time he took a sip of coffee. Not for amateurs, especially while driving. Years of practice had reduced it to mindless habit. Funny the things we get good at in life. With the coffee secure and his right arm free, he shifted the Bug into first. "I've got a feeling today is going to be a great day."

Interstate 90 in western Montana is one of those drives where you're content to just look out the window and watch the scenery. Unlike Idaho, with its tight turns and steep mountainsides rising up in front of you, the drive through central Montana is panoramic, with distant mountains north and south, and a middle ground of rolling green grass, visible for miles.

After last night's doubt and despair, today was radiant with hope. The darkness had become light. I wondered what had caused the shift. Maybe I'd just needed some rest. Or maybe my mood was somehow a reflection of the world around me. Last night, driving in the darkness, I felt lost, stuck in a car with a guy who had no desire to encounter anything, who just wanted to get this journey over with. But today, driving through the wide-open spectacle of western Montana, I felt back on track. I still wasn't sure where this whole spiritual journey idea was going, but at least I felt that it was going somewhere, and that allowed me to relax. To sit back and enjoy just being here.

"Now this is more like it."

Richard seemed to share my mood. "This is what I mean by spiritual benefit. Being someplace like this." It surprised me that he seemed to be thinking the same thoughts that I was. "This is exactly what I needed. A chance to step away from all the noise and commotion and find a little peace."

He was absolutely right. For all my fretting and complaining and resistance, it occurred to me that maybe I had something to learn from Richard. Maybe he was onto something that I'd overlooked. Maybe if I just shut up more and listened.

"Amen to that."

Whatever it was that he meant by spiritual, whatever it was that I meant by spiritual, I sensed that it might be something we had in common, some mythical golden fleece that we were both taking this journey to find.

In common. The word bounced around in my head, calling up its associates: Communication. Communion. Community.

We had entered Mountain Time just past Deer Lodge, losing an hour in an instant (demonstrating that hours are no less a figment of the communal imagination than borders.) By the time we passed through Bozeman and closed in on Livingston, where a road dropped south into Yellowstone, it was almost 11 AM.

Just before the Livingston exit, Richard asked if I wouldn't mind driving, claiming he had no patience for local traffic. That seemed a little odd. I couldn't imagine a town the size of Livingston having anything approaching traffic. Maybe he just wanted to symbolically turn over control of the helm for my little side trip. In any case, we pulled onto a small turnoff. The pit stop gave me another brief chance to be out in the clean Montana air. To the distant south, the mountains rose up until they disappeared into dark grey clouds. Yellowstone.

Richard didn't even bother turning off the engine. I got behind the wheel and shifted the car into first. Before we'd driven fifty feet, it started to lurch, making sudden jolts forward, like hiccups.

"What are you doing?"

"Nothing."

I merged back onto the interstate and shifted up, hoping speed might smooth out the problem. It didn't. The Bug continued to sputter and jerk forward. Then it gasped and glided. I pressed on the accelerator to no effect. It wasn't getting gas again. After yet another lurch, it died. I eased the car onto the shoulder.

"Crap." So much for a flawless day. This car was starting to get on my nerves.

"Not a problem," Richard reassured me, though I could tell the Bug's mysterious breakdowns were finally beginning to faze him. "I know what's going on here. The car's heated up and we're having the same vapor lock problem we had yesterday. That's got to be it. There's no other explanation."

I certainly had no other explanation. Richard got out and primed the carburetor yet again. I stayed in the driver's seat, turning the ignition on his cue. After two attempts, we got her running.

The surging symptom, in milder form, continued as I drove the last few miles to the Livingston exit. Then it got worse. I drove down the ramp and turned left onto Route 89. The car jerked and coughed its way past a stretch of tourist eateries and souvenir shops, including a place guarded by a life-sized grizzly bear chain-sawed out of tree trunks.

"It feels like it's gagging," I offered, trying to be helpful but not succeeding.

Richard didn't even hear me. He was lost in thought, like a doctor trying to assess a patient when he's not sure what's wrong, questioning his earlier, off-the-cuff diagnosis. The car ran for half a block just fine, then broke into another fit of backfiring and lunging forward. As we sputtered toward the southern end of town—the mountains of Yellowstone visible and looming in the distance—the car coughed a death rattle gasp and died. As it coasted to a stop in silence, I guided it onto the dirt shoulder.

Richard was having a hard time containing his frustration. He got out without a word and began the priming ritual. I sat at the wheel, awaiting his cue to start the engine, my eyes fixed on the mountains, beckoning, tantalizing, reminding me that this was why I came on this trip, to see America. And there it was. Towering in the distance. And here we were, on a dirt shoulder at the far end of Tourist Row, dead in the water.

Despite the day's upbeat start, the omens were getting ugly. For one, the dark clouds I had seen hovering above the mountains earlier this morning had grown even darker, into an aching, purple bruise, portending that the road to Yellowstone, a road no doubt leading up into far more serious mountains, also led into a storm, possibly a snow storm.

"OK, try it again," Richard huffed.

I turned it over. The Bug gave out a weak little roar that died even quicker than the last one, suggesting that we were draining the battery.

After a dozen attempts, the car was only growing weaker. And the gas can was nearly empty.

Richard set the can down, walked over to a small incline and sat down, staring at the car, perplexed. I got out and joined him.

He exhaled and shook his head. "This isn't making sense. I gotta think." The car just sat there. Sick? Defiant? Who the hell knew?

I wondered how Lewis and Clark would handle this breakdown? Back in 1804, you had to anticipate problems before you left home. No one would attempt a cross-country trip without first learning everything they needed to know to survive: how to find food, to make clothing, to secure shelter, to deal with medical emergencies and equipment breakdowns. If something went wrong, you either needed to know how to fix it or you were screwed. Meriwether Lewis spent two years preparing for the trip, learning medicine, geography, shipbuilding, botany, zoology, geology. He was already an expert hunter and frontiersman. William Clark was an expert mapmaker and navigator. They were dependent on no one.

Today, ignorance no longer stops people. We think nothing of driving a machine across the continent with only the faintest idea of how it works or how to fix it. In this complex world, we've lost the ability to solve our own problems. We operate on a faith so pervasive that we're rarely even aware of it. A faith that whatever happens, wherever we are, we'll find someone who has the expertise to fix it. Most of us can barely cook, much less hunt or forage for food. Few of us have any idea how to make our own clothing using a sewing machine and store-bought fabric, much less buffalo hide. Most of us have never slept outside under the stars. We wouldn't know how. The only way we know how to find shelter is with a credit card.

We live in the faith that whatever trouble we get into, someone will save us, that there's always an expert just a telephone call away. And we're right. We have evolved into a society where experts of every shape and size, specialists in every imaginable field, from transmission repair to open heart surgery, are distributed homogenously, thanks to the economics of supply and demand, throughout the population: a mechanic every two miles, a VW specialist every 100 miles.

I'm sure Richard would disagree. He took great pride in his self-sufficiency. Like Meriwether Lewis, he thought he'd brought along everything he needed, every supply, every bit of knowledge gathered from 30 years of owning VW Bugs. But as it turned out, all this amateur knowledge wasn't enough. He had reached an impasse.

Interestingly enough, Lewis and Clark reached a similar impasse not far from here. Lewis was aware that at a certain point on their journey up the Missouri River there was a series of waterfalls, collectively called the Great Falls, one of the few consistent details on the crude maps of the Louisiana Territory made by fur trappers. To continue up river, all their supplies would need to be portaged overland, around the falls. But there was no way to carry the heavy boats they had taken up river. So before they even left St. Louis, they knew they had a problem: how to get themselves and their supplies the rest of the way upriver to the Rockies and beyond to the Pacific.

Lewis's solution was to design and build a collapsible iron boat frame, which could be carried in pieces, then reassembled and covered with animal hides. His plan was to leave the larger boats below the falls and portage his iron boat kit. But he had no idea how to build a ship, much less a portable one. So he spent many months and many dollars studying shipbuilding, designing and overseeing the construction of this iron-frame boat, noting every minute detail in his journals. He became so obsessed with getting it right that the boat's construction delayed their initial departure by two months.

The disassembled boat, dubbed the *Experiment* by the apparently skeptical members of the Corps of Discovery, was hauled on a pirogue 2,000 miles up the Missouri. In the summer of 1805, over one year into their journey, they reached the Great Falls. A scouting mission revealed that getting past it would require an overland trek of 16 miles. Finally, Lewis would get to put his brilliant idea to work. The men hid the boats for their return trip, then proceeded to lug all their supplies and equipment, including the disassembled iron frame boat, up and over the rough terrain to the upper side of the falls.

Once they got it all there, Lewis began to reassemble the *Experiment* while the others hunted buffalo for hides to sheathe it in. Progress was held up for weeks as Lewis carefully prepared and sewed together dozens of buffalo hides, covering the frame, sealing the seams with a mixture of beeswax and tallow, allowing it to cure over a carefully tended fire. All in accordance with his arduously thought out plan.

In early July, he proudly recorded in his journal: "We launched the boat, she lay like a perfect cork on the water." That afternoon, a storm blew in and the seals that kept the buffalo skin seams watertight began to come apart. Lewis wrote: "She leaked in such a manner that she would not answer."

Time was running out. William Clark was eager to get over the mountains before winter set in. So Lewis was forced to abandon his brilliant idea. The other men, while they'd been waiting for Lewis to finish his iron boat, had been hollowing out tree trunks to make canoes. And it was in those roughhewn canoes that they continued west, abandoning the *Experiment* to rust in the shallows.

Richard and I had reached a somewhat less dramatic impasse, but an impasse nonetheless. The car was dead, and he didn't know how to fix it. We were stuck.

What happened next was one of those occurrences that restores the faith of the faithful, the kind of thing that would make a Christian perk up and say: "How can you say there's not a

God looking out for us now, huh?" It certainly felt like someone besides myself was writing this story.

Not five minutes after Richard quit trying to revive the Bug, a rattling pickup truck pulled up behind it. A local man in his sixties climbed out, bedecked in boots, cowboy hat, a silver and turquoise belt buckle, tanned and weathered skin, a loping walk and a bit of a beer belly.

"You boys look like you're having a problem."

He introduced himself as Delbert. Told us he used to own a Vee Dubya. Had to learn how to fix it 'cause nobody else in town knew how. In fact, if he recalls correctly, he had a '69 model. Had it for a year until he lost it in a lake.

Before I could ask about that, Richard launched into the telling of our particular tale: the fact that we hadn't seen each other in 30 years, were headed for a reunion in Jersey on Sunday, thought we'd take a little side trip through Yellowstone. Delbert nodded pleasantly as he soaked it all in. Richard stepped over to the open rear lid of the Bug. "We seem to have encountered a little problem." He described the symptoms and offered up his vapor lock theory.

Delbert bent down to get a closer look at the exposed motor. "Mind if I check out the points?"

"Go right ahead."

He asked Richard if he had a screwdriver. Richard fetched his box of tools from the front trunk and fished out a short flathead. Delbert used it to pry off the plastic distributor cap that covered the four spark plugs. Inside the cap was an elliptical plastic piece with two small strips of metal attached to the top. The two strips almost touched, creating a gap across which I assumed the spark from the plugs leapt. Apparently, these were the points. These points had not come up in any of Richard's theorizing about the car problem. They seemed to have no relation to the symptom of choked-off fuel supply. A skeptical Richard hovered over Delbert's shoulder with his arms crossed in protest.

"Looks like you've got too wide a gap here," Delbert declared.

"My mechanic set the gap just before we left. It can't be that off."

Delbert noticed a tiny black dimple on the one of the points. He scraped at it with the tip of the screwdriver.

"My suggestion is tighten the gap."

Richard wasn't buying it. "I'd prefer not doing that. Any chance there's a mechanic in town who can take a look at it?

Delbert took a moment to ponder Richard's question before replying. "There's Larry. I think he does foreign cars." He put the plaster piece with the points back in place and replaced the distributor cap. "Try it now."

More to humor the guy than for any other reason, Richard climbed behind the wheel and turned over the ignition. The car started first time.

"Oh, my God."

"I'd have him check your points."

Delbert also suggested we rethink our day trip into Yellowstone, offering an extensive list of good reasons: a storm was coming, my cell phone wouldn't work in the park, and it was a bad place to break down. "Don't know if you know anything about the government, but they're not the world's most responsive people."

He then told us how we could find Mechanic Larry: head back through town, past the tracks, past John Deere, turn right at the welding place, and he's right there. We thanked him, and with Richard back at the wheel, made a U-turn and headed off in search of Larry. Goodbye, Yellowstone.

Driving under the interstate, we found ourselves in something that actually resembled a town. There were houses, a fire station, even a main street, lined with classic Western false façades. I could imagine the long-gone wooden sidewalks. In lieu of Yellowstone, this was a place I wouldn't mind being stuck in for a day.

But our goal, at the moment, was to locate Larry. So we passed through town, crossed the set of tracks, went by the John Deere distributor, and passed a white stucco building that had *Welding* painted on the side in stark black letters. We made a right and half a block up found a garage surrounded by a herd of sick-looking Hondas and Toyotas. Overhead was a peeling, sheet metal sign: *Larry's Foreign Auto*. To me, it was a rare piece of luck: breaking down within a mile of what was probably one of a few foreign car specialists in a hundred miles.

Richard was far less reassured. The last hour had been a full frontal attack on his VW belief system. "I don't like this already."

He shut off the Bug and we went to find Larry. Inside was a large, dark open area with four or five half-assembled cars in a row. A guy smoking a cigarette and wearing a hopelessly grimy T-shirt had his head buried under the nearest hood.

"We're looking for Larry."

The guy glanced up at us, pausing for a second to decide if we were customers or trouble. "Think he went to lunch." Just before diving back under the hood, his eye caught a man emerging from the back office. "No. Hang on. That's him right there."

Larry walked towards us, wiping his hands on a paper towel. He was in his thirties, wearing gray overalls and smoking a cigarette. "Hey. What seems to be the problem?" Richard gave him an only slightly abbreviated version of our story. Old friends.

Old car. Cross-county trip. High school reunion. Larry didn't seem impressed. He said he was on his way to lunch, but he'd take a quick look at the Bug.

Larry opened the rear hatch while Richard explained his take on what was wrong, pushing his vapor lock theory, briefly mentioning Delbert and the points. Larry didn't seem to be listening. "See if it turns over."

Richard climbed into the driver's seat and turned the key. Damned if the Bug didn't start, first try. Richard shut it off and tried again, hoping the car would fail him as faithfully as it had just 15 minutes ago. It didn't.

Larry shook his head and delivered his initial verdict. "You know you don't have a heat shield on this thing." A heat shield, I learned, is a sheet of metal that is supposed to be between the back seat and the motor to keep car interior from getting too hot. For some reason, Richard's mechanic Mike had either forgotten to put it back or decided to leave it off.

Larry was also amused by the coat hanger.

"Never saw anybody try that before. The fuel line is supposed to come up and around over this way."

Lacking a symptom to diagnose, Larry had only Richard's description. He avoided getting into the vapor lock versus points debate. "Could be a lot of things. Dirt in the fuel line. Clogged valve." He said he was disinclined to start taking the car apart in the hope of finding the mystery problem. "I could change a few things, but a hundred miles down the road, you could run into the same problem."

He told Richard to figure out what he wanted to do. Meanwhile, he was hungry and it was lunchtime. He'd be back in an hour.

*   *   *

It was 12:30 and we had yet to pause for a decent meal since leaving Portland. Our car had just broken down and we had no idea why. We were in a state with few towns and many miles between them. I figured that, food aside, a break for lunch would at least give us the benefit of weighing our options. It seemed more than a little foolhardy to drive away from one of the few guys in this very large state who might be able to get us out of this jam.

Richard disagreed. He didn't trust Larry. A good mechanic should have been able to pinpoint the problem. He wasn't about to start throwing money into a "fishing expedition."

"I still say vapor lock," he proclaimed, like a zealot who, despite evidence to the contrary, refused to betray his faith. He borrowed my cell phone to call Mike back in Portland.

By now, my mind was in full backpedal. Delbert the Heretic seemed to be onto something with his points theory. And Larry the Local Wizard at least possessed the credibility that came from owning a foreign car shop: if he didn't know what he was doing, he wouldn't be in business. On the other hand, Mike the Mechanic, lord of the coat hanger rig, had dropped more than few notches on my credibility scale. I flashed on an image of a guy with a sign around his neck that read: "Will work for pot."

Richard got Mike on the phone, explained our situation, and ran through his argument for vapor lock.

"Ask him about the points," I butted in.

Richard waved me to silence as he listened to Mike's pronouncement, made entirely on the basis of Richard's more-than-skewed presentation. "Uh huh, uh huh, uh huh. Exactly. That's what I thought. Thanks."

He handed me the phone and headed for the car.

"What did he say?"

"Same thing I've been saying all along. Vapor lock. He said when we stop we just need to give it an hour to cool down."

We got in. The car started right up. Richard spun it around and headed towards the interstate. "It's running, and as long as it's running, I say let's keep pushing forward."

Earlier this morning, Richard and I seemed to be finally in sync. We were both living in the same story, so to speak, both in agreement as to what we should be doing and why. Two characters in the same movie. At least, it felt that way to me.

Now, a brief breakdown later, we were back in our separate worlds, working off different scripts. Richard had his story and I had mine. In Richard's story, he played a guy who believed in the power of Bugs, a belief reinforced by his minister mechanic. Bugs were simple. Bugs were reliable. Bugs didn't let you down. Bugs were machines that didn't require dependency on a world of strangers. Any evidence to the contrary was dismissed as blasphemy and only made him want to cling even more fervently to his story. Because within that story, his role was clear. The world made sense. He knew what his character did in that situation. Run. Get out of this heretic town full of skeptics and doubters, apostates and inquisitors. Flee all their confusing and conflicting advice. Never let reality get in the way of a good story.

I, on the other hand, was more conflicted. Until now, I was willing to accept the basic premise of Richard's tale, to play the follower, the unquestioning Gilligan. Richard knew this car, and I didn't. So my character deferred to his judgment.

But now *my* reality was conflicting with that story. The captain seemed to be coming unhinged. I saw him trusting people who rig fuel lines with coat hangers, while turning his back on people who scrape off points and actually get the car running again. I'm feeling like maybe I've boarded the *Bounty* here. This guy could get me in trouble, and I'd better start questioning his judgment soon, or I'm going to end up with my thumb out on a Montana interstate. In my story, there was something mysteriously wrong with this car that neither one of us understood or was capable of fixing. We had come face-to-face with the unknown. And when you are face-to-face with the unknown, the best course of action is to stop and assess your options. Stay put until we could get this car to die on us again, with Larry as our witness. I'd be happy to stay here overnight. Hell, maybe there was even still hope of seeing Yellowstone. If it were up to me...

This development shed a new light on my emerging philosophy of story-as-source-of-meaning. These stories of ours not only have the power to unite; they also have the power to divide. Much human conflict is triggered by incompatible stories. In *your* story, you may see yourself as making the best of a bad situation. Your story tells you to keep the faith. Hold course. But in *my* story, I'm being dragged down a sinkhole, asked to follow the judgment of a guy whose grip on reality I no longer trust. In my story, it's getting near mutiny time. Time to challenge the accepted wisdom of our little world. Time for a showdown.

Like so many friendships, so many marriages, so many nation states before us, events had caused our stories to diverge. The same reality was interpreted from different perspectives, seen in the context of different worlds with different rules, different values, different priorities, different ways of responding to problems. Neither of our perspectives made sense to the other person. The other person was acting crazy. I was left with three choices: fight, flee, or surrender. I wasn't ready to flee just yet, and I wasn't on firm enough ground to fight. My mutiny story was still a rough draft. Maybe I was missing something. Maybe Richard was right.

I also reminded myself, once again, that recent events could be viewed in the context of yet another story. In that story, I was on a self-proclaimed spiritual journey, the whole point of which was to let whatever happens happen, to turn off the stories and look out the window at raw reality. If we broke down in the middle of nowhere Montana and had to hitchhike to the next exit, so what? Maybe that would be the most revelatory experience of this whole trip. For the time being, that was a story I could live with. So, I chose surrender. I decided not to battle him over what to do about the Bug.

But I felt that I deserved a concession prize: "Can we at least stop and grab some lunch?"

Richard looked at his watch. "It's only 11:30."

Now, you may recall the small detail of our crossing into a new time zone earlier that day. By my watch, which I had reset to Mountain Time, it was 12:30. Everyone here in Livingston would no doubt agree with me.

"We're in Mountain Time. It's 12:30."

"I don't reset my watch."

"What?"

"I don't reset my watch. I'm always on Portland time. And I don't eat lunch before noon. So let's just get out of here."

Spiritual journey, I reminded myself. What is time, anyway, if not some made-up fiction we've talked ourselves into believing? Spiritual journey. Spiritual journey…

We turned onto the interstate ramp without another word.

———

\* \* \*

We drove another hour and a half to Billings, where Richard finally agreed to stop and eat, not because he wanted a sit-down meal, but because according to his Vapor Lock Theory, the Bug was due for its afternoon nap.

We took the last exit in Billings and landed at an up-and-coming franchise called *The Chow House*. In a gesture of goodwill, Richard decided that, this time, he would concede to actually going into the restaurant.

We went inside and got a booth. The hostess left us with two giant, laminated menus. Richard opened his as if it were some rare object of wonder. "Wow. Big." I recalled him telling me that he rarely went to restaurants. He searched the menu's dozen plastic pages for something that fit his narrow definition of healthy food.

"What's a chef salad?"

"It's a salad with a lot of stuff on it. Lettuce. Cheese. Some kind of meat, probably."

"It says it's got ham in it."

"You can ask them not to put ham in it."

"You can do that?"

"Yeah."

The waitress was a young Hispanic woman. Richard, feeling a socialist's discomfort at having someone waiting on him, started joking with her. No, wait a minute. Flirting with her. "Good afternoon!"

"Hello. Welcome to the Chow House. My name is Elani."

"Elani. That's an unusual name."

"May I take your order?"

"I'd like this chef salad here, but would it be a big problem to leave out the ham?"

"Not at all."

"Thank you. I appreciate that, because I don't eat ham."

"It's no problem at all."

"You're very understanding."

The waitress turned her attention to me.

"I'll have a club sandwich. With everything. Thanks."

Elani smiled and walked away. Richard followed her with his eyes until she disappeared into the kitchen. "Like I say to Meg, there's no harm done looking at all the merchandise on the shelves."

It was an unexpected remark coming from Richard. In high school, our little post-Hippie clique had a fairly pathetic record when it came to girls. Maybe it was the Catholic thing; maybe it was '70s feminism; maybe we were just geeky. I had had a few more-or-less girlfriends, but I couldn't recall Richard ever so much as expressing interest. He was the fat guy.

"Now that I think about it," I said, just to stir up a conversation, "back in high school, it seems we were all pretty much a bunch of losers when it came to women."

"I know I certainly was."

We began trading recollections of different girls from high school. I asked him if he remembered Lynn, a girl with long, thick, insanely curly hair. "I was crazy about her for the better part of a year. But she was going out with some guy from Florence."

"She was hot. I liked her. You remember Ginny?"

"No."

"Reddish hair. Always looked like she'd just fallen out of bed."

"Geometry class? She used to raise her hand to ask a question and wave it like someone shipwrecked." I demonstrated. "Save me, Mr. Plutarski."

"Yeah. I always liked her."

"She was a mess."

"But in a very erotic sort of way."

"Absolutely. You gotta love that in a girl. Remember Cindy?"

"The girl who looked like Linda Ronstadt?"

"Kind of. She and I were in the same art class, and we did an art project where we sat in a pitch black supply room with the door closed."

"Art project?"

"Yeah. It was sort of performance art."

He laughed. Then there was Linda, Anne, Jennifer, Ellie... I could only imagine what these poor girls thought of us.

And then there was Mindy. Mindy was this classic blonde who fluttered around the periphery of our tribe. Blue-eyed and long-limbed, she was our own little Siren, luring us one by one onto the reefs to break our boyish hearts. I knew of at least four guys who couldn't resist the temptation of her rocky shores. It turned out Richard was no exception.

"I've never told anybody this before, but I guess in the spirit of self-revelation we've got going here..." He stopped. Long, long pause.

I prodded. "Never told anybody what?"

"Were you aware of the note?"

"What note?"

"I thought everybody knew about the note."

Richard, in his adolescent turmoil, had written Mindy one of those it-seemed-right-at-the-time-I-was-writing-it, high-school-crush notes and slid it in her locker. It apparently didn't have the intended effect. Though she never mentioned it to Richard, she apparently showed it to half the school. Or at least to the two people who later advised Richard to give up hope.

"I could tell they'd read it."

High school boys are frequently dismissed as hormone-intoxicated sex addicts. Which is true, but doesn't do justice to the subjective side of the experience. Almost all of my friends in high school were oldest sons, lacking the corrupting influence of older brothers. All of us had been brought up in a Catholic culture where sexual desire, not to mention expression, was equated with weakness and sin. When nature sprang this strange obsession on us, we were ill prepared for it. We were junkies ashamed by our addiction, and clueless as to how to satisfy it. And it appeared that the wounds those years of bungling had inflicted upon us had not entirely healed.

I suppose they never do.


After its hour-long siesta, the Bug started up without complaint. I had to admit, maybe I was wrong. Maybe I could use a little more of Richard's faith.

I took over driving as we continued on from Billings, getting off I-90 and onto I-94, which led northeast into North Dakota. Richard figured we could reach the Montana border by sundown. I made a case for stopping for the night in Glendive, the last bold-type town on the Montana map, maybe 50 miles shy of North Dakota. Past there, we could get stuck having to drive all the way to Bismarck to find a motel. Besides, if we started tomorrow morning in Glendive, we'd make Fargo by mid-afternoon, just as Mars was getting off work.

Richard put up no resistance. The appeal of having a few hours of daylight to check out a town seemed to be gaining ground with him. Or maybe it was just that the apparent victory of the Vapor Lock Theory had put him in a generous mood.

Our conversation drifted back to the past. Richard asked me about the time I'd hitchhiked cross-country. Midway through that trip, I'd passed through Tulsa and hooked up briefly with Richard. It was my fourth day on the road. After my evening camped out in the backyard of the family outside Philadelphia, I'd spent one night in an eight-dollar motel, then a sleepless night in a trailer park, so I was glad to see a familiar face.

"What happened to you after you left Tulsa?" he wanted to know.

It had been such a long time ago. "I kept going west. Amarillo. New Mexico. In Arizona, I remember, a family from Oklahoma picked me up. They were driving one of those long, family station wagons with fake wood siding. Car loaded to the gills. A couple kids in the backseat. Said they were moving to California. But for some reason, they stopped to pick me up. Which is kind of unusual, for a whole family to give you a ride. Usually, it's just loners who want somebody to talk to. Anyway, the dad asked me if I'd ever been to the Grand Canyon. I told him no. I'd never been anywhere west of where we were at that moment. So he decides that I have to go to the Grand Canyon. Not to be missed. Experience of a lifetime. He was so intent that he actually got off the interstate at Flagstaff and drove 100 miles out of his way to drop me off at the entrance to Grand Canyon National Park. The wife and kids were just as into this as he was. They were all like 'Go for it. Go see the Grand Canyon.' I couldn't believe that for all they had going on, they would go to this much trouble for a total stranger."

"Wow. What did you do?"

"I went to the Grand Canyon."

"Did they go with you?"

"No. They dropped me off and headed back on their way. For some reason, it was just very important to them that I go to the Grand Canyon. They all waved goodbye like I was their long-lost son. It was quite amazing."

"So did you camp out?"

"Well, it turned out that the only campsite available was halfway down the canyon. So I hiked halfway down the canyon. It was beautiful. Everything the guy had promised. The next day, I hiked down to the bottom. And that was even better. I camped right by the river. I remember sitting there at night, thinking, 'Can you believe this? Here I am. At the bottom of the Grand Canyon.'"

"Did you eventually make it to California?"

"Yeah, a couple days later I was in San Francisco. I hooked up with another hitchhiker who let me crash for a couple days in Berkeley, then I found a room to rent by the week. One room, with a shared kitchen and bathroom. The only window looked out on a brick wall."

"What did you do for money?"

"I somehow convinced the landlord that I could do odd jobs, and so he hired me to paint. I eventually painted the whole building, inside and out. When I wasn't doing that, I was exploring the city."

"How long were you there?"

"A couple months. By Christmastime, the building was painted, and I felt I'd accomplished whatever it was I'd come to accomplish. Asserted my independence. Taken hold of the wheel. One day, I saw a sign stapled to a telephone pole for a bus service called the Grey Rabbit. *SF to NY only $50*. It turned out to be a converted school bus that two enterprising hippies would drive from Haight-Asbury to Port Authority in New York – like a hostel on wheels. They'd ripped out the seats so they could create more storage by raising the floor. So you had to lay on plywood for three days with 30, 40 other people. Trading war stories and germs. We landed in New York at 2 in the morning, and I took a bus from there back to Riverside." My hometown.

After that, I'd spent half a year in Jersey before heading back to a college in Ohio. I recalled that Richard had also eventually returned to Jersey after his self-imposed exile in Tulsa. But again, I was sketchy on the details.

"How long did you live in Tulsa?"

"About five years."

"Didn't you go back to Jersey for a while?"

"Yeah. At a certain point I had this realization like 'What am I doing here?' I was still working in microfilm, but nothing much else was going on. It occurred to me, I could have been in and out of college by now. So come Christmas, I ran home to Jersey like a whipped pup. I signed up at Burlington County College. I got a job at a microfilm place over in Cornwall, just north of Philly."

"Were you living at home?"

"No. I'd occasionally stop by the house, but my mom and I were keeping our distance. By then, I had officially become the black sheep of the family."

"So you were going to school and working at the same time?"

"Yeah. I'd take classes in the morning. Around three, I'd drive over to Cornwall to work the late shift. At first the job entailed driving around Center City with an old retired Philadelphia policeman to pick up boxes and boxes of documents to take back to the worksite. Then I was put on another COM machine, which was supposedly some highly skilled job. A crack addict could operate this thing. So I'm going to college, studying whatever, I can't even remember. I'm working full-time, I'm doing all these things not because I wanted to do them but because I figured, 'Oh well, I'll do what is expected.'"

"How long did that last?"

"About a year and half. I gradually realized that there was no way I was ever going to do what I assumed was expected of me. I'd given it a try, and it wasn't working. I was as miserable in Jersey as I was back in Tulsa. Then one day, out of the blue, Big John contacted me. He was passing through town with a huge tractor-trailer load of Alaskan king crab legs. So one night he stops at my workplace, at the microfilm company in Cornwall. I come out and I see the truck and I decide, 'Fuck it. I'm out of here.' I go back inside and tell the shift supervisor that I quit. It was quite dramatic. All my coworkers came out and saw me off. I jumped up into this semi with just the clothes on my back and the money in my pocket and took off for parts unknown. It was classic. Take this job and shove it."

"Where did you go?"

"We drove up to Bangor, Maine and went to some fruit juice distribution facility and picked up a whole truckload of some kind of juice bottles. And we took that load to Florida. And from there we picked up a load for California. That was a great trip, because the weather was nice, it was springtime, and I had just thrown off the shackles of that job and that whole Jersey scene. And I was going to places I had never been before. I got to see America on the thousand-mile-a-day plan."

* * *

Somewhere around 5:30 local time, I began feeling the need to stretch my legs and maybe get a cup of coffee. In Montana, that desire meant driving at least another 30 miles before hitting the next exit and then hoping there was something there. Richard checked the map. The next place big enough to have a name was a speck called Rosebud.

"Doesn't look promising."

"They've got to have at least a cup of coffee."

"Fine. Whatever."

Twenty minutes later, we reached the Rosebud exit. Rosebud was nowhere in sight. There was no gas station. Just a small, hand-painted arrow pointing left down a narrow paved road. I figured, "what the hell?" and followed it. Five miles later, we came upon a few beat-up shacks. No gas station. No coffee. No people even. If this was the town of Rosebud, its glory days were clearly over.

"Hey. At least we can say we've been to Rosebud."

"Which from the looks of it, puts us in a very exclusive group."

"Exactly."

Richard pulled out the map. "We can stop in Miles City. It's only another 30 miles."

I turned the car around and retraced our path back to the interstate.


As we closed in on Miles City, the car started surging again, especially when we were climbing hills. But this time, the surging was barely noticeable. I wrote it off as a struggling engine and didn't mention it to Richard.

I could tell before we even reached the bottom of the exit

ramp that Miles City was considerably more developed than Rosebud, big enough to justify the presence of all the major players. Stretching a good half-mile on either side of the free-way were a slew of motels: Comfort Inn, Best Western, Motel 8. And all the big names in fast food: McDonald's, Hardee's, KFC, Wendys, Pizza Hut, Taco John's. Representatives from every major oil company: Conoco, Exxon, Amoco, even Texaco. Clearly, a place where many travelers made an obligatory stop. A way station. But no sign of an actual town.

The sad reality of cross-country travel these days is that every town in America is starting to look the same. Local color that used to emerge from organic roots is becoming a thing of the past. All those mom-and-pop operations have been driven out of business by nationwide franchises, from Wal-Mart to USA Today, flexing the muscle of bulk purchasing, mass marketing, and predictable products.

It made me wonder what hidden forces lay behind this vast transformation. I imagined a roomful of suits in some glass metroplex tower, watching a PowerPoint presentation on the socio-economic tipping point that triggered the building of an-other Burger King. The real algebra of America: population den-sity, median income levels, hamburgers per capita. Plug the data into the equation, and *voilà!*

I imagined the designers of hamburgers, armed with a cook-book of data culled from focus groups, market surveys, and consumer purchasing trends. Guys in blue shirts, trying to quantify the ratio balancing the desire for novelty against the desire for predictability. Franchise overlords tying the hands of the locals by making every decision for them, supplying the raw materials, building identical kitchens that precisely matched the employee handbook, dividing preparation into easily repeatable steps intended to utterly usurp any inclination by Employee #456 to add his or her own touch. If you aspire to building a better burger in America today, you need a master's degree in marketing, not a talent for cooking.

From Richard's perspective, the good news was that Miles City had a Texaco station. While Richard refilled the gas tank, I went inside for coffee. As I paid for it, the guy behind the counter said, "Too bad, you just missed Luigi."

"Who's Luigi?"

"Luigi." he said, pointing out into the parking lot. "He runs the Koffee Kiosk. Except his name's not really Luigi."

I looked towards where he was pointing. It was a small, red and white shed. On the side was a sign that read *The Koffee Kiosk*.

"What's his name, really?"

"Frank. He just calls himself Luigi when he's working."

"Why is that?"

"I don't know. Makes him seem more Italian, I guess. He said that's what they suggested in the handbook."

I went outside to check it out. *The Koffee Kiosk* was a pre-fab shed with a counter running along one side. A metal gate closed it off for business. Inside, I could see a menu advertising the usual Starbucks fare: cappuccino, latte, espresso. There were at least two dozen bottles of those Italian syrups to create some authentic atmosphere: lime, strawberry, hazelnut.

I imagined this Luigi/Frank person was some ambitious local entrepreneur trying to get a foothold in the tourist trade. Perhaps inspired by a small ad in the back pages of *Franchise Magazine*: "A Franchise You Can Afford!" I could picture the whole thing arriving on a flatbed truck. Kiosk lifted off in one piece. Frank carefully opening up boxes of Italian syrups and arranging them in alphabetical order, having been instructed that such orderliness subconsciously reassured potential customers. I pictured Frank pouring over the thick manager's manual, memorizing every step necessary to launch a successful Koffee Kiosk franchise in his town, patiently learning how to concoct variations of espresso and milk, carefully testing the temperature of the steam, selecting an Italian name from the "approved names" list. All an act of faith that some expert somewhere knew something he didn't, understood the tastes of the average American with a scientifically proven assurance he could never argue with.

What baffled me was why the kiosk was closed. Maybe today was Luigi's day off. Maybe he was indulging in the Italian propensity for incredibly long lunches. Maybe it was just a seasonal thing. Maybe he was on the slow road to giving up. Funny thing about faith. It seems to require constant renewal.

By now, Richard was anxious to move on to Glendive. He decided that twenty minutes was more than enough for the Bug to cool down. It hadn't given us a problem since Delbert scraped that dimple off the points—though I kept that heretical observation to myself. So off we went.

With Richard back at the wheel, the Bug started, first try. We drove under the overpass and turned left onto the incline of the eastbound onramp. Twenty feet before we merged onto I-94, the car abruptly coughed and died.

By now, Richard had had enough. "Fuck this." He slid the Bug to a stop on the shoulder at the top of the ramp and exhaled. I didn't say anything. He started to think aloud, going over the options. "What the hell is going on here? We let it cool down. It started up fine. It shouldn't be doing this."

His Vapor Lock Theory had now, oddly enough, refined itself to exclude the carburetor priming solution. According to theory, vapor lock goes away when the car cools down. Dumping gas into the carburetor should have no effect (even though it had worked in the past). But alas, this is the tangled web we weave when our story trumps reality.

"Maybe we just didn't let it cool down enough. That has to be it." I opted not to interrupt Richard's conversation with himself. "Maybe we just need to sit here for a couple of minutes." He jerked up the parking brake and crossed his arms.

I got out and looked down the embankment at a trio of motels to the south. The Motel 8. The Holiday Inn Express. The Guesthouse Inn. The wind blew empty and ominous, like the soundtrack of some old Western. A few cars slowed as they passed us, the people inside offering nothing more than a curious glance. About two minutes went by, and Richard tried to start the car again. Nothing.

"Wait. You just have to wait," he advised himself. Having nothing of value to contribute, I stayed out of it, not interfering with the heated debate apparently raging in the chambers of Richard's head.

We waited another two minutes. Then he tried again. Again, nothing. In a sudden crisis of faith, he conceded to priming the carburetor, even though theoretically it shouldn't have anything to do with the problem. I stood back and watched him prime, then walk up to the driver's seat, reach in, and turn the key. Nothing. Prime and crank. Prime and crank. Repeatedly. Manically. For twenty minutes.

Finally, he gave up. He calmly screwed the top back on the carburetor, returned the gas can to the front trunk and then sat back in the driver's seat, staring out through the windshield.

I wasn't sure what was upsetting him. Maybe it was the realization that, as carefully as he'd planned this trip to go without a hitch, he'd overlooked something. He'd messed up. He'd dragged me all the way out here only to get us stuck. Or maybe it was the realization that his Vapor Lock Theory, after all his defense of it, was wrong. The sun doesn't revolve around the earth after all. And here we went and burned all those heretics. Sorry about that, Galileo.

Or maybe it was just embarrassment. It's one thing to face the fact that you've been kidding yourself. It's another to have to admit it to someone who trusted you—and your story.

Whatever he was thinking, it didn't take long for him to recover. After about a minute of rumination, he came back to life. Clicked into plan B.

"O.K. Let's get this thing off this ramp." He got out of the car to survey the terrain. Having made it up the ramp, we'd bought ourselves a little gravity, which Richard decided to use to our advantage. He wanted to put the Bug in neutral and steer it backwards down the ramp while I walked behind him, frantically flagging a warning to any oncoming traffic.

He pulled off this maneuver with remarkable finesse, expertly steering the Bug backwards and even capping it off by using the momentum to make an elegant U-turn into the driveway of the Guesthouse Inn. I jogged over and helped push it off to one side, until it came to rest.

Richard got out and asked if he could use my cell phone. He again called Mike the Mechanic. I stood there listening as he brought Mike up to speed on this latest turn of events.

"It's not Vapor Lock. It's got to be something else."

He listened and nodded. He answered questions. It was then that I remembered the Bug struggling to get up the hill just before Miles City. "I don't know if this will help, but just before we got here I noticed that the car was struggling to get up hills. Like it wasn't getting enough fuel maybe."

Though Richard seemed to dismiss this bit of evidence, Mike evidently heard me. They conferred intently and I could sense a new theory beginning to take shape, like a new creature emerging phoenix-like from the ashes. Richard nodded with increasing conviction. "Got it. Got it. I think you're exactly right. Of course. I can't believe I didn't see this earlier. Appreciate it. Thanks."

He hung up the phone and handed it back to me.

"It's the fuel pump."

I wasn't quite sure what that meant, but from what I could gather, it entailed finding a new part. That wasn't going to be easy. For starters, it was 7 p.m. local mechanic time. Long past closing time for any car parts stores. The chances of this little burg having an expert who knew VW engines were 50-50 at best. The chances of it having a car parts store that carried a 30-year-old VW fuel pump were considerably slimmer. And we couldn't go anywhere, because the car wouldn't start.

The only thing for certain was that this journey had just gotten a whole lot more interesting.

# 7

## THE CITY OF SURRENDER

The sun was sinking and the shadows were long. With the Bug in a coma and no hope of finding a mechanic at this late hour, the question of the moment shifted to where to stay the night. Fortunately, we had an abundance of choices within walking distance. We had pushed the Bug into the access drive for the Guesthouse Inn. It was a motel franchise that catered to the business traveler, with a banner stretched across the front that exclaimed a red-letter list of temptations: *Workout Room! Jacuzzi! Pool! VCR's in every room! HBO! Broadband Internet!* Compared to its rivals, a Motel 8 next door and a Holiday Inn Express across the street, it was the Waldorf. Plus, we wouldn't have to push the Bug to another parking lot.

For Richard, however, the choice was not so obvious. He had a hard-set policy of not forking over a dollar more than was absolutely necessary to any capitalist-pig corporation. It wasn't a question of money; it was a question of principle. For him, the obvious choice was the Motel 8.

I'm not sure why it's called the "Motel 8." I assume the "8" is intended to lure the naïve with the illusion that a room could be had for a mere $8—and the more worldly with the insinuation that, even though no room had gone for $8 in the past 30 years, they were still cheaper than the competition. That was enough for Richard. He was more than happy to push the Bug back down the driveway, into the street and up the block to save $10 a night.

"Look," I said diplomatically, not suggesting that this penny-pinching bullshit of his was partly the reason we were in this mess to begin with, "Let's do ourselves a favor. I'll pick up the tab."

"You sure? I'm happy to push the car down the street." It occurred to me that maybe I was the sucker here. But I didn't care.

"It's been a long day, Richard. Jacuzzi. HBO."

"I don't do Jacuzzis."

"Broadband Internet Access."

"I don't have a computer."

"They probably have one you can use."

"Really?"

"Yeah."

That did the trick. We pushed the Bug into the closest open parking space and walked into the lobby. A double went for a whopping $79 a night. As the Bug would hopefully be getting towed away in the morning, we unpacked all of our belongings and hauled them to the room.

Sitting on the edge of one of the beds, Richard opened up the night table drawer to find a Gideon's Bible and a thin phone book. The Yellow Pages listed two auto mechanics: Kelly's Car Repair and Silva's Auto. He tried both, but no one answered. So he left messages, trimming his usual long-winded explanation into a brief, "please call ASAP."

When he was done, I called Mars and told him that we'd run into a snag and might not make it to Fargo by late afternoon tomorrow.

"What happened?"

"Apparently the Bug is having some issues with its fuel pump."

"Where are you?"

"Miles City."

Mars laughed. "And you're hoping to get a new fuel pump by tomorrow?"

"Hey. We're optimists."

"Yes, you are. I've been to Miles City."

"Any sights we shouldn't miss?"

"I've only stopped there to eat. As I recall, there's a half-way decent restaurant on the second floor of a bank."

"Duly noted. We'll check it out."

"I'll see you guys when you get here."

"Stay tuned."

With the phone calls over, Richard decided that we should walk into town to get advice on which of the many choices of mechanics available was the guy who could be trusted. "I hate just pulling a name out of the phonebook. These guys can be squirrelly."

"Richard. We're in Miles City, Montana. There are two mechanics and we can't get in touch with either one of them. I'd say the phrase 'beggars can't be choosers' applies."

"It never hurts to ask."

"Fine. Maybe we can get something to eat."

I fished a jacket from the bottom of my carry-on bag, and we headed on foot back towards franchise row. It was dark enough that the lights were coming on, the electric glow of a 21st-century dusk. The air was clear and it felt good to walk. We passed under the interstate overpass, cars and trucks sweeping effortlessly over our heads, their fuel systems functioning without a second thought. Who is even conscious of any of our many support systems until they break down?

Emerging from the underpass, we walked by the Koffee Kiosk and the Texaco station, past a McDonald's and a video store, not sure where we were headed. Richard was in search of another human being he could trust. I was looking for a decent place to eat. No place seemed to have both. So we kept walking.

A car slowed down and honked at us. There were two women in the front seat, both roughly 30. The one on the passenger side waved and yelled, "Hey." I figured they mistook us for somebody else, but waved back anyway: "Hey." By then the car was half a block ahead of us, the girl's arm still waving out the window.

"What do you figure that was all about?" I said.

"Maybe they don't see a lot of new faces in this town."

On the next block, we came upon Lucky Lil's Casino & Steakhouse. From my experience the previous night, I assumed that a Montana casino was roughly the equivalent of what I called a bar. And sure enough…

Inside, cigarette smoke drifted like fog on a film set. To the right, couples sat at wooden tables working their way through various slabs of beef. To the left, a handful of men were perched at a long bar, settling into a slow night of drinking. A perky hostess in vaguely cowgirl attire confronted us from behind a podium.

"Table for two?"

Before I could respond, Richard jumped in, clicking into charming mode: "No. We're not here to eat. Actually, we're traveling across the country. Headed for New Jersey." Here we go again.

"That's a long ways away."

"Yes it is. I knew this guy in high school. Thirty years ago."

I nodded "it's true" to the hostess.

"Anyway, we ran into some car trouble and we were wondering if you could recommend a good mechanic. Somebody who isn't going to rip us off."

"I use Kelly."

"Yeah, we saw his name in the phone book."

"He's just right up the street." Somehow, I expected that everything in this town was just right up the street. "There's also Silva," she said, trying to be both helpful and diplomatic. "I haven't ever used him, but he's just up the street, too."

"Great. Thanks."

"You fellas interested in dinner? Tonight's special is rib eye."

"Not tonight. Thanks."

"Good luck."

"Thank you."

He turned to go. I smiled to the chipper hostess and followed him outside.

"There you go: Kelly. I'll call him first thing in the morning." Reassured that this scientific survey had revealed the most trustworthy of the town's many mechanics, he started walking back towards the motel.

I was still determined to get a meal. With the casino/steakhouse off the dinner list, and fast food not even worth mentioning, the only other choice was a Chinese restaurant across from the motel.

"You feel like checking out that Chinese place?"

"What Chinese place?"

"Across the street from our motel."

"Sure. Why not?"

On the way back, as we passed McDonald's again, a car screeched away from the takeout window and zipped directly in front of us, missing us by only a few feet, then suddenly braking to a stop to check for traffic, blocking our path. Inside were four big hooting guys in their early twenties.

"Hey, asshole," Richard barked, not two feet from the closest guy's face, "Don't you stop for pedestrians in this town?"

The driver ignored him, squealing into traffic. The guy in the passenger seat shouted back through the open window: "No, we don't."

"Then fuck you," screamed Richard. With that, the car again squealed to a stop. I thought, "Great. Let's get beat up. Perfect end to a perfect day." Confrontation is something I'm inclined, both by nature and by living in a culture of gun-crazy paranoids, to avoid.

Not Richard. He stood his ground, eyes locked on the stopped car, apparently ready to take on all four of them.

"Fuck you, too," the kid yelled back. And with that, the car peeled away.

Richard glared at it for another few seconds, then continued walking as if nothing had happened. No big deal.

"What was that all about?"

"What?"

"Yelling at that car?"

"That asshole cut us off. I don't take that kind of crap from anybody, especially a carload of punk-ass kids."

I asked him if that kind of reaction got him into many fights.

"No. I just don't tolerate people fucking with me." He reassured me that such confrontations rarely led to somebody actually wanting to fight. "I can tell when they're serious."

"What happens when they're serious?"

"One time," he said, laughing at the memory, "I was driving and this guy in a pick-up was holding up traffic trying to figure out what he wanted to do. So I shouted some abuse at him. I don't even remember what I said, but the guy all of a sudden gets out of his truck and comes storming back towards me, rolling up his sleeves, ready to go at it. So I wait until he gets within earshot and I say, 'Oh yes! Please assault me. I would love to own that nice pick-up you have.' The guy just stopped, frozen in the middle of the road."

"He wasn't serious?"

"Not serious enough to risk his truck. The only people you've really got to worry about are the people who have nothing to lose. Or drunks."

"So you've never gotten into an actual fight?"

"Once or twice. Most of the time, people avoid fights."

"But not you?"

"No. Never. I've never backed away from anybody. I don't let people fuck with me."

Somehow, I didn't find that hard to believe.


By then, we'd reached the Chinese place, a stucco box painted black and red in a half-hearted attempt to be exotic. *Chang Lo's Chinese Buffet. All You Can Eat.*

Inside was an imitation-rock koi pond that held two obese, splotchy orange carp. Behind it was a large, open banquet room with at least 30 tables, all with pink tablecloths and paper lanterns. Along the walls were a smattering of Chinese decorations: a few paper screens, a few bamboo wall hangings. Off to one side was a steam table with a thin collection of uninspired Chinese fare. There were only a few customers, and no hostess. An embossed plastic sign read: *Seat yourself*.

So we did. I went for the buffet. A waiter eventually appeared and Richard ordered fried rice off the menu and used my cell to update Meg on the latest turn of events. As he talked, I watched the other customers.

Not far from us, a sour-faced man in his late twenties kept nervously adjusting a NASCAR cap on his prematurely thinning head. He was sitting with a world-weary older couple whom I took to be his parents or in-laws. They said nothing, made eye contact with nothing, just ate their food with a sad, catatonic resignation. Orbiting around them was a girl who appeared to be just out of high school, chasing a toddler. The kid kept trying to run under the table or take a dive into the koi pond.

"Can you watch him?" she asked NASCAR man, apparently her husband, "I'd like to eat, too."

"I'm not finished yet," he shot back, not even looking at her, not eating. The threesome sat there speechless, a living monument to life turning out badly.

At another table, a hefty couple wolfed down heaping platefuls, taking full advantage of the all-you-can-eat buffet. Two plates at once, with more dirty plates in a discard pile beside each of them. They ate like people you see in Vegas at slot machines, obsessively, without a hint of enjoyment, unable to stop themselves. Next to them, an elderly woman sat alone, her fork hand trembling, the expression on her face suggesting she was desperately trying to remember something, but despite all her effort, she couldn't.

The whole scene just made me think that a lot of people lead a hard life, a life that sucks all the desire and kindness and joy out of them, a life that leaves them ever on guard, watching warily, bracing themselves for the next blow.

After dinner, we crossed the street to the Guesthouse Inn. Richard decided to give the Bug one last shot before dark. "It's got to be cool by now." I stood there hoping that it wouldn't start, fearing he'd be tempted to head out tonight.

He got in and turned the key. Crank, crank, die. Crank, crank, die. By now, the battery was too weak to support life.

Fortunately, Richard wasn't fazed. He was happily in the embrace of a new story. "Fuel pump. Got to be."

Inside the lobby, I noticed a stack of videos behind the front desk and figured we both could use some cheering up. There's something about comedy that takes the edge off dire situations, that helps us laugh at the disconnect between story and reality. I picked *There's Something About Mary*.

The next morning, I was awakened at 7:30 by Richard already on the phone with Kelly the mechanic. "Hey, yeah, Kelly. I got a '69 Bug here in need of a fuel pump. I wonder if you could take a minute this morning to pop one in for me?"

His upbeat tone descended through an increasingly dark series of "uh-huh's". "Uh-huh. Uh-huh. Uhhh-huh. Uhhhh-huhhh. You're sure? All right. All right. Thanks."

"That didn't sound good."

Richard paged through the slim phone book. "He says he can't get to the car until the end of the week. Maybe Thursday, probably Friday." Today was Tuesday. Richard had hoped we'd be

in Jersey by Friday, another 2,000 plus miles away. "I guess that means we're gonna have to go with Silva," he said with a certain resignation as he dialed the number.

The word from Silva was only relatively better. He couldn't look at the car today either. But maybe tomorrow.

Richard dug down to the next layer of options. There was a NAPA car parts store in town. Maybe we could fix it ourselves. "I've got tools in the car. If we need something I don't have, maybe I can borrow it from one of these guys."

So he called the NAPA store to ask if they had a fuel pump for a '69 Volkswagen Beetle. I could hear the guy laughing from across the room. Richard didn't find it funny. "Do you know where I *can* find one?" There might be one in Billings. If so, it could be here by tomorrow. Maybe.

Richard wasn't ready to take "tomorrow" or "maybe" for an answer. "There has to be a way out of this." We could rent a car, drive to Billings (150 miles east), drive back, fix the pump ourselves and be back on the road by late afternoon today.

Sorry. No place in Miles City to rent a car.

Then Richard remembered that he had free towing on his car insurance policy. Maybe we could tow the car to Billings. Have somebody pop the fuel pump in there. "This could work." He called the 800 number on his insurance card and was informed that the free towing was only on his wife's policy.

The first bit of good news came from a car parts store in Billings. They did have a fuel pump, it only cost $33, and they could get it here by tomorrow morning.

Richard called Silva back to ask if there was any way to get the car at least towed to his place this morning. Silva couldn't do it, but he knew someone who could. Randy. So Richard called Randy. And Randy said fine. He'd be here in ten minutes. It wasn't perfect, but at least it was a plan.

Richard hung up the phone and exhaled his frustration. "So I guess we're spending a day in Miles City."

"Yes, I guess we are."

Ten minutes later, we were standing outside the Guesthouse Inn watching a flatbed tow truck pull up the access drive. It was big enough to carry a tractor. Two tractors. Randy, a guy in his twenties with a quick smile and a hearty handshake, climbed down from the cab. Richard launched into another retelling of the whole long story as Randy nodded and smiled and attached chains to the rear bumper of the VW. Without further ado, he hit a lever and away the car went, dragged backward up the ramp. Perched on the vast expanse of flatbed, it looked more like a bug than ever.

Richard decided to go with Randy to Silva's. Check the guy out.

"After all, he doesn't exactly come highly recommended."

Whatever. I wished him luck, and off they went.

On the way back to the hotel room, I remembered an empty notebook I'd tossed into the bottom of my carry-on. Putting words on paper was, for me, a private conversation, a way of pinning down the chatter in my mind, combing my messy head in the mirror of words. Until then, I'd neither the time nor the inclination to write. But Richard's absence provided a chance to pause and reflect.

So I dug out the notebook and fished a ballpoint pen from the desk drawer. Sitting on the bed, propped against the wall, I decided to write down what had happened—just the facts, the surface details of the last two days. But where to begin?

In my head, opening sentences auditioned for the empty page: "I woke at 7:23 AM." "As the flight to Portland left the ground…" "Three months ago, I got an e-mail out of nowhere…" "The Richard who got out of the pale blue Bug was not the Richard I remembered from high school."

The act of writing is not a simple matter of recording facts. It is an act of interpretation. Or maybe even, of creation. From the first sentence, I found myself setting a stage, selecting an arbitrary beginning for a sequence of events plucked from ever-flowing life. As each sentence built upon the last, some part of my mind was shaping the experience, dressing up memory in the clothing of language, embellishing half-recalled details, choosing what to include and what to ignore, hanging happenstance upon a narrative frame. Without intending to, I was transforming the sensory stream of the last few days into a story.

It made me realize that the process of converting the stuff of experience into the stuff of story had begun well before now. My mind had already done a fair bit of unconscious editing. Certain episodes came back vividly, while entire miles of road had faded and disappeared. Why is it that I could recall the fine details of my chicken meal at the Kwiky Mart, but my recollection of driving through Spokane was less than a blur? The mind is not a video camera or a tape recorder, faithfully recording every passing moment. It chooses what to remember. Even at the moment of experience, it chooses what to perceive, where to focus the lens of consciousness. And then the mind attempts to assemble it all into a coherent, emotionally engaging version of what happened. My writing those memories down was only a further revision of the story my mind had already created.

Working in TV, I'm perhaps more conscious than most of this storytelling tendency. The first commandment of television is to tell a good story. The guiding principle for organizing hours of footage, be it archival clips of ex-presidents or verité video of police raids, is to find the story. Viewers don't want a lecture or a recitation of facts or a string of pretty pictures. They want a story.

This is nothing new. Humans have always had a hunger for stories. Before there were flat screens and multiplexes, there were stages, amphitheaters, wandering minstrels, tales traded around campfires. Novels, legends, folktales, bedtime stories. Human have been drawn to stories ever since they've been able to talk. There's even a theory that language itself emerged out of the desire to tell stories (see Merlin Donald's *Origins of the Modern Mind*). Why is that? Why do stories have this power over us? What do I even mean by this word *story*?

The English class answer is that a story is the tale of a protagonist (the hero) whose world is disrupted by an antagonist (the villain). To restore the peace (heal the wound, soothe the aching heart, save the planet), the hero must confront and defeat the villain. Good must take on evil. In any well-told story, this is rarely easy—complications ensue, stakes rise, odds get ugly. This all climaxes in a showdown in which the hero (usually) wins. The planet is saved. The deformed psychopath is shot down in a hail of automatic weapon fire. The lovers overcome whatever petty prejudice plagues their particular social group. The dent in dad's car is fixed.

Or not. Stories can turn out badly. Some tales end tragically. Heroes can be defeated. But in most cases, the story sheds light, be it subtle or glaring, upon some assertion of how the world works: persistence pays off, patriotism is honored, compassion trumps cruelty, justice prevails, love conquers all.

Life, of course, rarely offers the heightened action and dramatic clarity of a TV drama. My life, at least, was not so neatly polarized. There were no obvious heroes or villains. The planet wasn't at stake.

Considered on a more basic level, a story is a disconnect between experience and expectation, a conflict between objective and subjective reality. Objective reality (*context*) is everything outside me: my external environment including nature, culture, politics, economics, the furniture in this room, Richard and his broken-down old Bug, even my own body, my grumbling stomach and my aching head. Context is the world "out there".

Subjective reality (*content*) is everything inside my head: my ideas, my memories, my emotions, my hard-wired genetic propensities, the neural residue of all my education and experience, my encounters with cultures and customs, with superstition and science, fantasy and fact, success and failure. Somehow all of these experiences have left their mark on my brain, creating the unique neurological model of the reality that is me.

Life is an ongoing interaction between these two realms. I interpret what I experience in terms of what I know, filtering the *context* I perceive through the *content* of my mind. When these two worlds are in sync, my mind churns like a smooth running engine, providing automatic interpretations and responses to my reality. But when I experience a discrepancy, or an ambiguity, then a warning light appears on the dashboard of my consciousness: to avoid a breakdown, take action now!

I hear a bump in the night. The warning light goes on: "What was that?" The debating team inside my head pages through the contents of my mind and suggests several possibilities: the wind, the house settling, an intruder. Recommended action: get more information. So I listen intently, hoping to hear it again, hoping more data will allow the content team to make a definitive interpretation. But I hear nothing. The debate team huddles. If it is an intruder, I should hear a second step. Or maybe not. Perhaps he heard me and froze.

The mind cannot rest until the warning light goes off. It will continue to pay attention and suggest actions until the problem is resolved. What do I do? Do I try to go back to sleep, dismissing the noise as nothing? What if I'm wrong? Do I hide under the bed to protect myself? Do I go to investigate? What if there is someone there? What do I do then? Sometimes the problem resolves itself easily. But other times, it doesn't. The warning light remains on. The initial theory proves wrong. The solution that should work doesn't. The Vapor Lock Theory falls apart. The old Bug breaks down and can't be restarted. The conflict between content and context can escalate to the point that one or the other has got to give. I have to either change the world or change my mind. This can be accomplished in several ways. I can exert energy to force the world to submit to my expectations (fight). Or I can run away from the problem (flight). Or I can find some way to explain what I'm seeing so it fits my model (denial). Or I can ignore my preconceptions and open my eyes (acceptance). Abandon old ideas for new ones. In either case, I can't rest until I find a resolution. Until I shut off the warning light. Until I find some way to bring the story to a resolution.

So here's my tentative definition of what I mean by *story*: a story is what happens when the content of a particular character conflicts with the context of a particular situation, place, and time. The story begins when an incident disrupts the peaceful co-existence between these two worlds. When an expectation isn't met. When an intention goes awry. When the warning light goes on. The story tracks the escalating chain of actions and reactions until the conflict is resolved.

What's at stake is whatever it is that motivates our hero into action, whatever is potentially threatened by the disruption. At the most basic level, what's at stake is life itself. But, as we all know, there are many things characters are willing to risk their lives for: their family, their tribe, their nation, freedom, justice, a way of life, love, pride, money, fame, God.

Stories are not disembodied ideas, not abstract theories, not logical arguments. Stories are inherently personal. A story is what happens when one individual's beliefs confront an uncooperative reality.

Stories are also inherently emotional, perhaps because it's just such confrontations that trigger emotions. Emotions urge us into action or into retreat. They are genetically programmed responses that improve our chances of survival in countless obvious and not so obvious ways. Perhaps they are the mechanism by which living beings resolved conflicts, before language and rational minds came along and created stories. Emotions still greatly influence nearly everything we humans do. They play a primary role in how we respond to the warning light. Resolving conflicts is at least as much an emotional experience as it is an intellectual one. And so, stories are also about emotions. Perhaps the power of stories is that, unlike abstract theories or philosophical propositions, they do a much better job of capturing the subjective, emotion-drenched experience of being human.

Come to think of it, much of what I'm calling the content of my mind consists of stories. Stories are great teachers of what works and what doesn't, of how to navigate the treacherous waters of life. Stories dramatically illuminate what is meaningful. When confronted with a conflict in my life, I turn to the stories in my head to see what happened when characters confronted similar conflicts. And when these stories conflict with experience, they generate new stories, like a Russian nesting doll. How many of the conflicts in the world today are fueled by a disconnect between a changing reality and a story that people refuse to let go of?

There seems something inherently delusional about this. I don't like to think of myself as living in a story. Reality is real. Stories are fiction. But is it really that simple? A couple gets married and raises a family. A student aspires to a career. A soldier goes off to war. All these people are undeniably doing real deeds in a real world. But what is motivating them, creating and sustaining their world, is a story.

Power and status are stories. Wealth and fame are stories. Romance and marriage are stories. It is our mutual belief in these "realities" that makes them real. Without it, the powerful are just people, the famous are just folks. Money and love are just paper and pangs.

This holds true not only for individuals, but also for communities, societies, and entire nations. The stories people collectively believe are what give their society its values, its identity, its structure, its institutions, its boundaries, even its physical reality. Belief in mythical Egyptian deities led to the building of very real pyramids. Out of such fiction was civilization born.

The world's major religions are based on books that are compilations of stories: Christianity, Judaism, Islam, Hinduism. And who can deny that those stories have spawned countless concrete realities, from cathedrals to crusades, from vast institutions to innumerable individual acts of worship?

Much of what we value and believe in as Americans – family and country, democracy and freedom, the presidency, the law, skyscrapers and satellites – owes its existence to stories deeply rooted in our communal mind. The trick to successfully engaging in life isn't finding a way through this thicket of fiction to some undeniable reality. The trick is in finding a story I can believe in. A story that resolves the content and the context of my world. A story that isn't riddled with inconsistencies. A story where the hero can act clearly and forceful without having to constantly weigh the evidence and question his intentions. A story where the stakes are clear.

The problem is that believing in any story ultimately requires a leap of faith. The one thing that I know for certain is that I don't know everything. No matter how smart I am, how complex my model is, how many years of education I've had, I didn't sit in on every class there is. I haven't read every book. The neat little packages of ideas by which I sort the world are only one of many possibilities, all of which are human creations, subject to revision at a moment's notice. The stories that illuminated the world a hundred years ago have all been radically revised, if not outright dismissed, and who among us is willing to bet on what people will believe a hundred years from now?

Content and context will never be precisely aligned. The world out there is never fully knowable, because it is both infinite and ever-changing. The ideas in our heads are ultimately fallible human creations. Whatever action (or in-action) I decide upon, I can never be sure, never be guaranteed, of the result. I can never predict the future with absolute certainty. Every action is a gamble that what I believe is true, that what's at stake is real, that life means something. Once I take that leap of faith, the course becomes clear, and life has significance and purpose. The problem is taking it.

In these post-modern times of ours, you don't need a degree in philosophy to see everything as bullshit. Ask your average teenager. It's very easy to stand a cynical step removed from life, to dismiss everything as phony. To see through the story.

Taking a leap of faith in such a skeptical environment leaves you vulnerable to all those critical eyes who see through you, who say that you're only kidding yourself, that all that trouble you're going to doesn't make any difference...because in the end, nothing really matters. It's all just a story.

To me, this dismissive attitude has a far more corrosive effect on people and on society than the loss of religion. It leaves people stranded, paralyzed, embarrassed to take a step in any direction. As individuals and as a society, I suspect we can survive without religion. Many of the benefits of religious faith can be replaced, as many of them already have, with new beliefs.

But we cannot survive without an ability to believe in stories.

For me, belief in God was a belief in a story that had the power and scope to touch my darkest fears, my deepest insecurities, my highest hopes, my loftiest dreams; a story that gave meaning and purpose to both life and death. But, sadly, it is a story that I can no longer believe, no longer surrender to. Its content doesn't fit my context. Too much needs to be explained away. I am not willing to do that. I *couldn't* do that, even if I wanted to.

Perhaps what I'm seeking on this self-proclaimed spiritual journey of mine is a story to replace it with, a story with that same power and scope, a story that embraces all the new ideas of the last two thousand years, that welcomes all of this vast circus of a world I have come to live in, where Darwin can dine with Jesus, Nietzsche can trade jokes with Mohammed, and Bob Dylan can sing a duet with St. Paul. Wouldn't that be something?

Richard returned an hour later with a big shit-eating grin. Silva had made a good impression. To Richard's delight, he'd confirmed that the problem probably was the fuel pump. If we could get one from Billings first thing tomorrow, we could be back on the road as early as 9 a.m.

Even better, Richard had discovered an actual town on the far side of franchise row. It had a courthouse, a main street, saddle shops, taverns, the whole works. It wasn't exactly Yellowstone, but it was at least *someplace*, and I was downright eager to check it out. Though Richard had just come from there, he was more than willing to head right back. And so off we went.

By then, it was mid-morning. The day was bright and warm and receptive. As we made our way on foot beneath the interstate overpass, Richard told me that Randy, the tow truck driver, had just moved back here after a jarring year in the big city of Billings.

"Said he couldn't take it. Too many people. Too much noise. Plus, his Camaro kept getting trashed by the local hoodlums. Apparently it's a form of entertainment in Billings to pour paint on cars. Said after the third time, he packed it in and headed home."

"Spray paint?"

"No. They just opened up a pint of paint and poured it on

his hood."

That was a new one on me. "Must be a Montana thing."

"I guess."

We retraced last night's walk to the casino and kept on going. Within a few blocks, the franchises gave way to less familiar motels and eateries. We came upon a collection of buildings, still under construction, that I would have assumed was a school, were it not for the razor wire fence and windowless walls. A temporary sign on the chain link explained: *Future Home of the Eastern Montana School for Troubled Youth.* No doubt all those paint pourers from Billings would soon be following Randy's trail.

A broad street, angling off to the left, led into the town proper. This street had an entirely different look and feel than the commercial strip we'd just come down. For one, it was lined with trees: large, plush oaks that gave off an aura of endurance and history. Set back behind the trees were humble but solid houses, no two identical: this one brick, that one aluminum-sided. The front yards were cultivated by the people inside, daffodils popping out of flowerbeds, fruit trees in bloom. This was not a street that emerged from a blueprint, bulldozed and subdivided by unseen planners in some faraway corporate headquarters. This was a street shaped by the people who lived here, formed by years of personal aspirations and making do—an organic neighborhood.

A few blocks up, we came to a courthouse. I started to go inside.

"Where are you going?" Richard wanted to know, stuck on the sidewalk as if he had an allergy to legal institutions, however benign they may seem.

"Let's check it out. Maybe there's a trial we can sit in on."

He shook his head and followed me up the granite steps. Inside, the stone foyer was empty and quiet. A wide marble staircase led up to the second floor. Along one wall was a display case with photos from the Annual Cowtown Beef Breeders Show and Craft Expo and a folding table that offered various local flyers and brochures.

One gave a brief history of the town. I'd figured Miles City was a not very imaginative name for a road stop along the wagon trail. Turned out I was wrong. It had been named after Colonel Nelson Miles, commander of a nearby U.S. Calvary post that was established in 1876 on the Tongue River after the battle of Little Big Horn. The town had popped up an arm's length away to supply the troops with the necessities of frontier life: alcohol and "soiled doves." When the fort moved a year later, the town followed "lock, stock and whiskey barrel." Hoping to score some political points, local proprietors named the new town after the good Colonel, but he was evidently unmoved by the honor. Being "a temperate man", he insisted that the town that bore his name remain a discreet two miles from the fort.

Richard followed me up the wide, stone staircase to the second floor, passing leaden portraits of retired judges. Upstairs was an antiseptic government corridor with an empty traffic ticket window and a Dutch door labeled *County Records*. At the end of the hall, we found a small, down-to-business courtroom. A bailiff, busy straightening chairs, informed us that we'd arrived too late for the day's only trial.

So we headed back outside and continued up main street. The downtown area was mostly depression-era brick buildings with stores at street level and offices on the second floors. The businesses were geared to a cattle economy: feed stores, a boot shop, a saddlery, farm equipment. There were several saloons with names like *Texas Club* and *Bison*, ass-kicking cowboy bars that no doubt came alive on the weekend. An enduring tribute to what had put this town on the map: male orneriness.

In other aspects, however, downtown was downright subdued. We passed a place called the 600 Café, a local luncheonette named after its address. Peeking through the window, I felt the urge to make myself at home. "Let's have us a piece of pie."

Richard was clearly not big on wandering impulsively in and out of places, but as we had nowhere to go and nothing better to do, he didn't put up much of a fight.

Inside, a sprinkling of locals lined the counter or sat at the red-checked tables. There was a fair contingent of cowboy hats. At a table by the window, a man in a business suit, wearing a string tie, was going over paperwork with an alert woman in a red jacket. He waved an eager, gesturing hand and she nodded, her bug eyes locked on him like a tracking radar. Across from them, an old man sat at the counter quietly absorbing the local paper over a cup of coffee. Richard and I took the two empty stools beside him as a waitress, coffee pot in hand, beelined towards us.

"What can I get you boys?"

The comforting feeling of having arrived settled over me. This was what I loved about driving across country. To sit at this counter and have a waitress say exactly that.

"What kind of pie do you have?"

They had seven kinds of pie. I picked apple rhubarb, not because I especially liked it, but just because it was there.

"This is what traveling is all about for me," I gushed, "Coming into a place like this and just being here for a while." Richard agreed, loosening his moral belt enough to order a piece of pie for himself.

I walked back to the door and picked up a copy of the local paper from a stack on the window ledge. The cover story was about a Miles City man who had survived the Battle of Midway, 60 years ago today. "We should go look him up. Tell him we came all this way just to congratulate him."

Richard shook his head and bit into his pie. "Let's not."

After pie and coffee, we headed back out onto Main Street. Maybe it was the sugar, maybe it was just being free of the car, but I was downright giddy. Not a trace of tourist ennui, experiencing everything as not quite a postcard; not a hint of that smug audience-member mockery our generation seems to have picked up from so many hours of watching television. I was just feeling immensely content. Present.

We passed under a massive, Montana-shaped neon sign that announced *The Montana Bar*. It didn't look open this early in the day, but I decided to try the front door anyway. Sure enough, it was locked. But through the smoked glass window, the place appeared to be straight out of a John Ford movie.

"Wanna see inside?" The voice came from behind us. I turned to see a guy in his late thirties approaching, clean cut and looking a little out of place in a button up shirt and khakis, pulling a key out of the pocket.

"Sure."

He introduced himself as Kyle. Turned out he was the owner. Took the place over from his father last year. Was still working on restoring it. He unlocked the door and let us in. "This place has been a working bar for over a hundred years."

The floor was a handcrafted blue-and-white tile mosaic; the ceiling, molded tin; the walls, solid redwood. The bar itself was a work of art, 40 feet long, carved out of solid mahogany. A long back shelf full of bottles framed a mirror that had darkened with the years, giving our reflections the smoked glass look of old photographs. Kyle told us that his great grandfather had brought the bar up the Missouri from St. Louis just before World War I.

Kyle had moved back to Miles City after an extended foray into the wider world. "Couldn't find anything better to do than this. Plus, I hated the thought of the old place going to hell, so I came back. Now I spend my time and money fighting off the ravages of time." Don't we all?

I envied the guy. In a world so focused on the next novelty, the next form of fleeting entertainment, there was something to be said for preserving a tradition. It reminded me of an old church, this bar, the embodiment of a certain community spirit that was fading, but had not been entirely lost. We promised to return after sundown, when it was open for business.

Next, we wandered into a store that sold western wear: two stories of leather boots, multi-colored shirts, and belts with giant buckles. There was an entire room dedicated to nothing but cowboy hats. Behind the counter was a plump girl with a big smile and rosy cheeks, meticulously folding T-shirts.

"How y'all doin'?"

"Just fine, thank you very much," I said, wandering into the room of cowboy hats. "Why so many hats? Isn't one cowboy hat pretty much like another?"

"Oh noooo…" She tried her best to explain the subtle variations in cowboy couture: the ranch-owner hat versus the ranch-hand hat, the spring hat versus the fall hat. They had hats made of felt, hats made of straw, cattleman hats, old west hats, pre-soiled hunting hats. I tried on a Stetson Tom Mix hat with a ten-gallon dome top and its own solid plastic carrying case.

After that, we walked a mile west to the Tongue River, then turned back, cutting through a residential neighborhood with tree-buckled sidewalks and kids' toys on the front lawns. There was a handful of apartments, but mostly single-family homes, all unique and custom built, many easily a half-century old, each with its own archeology of repairs and improvements. A community.

The experience was a great example of what I enjoy most about traveling: the chance to encounter the unexpected. To me, rushing through some place, or just going to see where the guide-book pictures were taken, is missing the point. It does both the place and you a disservice. Because it only confirms what you already know—or think you know.

Here's my recommendation to anyone who really wants to see what this country—or any country—is all about. Take a two-week road trip. Have no destination in mind. Just drive wherever the road takes you. When you get tired of the road you're on, turn onto another road. The smaller, the better. Maybe you'll go 1,000 miles. Maybe you'll go only 10. Stop anyplace that grabs your curiosity. At night, stop wherever you end up. Never stay in a hotel that has an identical cousin somewhere else. Never eat in a restaurant where the menu wasn't written by someone who works there. Throw out the guidebook. Talk to at least 10 people every day. Ask them to tell you something interesting about wherever it is you're at: history, geography, economy, favor-ite hangout, local legends of crime and bad behavior, anything. You'll be amazed at the thrill of simply *being* somewhere.

Muslims are obliged to visit Mecca at least once in their lives. Perhaps we Americans should feel it is our duty and obligation to the spirit of America to drive across the country at least once in our lives. Take a jarful of one ocean and pour it into the other.

Back in town, we found the restaurant Mars had mentioned, the converted upstairs floor of a bank: Club 519 (it was apparently a trend among food establishments in Miles City to take their name from their street number). A back stairway led up to a bar with a few booths and a dance floor. The bartender was cleaning glasses, getting ready for tonight. "Can I help you boys out?"

It was only late afternoon. "You open for dinner yet?" I asked him.

"Restaurant's that-a-way," he nodded toward a door that led into a near empty restaurant, with tables set along the floor-to-ceiling sash windows that overlooked Main Street. A girl not long out of high school made her best attempt at being our "waitress for this evening." I ordered a gin and tonic, snacked on the celery stick appetizer and ordered pan-fried trout.

"I don't know about you," I said to Richard, "But I am very glad we got to take a break and be somewhere for a little while."

"Yeah, me too. This has been good," he said as he checked out the celery plate, "I know I can be pretty manic sometimes. I apologize for that." He picked out a stick and bit into it. "I think a lot of times I try too hard to make things happen instead of just letting them happen. But I think," another bite, a pause to chew, "I think I'm finally getting a handle on that. In a way, you could say this trip is my way of letting go of that particular mania."

In our relationships with the other people, we often have the illusion that they are far more set in their ways than we are; that they're much clearer about who they are and who they're not, what they believe and what they don't. But they're not, really. They're the same tangle of conflicts that we are. The closer you get, the more the plot thickens, and the more you discover that, just like you, other people are an ongoing tangle of becoming.

I sensed that for Richard, the reason he was making this journey had a lot to do with the reason he had not returned home in almost a decade and a half. Until now, I had figured that if and when he wanted to talk about it, he would. But I was beginning to sense that he didn't know himself; that his motivations were even less clear to him than they were to me; and that maybe, as his friend and traveling partner, I ought to help him figure it out.

"You've never really told me what made you want to take this trip in the first place."

"I wish I could."

"What do you mean?"

"Just how the whole thing came about was a very weird experience for me."

"How did it come about?"

"Well, last winter, March I think, the floor fell out of my old car and for a while I was without one. I was pretty much stuck at home. That's when I started my daily walk to the top of Rocky Butte, just to get out and get some exercise. I'd follow the same route every day. I got into this routine: 10:30, every day, I'd go for this two-hour hike. Then one day, I went outside and the sky was a just-about-to-rain grey. I was feeling borderline sick and I didn't want to get stuck up on the mountain in a big storm. So I started walking in a direction I had never taken before. Just through the neighborhood. I walked a couple miles, maybe, and by then, I wasn't even sure where I was. And that's when I came upon the '69."

"The old Bug?"

"Yeah. That's how I found it. Parked on some guy's lawn with a *For Sale* sign. If I hadn't taken this new route, I would have never found it. I checked it over and it looked to be in O.K. shape, so I went up to the house and knocked on the door. The owner was home. Nice guy. He took me for a test ride, and I bought it from him that night. It was like *it* found *me*."

Our dinners came and we started eating. Outside, the day was beginning to wane. Richard continued with his story. "Shortly after I bought the car, within a day or two, I woke up one morning and I had this realization, 'It's time.' Like a light bulb going off in my head. 'It's time.'"

"It's time for what?"

"Time to make this trip. I hadn't been consciously planning it or anything. I bought the car. Then a few days later, I woke up thinking, 'It's time.'"

"So what did you do?"

"Well, that's what I'm saying. Normally, I would have just gone back to sleep. Dismissed it. But that morning, for whatever reason, I didn't. I just accepted it. It's time. Which is *not* my usual way of operating. My usual way of operating would be to plan something like this for a year, go over every detail, and make a million phone calls. Know exactly what I was getting into. Tie myself up in knots until I was sick to my stomach. But this time, I just went with it. I got up, and Meg was in the kitchen and I told her I was thinking of driving back to Jersey. I figured she'd find some perfectly good reason for me to forget about the whole thing, and I'd be off the hook."

"What did she say?"

"She said, 'O.K. If that's what you want to do, you should do it'"

Richard took a long sip of water to empty his glass when he saw the waitress heading towards us with a water pitcher. She gave us a refill and asked if everything was O.K.

"Everything's great," I said. She smiled and walked away.

Richard went on with his story. "It was later that morning, I wrote you that e-mail."

"That morning? Really?"

"Yeah. Like out of nowhere. I figured, why not?"

"Wow. I had assumed a lot more thought had gone into it."

"No. It was total impulse. I almost fell of my chair when you wrote back."

In a life where there is usually a logical explanation for everything, here was a mystery. Both of us had signed onto this journey for reasons we ultimately did not understand, for motives we could not put into words, but were compelled to follow anyway. This sort of thing happened all the time in legends and myths, but not in 21st century America. In our world, people didn't make a habit of following mysteries.

I wanted to know more. "But why me? I admit, I was kind of flattered, but we hadn't seen each other in years. You must have friends in Portland who'd go with you."

"I do. But it was one of those crazy things again. The idea wasn't a couple hours old in my head and I'm sitting at my computer, thinking that maybe this wasn't something I should do by myself. And then I thought of you. I thought back on those crazy plays we used to do in high school. Remember those?"

"Yeah." Funny, how we'd both gone back to the same experience. For all that those crazy plays had meant to me, it had never occurred to me what they meant to him.

"You were the only guy I could think of who might say yes. So

I dug up one of your old e-mails, found your address, and sent you that message. And then I just let things happen. Next thing I know, you're on board. This high school reunion appears out of nowhere. My sister starts organizing a get-together and invites the whole family. It was weird. Because I didn't feel like I was doing anything to make any of this happen. I was just getting out of the way."

"Captain Karma."

"Yeah, Captain Karma, exactly," he agreed. "The power of just letting things happen. Surrendering to the mystery of it all."

I raised my water glass in a toast.

"To the mystery of it all."

"Here, here."

After dinner, we walked over to the Montana Bar. It was still early, but a handful of people had already started drinking. The bartender was a guy in his twenties named Kenny. We told him about running into Kyle earlier and about being stranded by car troubles, and spending the day walking around Miles City.

"So tonight, we're just celebrating being here."

"Amen to that," Kenny pronounced.

"What's good to drink?"

"Funny you should ask."

He recommended a local, dark ale, which he poured from an unlabelled vat set on a folding table beside the bar. I asked him where it came from and he said he brewed it himself. Kenny's homemade beer. You can't ask for much better than that. This was turning into a night for toasting.

"To Miles City."

"And to the broken fuel pump that got us here."

"Cheers."

There was a pool table in the back room and Richard suggested we give it a whirl. I play pool maybe twice a year, and I'm one notch up from pathetic, but I figured, why not? He racked up the balls and let me break. I sank the four, then missed my second shot.

Richard paused to chalk his stick as he surveyed the table. He lined up a long shot, then with a quick snap, fired the seven ball into the corner pocket, the cue ball stopping dead on contact, precisely lined up for a shot at the three ball. I never got another turn. Richard cleared the table of stripes with one effortless shot after another, always leaving the cue ball exactly where he wanted it, calling out each shot with an understated calm. "Eleven in the far corner. Five in the side. Combo off the six. Nine in the corner."

"I take it you've played before." I'd settled onto a barstool, conceding defeat and shifting into spectator mode.

"Once or twice."

The next game, he broke, the cue hitting the racked balls with a shattering smack that sent two solids into the corner pockets. He worked the table like a pro: down the table shots, combinations, angles off the bumpers. Playing the game with a precision and finesse that was beautiful to behold. I asked him where he'd learned.

"After I went back to Tulsa, I was driving a cab, working microfilm again," he told the story as he continued to clear the table. "Underneath the Tulsa Tribune Building there was a pool hall: Boulder Billiards. They had these really old, flat-railed Brunswick tables with leather thong pockets. There was this old guy who ran the place, Benny. He didn't own it, he just managed it during the day. He and his wife came in every morning and opened the place up. She vacuumed the carpets and cleaned."

He lined up a bank shot, sending the three off the bumper and gently into the side pocket. "I would wake up and go down there at nine in the morning. This is when I was working four to midnight. I'd get up in the morning. I'd go have my coffee at this pool hall. For me it was just a comfortable place to hang out. Sometimes, I'd shoot with whoever was there; sometimes, just by myself."

The cue ball flew diagonally across the table, coming to a dead stop as it hit the nine and sent it careening, with a sharp crack, into the corner. "Anyway, Benny eventually took me under his wing. For my first dozen lessons, the cue ball was the only ball on the table. Benny would touch a spot with his finger and say, 'Put it here.' He taught me how to stand. How to line up shots, how to follow through, use English, see one shot ahead, then two, then three. Nine Ball, straight pool."

It reminded me of playing the piano, a skill I have always desired, and have occasionally attempted to acquire. Another of those skills that take years to hone, that you can never be too good at. A skill that, in the scheme of things, doesn't get you much, unless you turn pro. It's like any sport. Any game. Any art. Shooting hoops. Playing chess. Climbing mountains. Painting pictures. Singing songs. For we, the vast army of amateurs, these activities rarely make us any richer or carry any other obvious benefit for survival. The attraction is just the sheer beauty of being able to do it.

I tried not to think too much about playing pool that night in Miles City. I tried to quiet my yammering mind and simply surrender to the experience of being there.

8

AT FAITH'S TOLLBOOTH

W e woke early the next morning, eager to get moving, but with little to do but wait. Richard called Silva the moment his shop opened at 8 a.m. Silva was already working. The fuel pump had come in. All he needed to do was install it. Piece of cake.

So we waited. We went downstairs and had the free breakfast in the motel's small dining room. 8:35. Richard decided to check out the "Business Center," a tiny room off the main lobby that had a small desk with a single computer, plugged into what was advertised as "Broadband Internet Access!" I went back to the room to read the complimentary *U.S.A. Today*.

Nine o'clock came and went with no word from Silva. Our goal for today was to reach Fargo, 450 miles away, by evening, early enough to get together with Mars. Realistically, that was an eight-hour drive minimum. If we left by ten, that would put us there by six. Add another hour for the mid-Dakota time zone crossing and that pushed our E.T.A. to seven at best. Not great, but good enough to get us back on track.

At nine-thirty, Richard came back to the room all antsy. He couldn't figure how installing a fuel pump—which by his estimation should have taken 15 minutes tops—was taking hours. But, adhering to some unwritten VW mechanic protocol, he held off calling Silva until 10.

The news wasn't good.

Silva had replaced the fuel pump, but the car still wasn't starting. He'd managed to trace it to a "defect in a sleeve," somewhere in the accelerator. The defect was "breaking a vacuum," which was somehow keeping gas from going through the fuel pump. He did not have a replacement sleeve, but was trying to cobble together a solution. He'd call us when he'd either succeeded or given up.

This news had a cascading effect on our plans. It meant we'd never get to Fargo in time. Even worse, we could be stuck in Miles City for another day, maybe more, meaning we wouldn't reach Jersey by Saturday. Richard, in a rare crisis of faith, asked Silva if he thought the car could even make it to the east coast and back: another 5,000 miles. Silva said he'd have to look it over more closely. Suddenly, the entire trip was in jeopardy. Richard suggested I start looking into contingency plans for getting home on my own.

The thought of giving up now was disheartening, to say the least. After our day in Miles City, the journey had started to jell for me, to take on some depth and resonance. But Richard was right. I didn't want to spend another day in Miles City, much less the rest of the week. I had little desire to go to Jersey if it meant missing the reunion. Maybe it was time to break out the alternatives.

I went down to the Business Center and logged onto Expedia to check out the airline options. Within minutes, I discovered, to my surprise, that Miles City had been hiding a commuter airport somewhere on its outskirts. I could get home today for the low cost of $777 and 10 hours, with only three connecting flights. Or I could fly to Philadelphia for a little more, go to the reunion on my own, and use my existing ticket to get home. Easily doable.

But both options felt like defeat. And I wasn't ready to give up yet.

I went back to the room, where Richard was still trying to digest the latest lump of bad news. Oddly enough, he wasn't all that worried about the car or about himself. His biggest concern was what would happen to everybody in Jersey if we didn't show up. Would the people traveling from out of town still come? Would the reunion still happen? It seemed very important to him that it did, even without us, even though we were the main event. The party had to go on.

For my part, I was hoping for a miracle while preparing for a loss. I was disappointed that we would miss seeing old friends. I was disappointed that we would miss seeing Mars in Fargo and Bill in Cincinnati. But mostly, I was disappointed that the journey would end unfinished. Unresolved. A story without an ending. We both sat there for the next hour, out of ideas, sulking, in the dark place of soldiers realizing that the battle had turned against them.

At just after 11, the phone rang. It was Silva. Good news. He'd found a German guy who'd "borrowed" a replacement for the damaged sleeve from one of the few other VW's in Miles City. The car was running. Come and get it.

———

"Yes!" It was like seeing the cavalry appear on the horizon.

Silva had no one who could pick us up in the next hour, so Richard said he'd walk. He was out the door in less than a minute. I stayed behind and phoned Mars to give him the update. I caught him before he'd left for work. "We're running late, but there is still a fair-to-middling chance we'll be in Fargo tonight." He said that whenever we showed up was fine. He'd be back from work at 3. We were welcome to stay at his place.

Eager to do something, I went down to the lobby, found a luggage cart and, with a little more looking, a service elevator. Up in the room, I piled all our half-packed stuff on board and got it downstairs. Then I sat under an awning outside the front lobby, on the edge of the cart, waiting.

Twenty minutes later, the pale blue Bug appeared below the underpass and turned into the Guesthouse Inn drive. It was an oddly glorious sight. Unable to hold back a smile, I rose to my feet, even raised my fists in victory as Richard steered the old Bug toward me. It was a scene right out of a Hardy Boys novel.

Richard was grinning from ear to ear, bursting with news. Silva had called in a guy he knew named Wilhelm, who wasn't exactly a mechanic, but who was at least German. They had taken something called a push rod sleeve out of the only other VW beetle in town, a retired '73 that was up on blocks in the backyard of a friend of Wilhelm. Even more amazing, the total bill came to a mere $150 : $61 for parts, $40 for towing, $49 for labor. Richard had asked Silva how he could afford to do the repairs so cheaply. Silva said he liked to sleep at night. To top it off, he'd given the car a good bill of health and wished us a safe and successful journey.

We loaded up, and with a whoop of victory, launched from the shores of Miles City, once again headed east. It was just past noon, and with any luck, we'd by in Fargo by nine.

It was a brilliant sunny day, with the temperature easily in the upper 80s. Our mood had risen from the nadir of earlier this morning to an exhilaration that carried us up like a pendulum swinging. There's something about the shared experience of duress that brings people together like nothing else. Here we were: two hard-core individualists becoming an *ad hoc* team, united by the common, admittedly goofy, goal of sailing this ancient car cross-country by Saturday. For me, that made today's victory over the forces of mechanical failure all the sweeter, because it wasn't just me who won, it was us.

Unfortunately, our exhilaration was to be short-lived.

We weren't 10 miles down the road before a new problem popped onto the radar. VW's are infamous for their bare bones heating systems. Heat is drawn off the engine through ducts in the floor to vents in the dash. In theory, there is a control on the dash for regulating this heat flow. Disdaining anything so bourgeois as a thermostat, the VW designers had opted for a solution more appropriate to the common Volk: a sliding vent cover. Open, close. More heat, less heat.

When Richard and Mike the Mechanic had removed the dash to replace the windshield that Mike had accidentally cracked (oops), they'd removed the sliding vent covers. Befitting their minimalist philosophy—or maybe just out of ignorance—they didn't replace them. So now, hot air rushed uninhibited out of every vent. This was not a problem on the relatively cool days we'd experienced until now. But on a hot day, like today, this blast of hot air turned the car interior into an industrial sized clothes dryer. To keep from passing out, we rolled down the windows, which pretty much obliterated any audible conversation.

Richard assured me (shouting over the 50-decibel roar of the wind) that this was an "…EASY PROBLEM TO FIX."

"HUH? WHAT?"

"I CAN FIX THIS!"

"FIX WHAT?"

"THE HEAT. I CAN SHUT OFF THE HEAT!"

"HOW?"

"WE'LL STOP AT THE NEXT GAS STATION."

"WHAT?"

The next gas station was another 30 miles down the road, in Glendive, the last town of any size along the interstate in eastern Montana. In a blast of heat and a roar of wind, Richard headed up the exit ramp and steered to a stop beside the pumps. The sudden silence was jarring.

"That was fun," my sarcastic streak couldn't resist.

"Easy fix. Give me five minutes," Richard said as he got out and crossed to the front trunk lid. He dug through his cardboard box of tools and came up with that classic American solution of last resort: duct tape.

While I topped off the tank, he began taping over every vent. I wandered into the Quik Mart, bought a bottled lemonade and a pack of peanut butter crackers, and watched him splayed out under the dashboard, ripping off pieces of gray tape with his teeth. As he worked, he launched into another pitch for VW's claim to greatness: "Simplicity. That's the key. That's what's missing in our world today. Simplicity."

By the time he was finished, the interior had been transformed to a new level of "you've-got-to-be-kidding" style. Two- and three-inch-long strips of duct tape covered the dashboard like a low-budget patchwork quilt. Band-Aids on a bleeding beast. Dutch boy fingers in a bursting dam. I groped for a more encouraging metaphor.

I drove the next leg while Richard obsessively taped any vent holes he'd missed and re-secured those which hot air was still seeping through. Despite his diligence, the car remained an oven and we kept the windows open. A mile or two down the road, I noticed an interesting new addition to the roar and swelter: the distinct odor of gasoline.

"I SMELL GAS. DO YOU SMELL GAS?"

He did, but he dismissed it as the residue of a splash that had hit the front fender while I was topping the tank. "IT'LL GO AWAY IN A COUPLE MINUTES." Exhausted from the frantic morning, he closed his eyes and went to sleep.

After a couple of minutes, the smell did seem to get less intense, so I decided to accept Richard's explanation and ignore it. I was still happy to be moving, to be back on track. I tried to also ignore the heat and the noise, keeping myself focused on the road ahead, falling into a trance-like lull in which the miles and the hours melted by.

Meanwhile, somewhere behind the curtains of consciousness, my mind was experiencing a communication breakdown. Of all the five senses, smell is the quickest to get the brain's attention. Nothing stops you faster than a foul smell. The sensory signal doesn't even bother going through the upper cortex for any fancy "what's that smell?" analysis. It heads from your nose straight to the alarm bell.

Coincidentally, smell is also the first sense the brain tunes out.

It's the olfactory equivalent of white noise. Foul, putrid, and rancid scents send you instinctively rushing for an exit. But if, for some reason, you fail to heed the initial warning—say, you're a sewer worker or you're stuck in a moving vehicle and can't escape the stink—your brain shuts off the signal: "I warned you once, I'm not going to say it again." And such is the case, apparently, with gasoline fumes.

Two hundred miles later, as my head started bobbing like a cork on a pond, the message finally got through that I was slipping into unconsciousness. Somewhere in the cubicles of my pre-frontal cortex, an internal memo went out, suggesting that maybe, just maybe, those gas fumes had *not* gone away. A glance at the fuel gauge confirmed this conclusion: it was nearly empty. We'd just filled it up and now it was nearly empty. Not good.

"HEY, RICHARD?"

"WHAT?" He was half asleep.

"DO YOU STILL SMELL GAS?"

He sniffed. "NO." He closed his eyes to go back to sleep. Or was he also losing consciousness?

"CHECK OUT THE FUEL GAUGE."

He forced his eyes open and leaned over to see where my finger was pointing. That got his attention.

"WE FILLED IT LESS THAN TWO HUNDRED MILES AGO. SOMETHING'S WRONG."

He sniffed the air again. "I THINK I DO SMELL GAS."

By then, we'd nearly reached Bismarck. I took the next exit and emerged at the edge a vast truck stop, an asphalt plain of grazing semis. I steered our little Bug into an empty parking space and stopped, my woozy head bobbing as I shut off the engine and finally focused on something besides driving. "Man. I'm dizzy."

I got out and gulped down fresh air like a dehydrated cowboy plunging his face into a clear stream. Richard climbed out of the passenger side and began circling the Bug, looking for signs, going through his mental checklist. "I don't get this. Where could it be coming from?" The gas cap was in place. He knelt down to look under the chassis for leaks. Nothing.

Finally, he lifted the rear hood to check the engine. "Holy shit. This isn't good. This isn't good at all." Having aired out my foggy head a bit, I walked over and stood next to him. The engine was soaked. From the smell, obviously with gasoline. There was so much of it that it was hard to tell where it was coming from.

Richard asked me to start the car.

"Won't it blow up?"

"If it was going to blow up, it would have blown up already."

There was certain logic to that. Just in case, I reached in the driver's window to turn the key, figuring being blown backwards was better than being trapped inside a burning car.

The Bug started immediately. Without blowing up.

"Check this out."

I rejoined Richard behind the car, where he still stood, calmly gazing down like a detective who had just found the crucial piece of evidence. He pointed to the new fuel pump. A steady spray of gas was shooting out from where it was attached to the engine. Richard stepped over to the driver's door, reached in and shut off the car. "That yahoo didn't tighten the bolts."

When the spraying stopped, I bent down to get a closer look at the fuel pump. Between the pump and the engine block, I could see a thin, soggy layer of gasket sandwiched like a slice of baloney. The pump was held in place by six bolts, only four of which were easily visible and accessible.

Richard crossed to the front, pulled out his box of tools and set it on the ground behind the car. This was my first good look at our emergency tool inventory. It was a shoebox with no lid and one torn side flapping open. It contained two screwdrivers (one flat, one Phillips), a pair of needle-nosed pliers, a hammer, and duct tape.

"That's it?"

"What do you mean 'that's it'"?

"That's all the tools you brought?"

"That's all the tools I need." Richard took out the needle-nosed pliers and made a sad attempt to grip and tighten the bolts. Even I knew it was pointless. What we needed was a socket wrench. This being a German car, make that a metric socket wrench.

"You don't have socket wrenches?"

"No. Too expensive. When I need any fancy tools, I borrow them."

A decent set of metric socket wrenches costs maybe $20. You can buy them at a yard sale for $5. But not Richard. Not let's-see-how-far-I-can-go-out-on-a-limb Richard.

The good news was that we were at a major truck stop. The bad news was that it apparently had no service center. And there were no other gas stations in sight. Our only hope was across the street: a Goodyear dealer that sold truck tires.

"Why don't I go over to that tire place and ask if they have a socket wrench?"

Richard glanced up from the engine to see where I was pointing. "Good idea." He tossed the pliers in the shoebox and restowed it. "I'll come with you." He locked the car and we walked across the vast parking lot to the Goodyear store.

The place had several large bays, only one of which was open.

Inside was a vast, mostly empty space, in the center of which two men in Goodyear overalls stood beside a truck cab that was raised on a hydraulic lift. One of them was using a pneumatic wrench to re-bolt the wheels to the axles. The other was holding the nuts. The wrench's abrupt whir shot out like a shrill banshee scream. *Wheeeer. Wheeeer.*

I followed Richard as he walked over to them, shifting into truck driver mode. "Hey…"

The guy holding the nuts looked up. The other guy didn't. *Wheeeer. Wheeeer.*

Richard kept talking. "How's it going? We ran into a little problem with a loose fuel pump. Any chance you got a metric socket set we could borrow for a couple minutes?"

The guy with the nuts remained silent. The wrench man took the last nut out of his hand, held it over the last bolt, and raised the pneumatic. *Wheeeer. Wheeeer.*

I glanced around. The walls were lined with cabinets filled with tools, shiny Craftman boxes, steel tables strewn with tools of all description. The place had more tools than a NASCAR pit crew. An encouraging sign. These guys had to have a $20 set of socket wrenches. Didn't everybody?

The wrench man set down his pneumatic and wiped his brow before finally turning to face Richard. "What do you want?"

"A set of metric socket wrenches."

The guy thought for a moment, never taking his eyes off Richard. I couldn't tell if it was genuine or just for dramatic effect. Finally, he sniffed slightly and shook his head, "Sorry. Ain't got nothing metric." He broke glance and returned his attention to the wrench.

Richard was not about to give up this easily. "You're sure?

In this whole place, you don't have a single set of metric socket wrenches?"

"Nope," he walked around to the other side of the truck cab, making it clear that we had been dismissed. The mute nut holder followed him.

Richard looked at me. "Can you believe these guys?" *Wheeeer. Wheeeer.* "Fuck them. Let's go. Somebody in this hood has got to have a damn socket wrench."

For the next fifteen minutes, we walked up and down the street. This was a major intersection with a major interstate highway. Surely, there had to be one stinking mechanic. Or a Pep Boys. Or a Wal-Mart. But no. There were donut shops, foam insulation suppliers, Diller's Ducts, a closed muffler shop, but no place likely to have a metric socket set for loan, lease, or sale.

So we went back to the Bug. It appeared that our only option was to start driving—gas spraying, fingers crossed—and contine looking. To keep things interesting, we'd just passed into the Central Time Zone, so it was now 6 p.m. local time. Bismarck didn't strike me as a stay-open-late kind of town.

On the other side of the interstate, we found a gas station/ convenience store, but no mechanic. Richard went inside to ask, just in case. Through the window, I could see him talking to the clerk, getting nowhere. I asked a guy filling the tank of his pickup truck if he knew of any mechanics nearby.

He looked up at me, considering for a moment if I were friend or foe, then said, "You're in luck." He not only knew of a VW mechanic, but he knew of one whose shop was two blocks away. "Left on Windward, right on Industrial Park Road Number 2."

Go figure.

So off we went. Two minutes later, we turned right on Industrial

Park Road Number 2. Befitting its name, it was a boulevard of anonymous, corrugated steel boxes. A block down on the left, my eye caught three vintage Bugs. "That must be it."

We pulled into the lot and parked beside the other VW's. A small sign on the building read *VW R Us—Bismarck's ONLY VW specialist.* Our latest dark cloud seemed to have lifted. "Who'd a thunk it? Just when you figure you've run out of options…" I said, all upbeat, as I got out and walked to the front door.

"Never say die," Richard agreed.

The door was locked. The place was closed.

"Crap."

"What's wrong?" Richard was checking out the other VW's.

"They're closed. Hang on."

There was a phone number on the sign. I dialed it on my cell phone and got a pleasant enough voice telling me their hours were 7:30 a.m. to 6 p.m. "It's a machine. Says come back in the morning." But I wasn't quite ready to give up. "Maybe there's somebody else around who has socket wrenches."

At first glance, it was hard to tell if any other businesses along the street were open at this hour. There were few cars, and no signs of life. But having no other obvious choice (I see that smirk on all you card-carrying AAA members), we started walking down Road Number 2, knocking on doors. Richard took one side of the street and I took the other. True to the Midwest's early-to-bed reputation, nobody worked late. Everyplace was shut up tight. Except for one.

I noticed the open garage door from a block away. There was a battered stock car on a trailer out front. Inside the open door was an eclectic chaos of car parts, cardboard boxes, sooty lawnmowers, rusted appliances, and cryptic machine tools.

I looked around, but saw no one. Still, the door *was* open.

"Hello!" I banged my fist against the side of an old refrigerator. "Anybody home?"

A man's voice came faintly from behind a set of lockers.

"I'm in the shower."

Hmmm. OK, maybe I'll just wait.

Not a minute later, a man's head popped from behind the lockers. He was soaking wet and buck-naked. "What do you want?"

I tried to explain in as condensed a form as possible our situation and need for a set of metric socket wrenches. He said he didn't have any metric wrenches, but then told me to hang on.

Richard came from across the street. "Is there anybody here?"

"Yes, and he might be able to help us, but first he needs to get dressed."

"What?"

"Don't ask. Go get the car."

From the look of the garage and the complete lack of any signage, it was impossible to figure out what kind of a business this was—or if it was any kind business at all. It appeared to be a pack rat's storage facility.

A couple minutes later, the shower-taker reappeared, wearing filthy, half-zipped, orange overalls. He was a wiry, hyper-alert man I guessed to be in his fifties. "I was just showering to go home. Wife hates it when I come home dirty."

By then Richard was back. He explained our situation as he led the guy over to the Bug and lifted the rear hatch to show him the leaky fuel pump. "I just need to tighten down these bolts with a metric socket wrench."

The guy scratched his chin. "Now that I think on it, I might have a set. I remember I lent it to a friend of mine a few years ago and when I got it back, a lot of the pieces were missing. So even if I *could* find it, I can't guarantee anything."

He retreated inside and began rooting through the piles of undifferentiated junk. Richard and I exchanged wary glances— what the hell? Journeys sometimes take you to strange places. We'd made it this far. We'd survived Miles City. Maybe our luck would hold out. Maybe the gods were just testing our faith.

Sure enough, our hero emerged with a handful of loose sockets (none of them metric) and a speed ratchet. Richard took them and, one by one, test fit them to the fuel pump's bolts. Miraculously, one of them fit. "I think we're in luck."

Richard tightened the four outer bolts, but couldn't reach the two hidden ones. Ever hopeful, he turned on the engine to see if this partial solution was enough to fix the leak. It wasn't. If anything, it had made it worse. Gas was spraying out with more force than ever.

To fix it, Richard decided, he needed to tighten the two bolts inaccessibly buried behind the pump. "That's probably what the whole problem has been all along." But the only way to get the socket down to them was with a socket extender.

"Any chance you've got an extender?"

"How long?" the guy asked.

"Two inches would be perfect."

"I doubt it. But I'll look."

And so our Good Bismarckian headed back into his chaos and, sure enough, he found an extender. And not just any extender, but a two-inch extender. Just what the doctor ordered.

Richard and I were both in unspoken awe at the miracle unfolding before us. This string of coincidences would never work in fiction. Nobody would buy it. But here it was, just when we seemed again to have run out of options, an unexpected plot twist that was getting our journey back on track.

Even with the extender, it took Richard nearly half an hour, bent over the engine, to tighten the back bolts to his satisfaction. Finally, he stepped back, his face streaked with engine grit and sweat. "I do believe I've got them tight."

He handed the socket wrench back to the Good Bismarckian and got in the car. He turned the key and the Bug started up without hesitation.

"Check the engine. Is it still leaking?"

I stepped behind the car and looked into the open engine compartment. It seemed fine. "No. Looks good." Then, after giving me that moment's pause to get the words out, the fuel pump began shooting out a fresh stream of gasoline.

"Hang on. Hang on."

"What?"

The Good Bismarckian shook his head at our foul luck, slowly backing away from these cursed visitors.

"It's still leaking."

"Damn it," Richard pounded the steering wheel and climbed out of the car to get a look for himself. "Damn it, damn it, damn it."

Having just sipped hope, defeat tasted all the more bitter. Especially after what we'd endured and overcome in Miles City. This was not supposed to happen. We'd had our crisis, our dark night of faith. We'd hung in there. That plot point was over. Now we needed to be driving. We certainly didn't need to be toyed with like this. It was as if the gods on Olympus were amusing themselves by squashing our hope in new and ever more diabolical ways.

Richard cursed a few times before shifting back into thinking mode. Once again, another theory he had propounded so zealously had turned out to be wrong. It wasn't a loose gasket after all.

"It has to be a defective fuel pump!" These definitive declarations were beginning to get tiring. In Richard's way of thinking (or at least in his way of expressing himself) there was never a "might be" or "could be" or "slight probability of." It was either "is" or "isn't". Black or white. No gray. And when white turned out to be black, he quickly painted something else white. "Has to be" indeed.

Perceptive fans of ironic plot twists will no doubt recall that there had been nothing wrong with the original fuel pump. When Silva replaced it back in Miles City, the problem turned out to be a bad push rod rod sleeve in the alternator. But as he'd gone to all the trouble of having a new one shipped from Billings, he installed it anyway. Couldn't hurt, right? Of course, it never occurred to him to give us the old one back. It never occurred to Richard to ask. In his mind, that fuel pump was evil and deserving of eternal banishment.

Now, half a day and half a state later, what this meant was that we needed to find yet another fuel pump. And that meant we weren't leaving Bismarck tonight. We'd have to wait until the VW repair shop opened in the morning and hope they had one in stock.

Again, all our careful plans toppled like dominoes. Because we'd already lost a day and half in Miles City, it meant that there was no way we'd reach Jersey by Friday night. We still had 1,800 miles to go, two-thirds of the trip, and only two days to do it in — and that scenario optimistically assumed we got an early start tomorrow. Driving all day Saturday meant that Richard would miss his family get-together.

It also meant that we wouldn't get to see Mars, and probably wouldn't get to see Bill either. Mars worked until three in the afternoon. Fargo was two hours away. If we got out of here by 10, that would put us there around noon and there was no way we could afford to waste a day hanging out, waiting for him. Picking up Bill in Cincinnati meant adding at least another two hundreds miles to the trip.

The one upside was that we'd already found one of the few, perhaps only, VW repair shops in all the Dakotas. It seemed safe to assume that whoever ran the place would know how to solve our problem.

So we thanked the Good Bismarckian, gave him back the pieces of his socket set, and set off in our leaky ship, inhaling gas, driving in gloomy silence to find a safe harbor for the night. This latest downturn was harder to take than the one in Miles City. Instead of feeling like a test, it felt like a curse, a cruel deathblow to a plan that had come so magically together. The Captain Karma thing was officially over. Fate had lured us into an ambush. Back in Miles City, I'd taken a bite from the tempting apple of surrender and I now had a sudden hunger for more. This whole spiritual journey thing was getting old.

Richard was trying his level best to not kick himself. It's one thing to have to watch life's disappointments from the bleachers, seeing your team slip down another notch in the race for the pennant. It's quite another to have to face them on the field, where, one short inning ago, you'd gotten a hit. Been on base. In scoring position. Now, mid-game, you'd returned to the mound to discover that your pitching arm had gone lame. The opponents were chipping away at our lead with a walk, then a hit, then a double. It's one thing to quietly believe in something and have it turn out not to be true. It's quite another to publicly believe, convince other people to follow you, then realize you're wrong. You've let them down.

We got a room at a Hampton Inn across from the truck stop. After lugging our stuff upstairs, we decided to check out the Trucker Special Buffet Dinner (only $7.89!) We walked across the great plains of the parking lot to the restaurant, and found seats at a bar they had discreetly tucked away in the back. The room was full of mostly silent truck drivers, road-weary men, miles away from home and family, alone tonight in North Dakota, taking a brief pause before mounting up and heading out again.

I ordered a beer, and Richard said to make it two. He sipped at the beer and stared forward into blank space, lost in thought. He hadn't said but a handful of words since the socket wrench incident. I wasn't much in the mood for talking either, but tried anyway to get a conversation going. "Have you ever been in this place before? During your years on the road?"

He didn't even bother looking around. "I've been in this place most of my life."

I let it go at that. I headed over to the buffet table and Richard followed behind me. I had meatloaf and mashed potatoes. He allowed himself a piece of chicken fried steak with gravy. We went back to the bar and ate in silence. On a television suspended from the ceiling, the Lakers, barely breaking a sweat, got another game up on the New Jersey Nets.

\* \* \*

I was reminded of Job. Of all the Bible stories I'd been told in my Catholic youth, the story of Job was one that stuck. It was the one book of the Old Testament I'd been inclined to read, in part, I suppose, because it was the one book where God plays the villain.

For those of you unfamiliar with the details, the Book of Job is the tale of man whose faith is put to the ultimate test. Satan and God get into a discussion about faith (this was back when they were still talking). Satan claims that faith is fickle, and that even the staunchest believer, under enough duress, will give up on God. God, in an uncharacteristically scientific mood, offers up as guinea pig the most faithful guy they can find on short notice, a pious and prosperous family man named Job.

Satan begins his experiment by killing off Job's thousands of sheep and camels. Job's faith doesn't waiver. So Satan kills off his ten kids. Still nothing. Satan then covers Job's body with painful, oozing boils. This gets a response. Job's wife curses God. Job curses the day he was born. But he stops short of cursing God (though he does begin to wonder what he did to deserve all this abuse).

Along come three friends to console him, a trio blessed with some of the best names in the Bible. Eliphaz the Temanite tells Job that his suffering is due to the fact that everyone is guilty of some sin. Job doesn't buy it. Bilbad the Shuhite declares that the cause of Job's misfortune is his wicked children. Job doesn't buy that either. Zophar the Naamathite suggests that Job must be hiding some sin and ought to just come out with it, confess the crime, and throw himself on the mercy of the court. Job insists that he's innocent—God can do what he wants, but he's is not copping to any crime he didn't commit.

Finally, a fourth friend, Elihu the Buzite, comes along and tells Job that his sin was to question God's judgment in the first place. Just submit. Accept it. To reinforce the point, God himself makes a dramatic appearance, speaking out of a whirlwind, asking Job (I'm paraphrasing here), "Who are you to question me?" (God conveniently forgets to mention that the real reason why he'd allowed this hail of misfortune to befall poor Job was to win a bet.)

Confronted by God's direct accusation, Job decides not to argue and concedes the point. God pats him on the back, and like the host of a heavenly game show, rewards him with a new family, new livestock, and twice as much stuff as he had before.

I was reminded of Job because I so wanted to blame these latest setbacks on somebody. Was it my fault? Was this a dumb idea to begin with? Was it naïve to think that we could really make it across the entire country in five days in a stripped-down, 30-year-old car? Was it Richard's fault for not buying a set of metric socket wrenches? Was it Silva's fault for trashing a perfectly good fuel pump? Was it the fault of the factory worker who allowed a bad fuel pump to slip past quality control? Or maybe God was just messing with us?

On the scale of human trials and tribulations, these mishaps barely register. There are people suffering from all varieties of illness, people cruelly crippled by blows that have fallen from out of nowhere, people who've known losses I can't even imagine. In the face of such ordeals, it must be tempting to blame somebody, to find some target for your rage and anger. These things don't just happen. Someone—or something—screwed up. Life isn't random.

Perhaps that's another benefit of religion. God, for better or for worse, provides the comfort of feeling that at least someone's in control—our setbacks and suffering are not just pointless bad luck. Though his motives may be inscrutable to us mere humans, God has his mysterious reasons for allowing pain and suffering to occur, as well as his mysterious reasons for making things right. It's all part of God's big plan. Our misfortunes are just a chapter in a larger story, a story where everything comes out right in the end. We may not understand what's going on, but believers take some comfort in assuming that at least God understands. The curious part of this is how God gets credit for the good stuff ("My cancer is gone!"), but is rarely blamed for the bad stuff ("My cancer is back!"). The sufferer, like Job, must finally accept that he's not in a position to ask questions.

Sitting there at that truck stop bar, broken down in yet another town, our well laid plans going rapidly down the drain, and not knowing what tomorrow was going to bring, I sure felt the need to blame somebody. But I wasn't about to blame God or any other cosmic, karmic force. And it didn't feel right to blame some factory worker or Silva or Richard or even myself. To put it bluntly, shit happens. It's nobody's fault.

Maybe there was a different way to look at our predicament: what if I were to think of Richard and myself as a kind of tiny, two-man community? Isn't a community, at its most atomic level, just two people bound by a common intent: security, survival, curing cancer, playing chess or, in our case, getting to Jersey to reunite with some old friends and family, and perhaps in the process, coming to some better understanding of ourselves?

The heart of any community is this common goal. Sometimes, accomplishing the goal is easy, a no-brainer. All you have to do is show up. Other times, you run into unexpected hurdles, setbacks, breakdowns. Cars stop running. The best-laid plans go awry. And these breakdowns test your commitment to the community. They test your faith in the community's ability to achieve its goal. Maybe the problem is a lack of money, or talent, or strength, or will. Maybe the problem is the goal itself: it's unrealistic or unattainable or not what you wanted after all.

When such breakdowns happen, you have a choice: do I stay or do I go? Do I bail on this "community" (this friendship, this job, this marriage) before I waste anymore of my time and energy? There's always the option of jumping ship, crossing the border, spiraling away from a community's gravitational field in search of greener pastures.

I realized that I was facing that choice now. It was the same choice I had faced yesterday, and this morning, and that I would no doubt face again tomorrow. Am I in or am I out? Do I sulk and despair and make accusations? Do I get on a plane and fly back to L.A.? Do I choose to stop believing and let this community vanish like a figment of the imagination?

*Was it* just a figment of the imagination? Or was it something real? Haven't all the accomplishments of civilization, from a mud hut to a skyscraper, started out as just such figments of the imagination? Haven't they *become* real because a group of people took a leap of faith that someone's farfetched idea could be "realized?" And didn't this act, this process of "realization," with all its rocky stretches and breakdowns and disappointments, test their faith in exactly the same way that my faith was being tested by this constantly breaking-down Bug?

The essential ingredient for making the leap from imagination to reality is faith. A community's very existence depends upon the faith of its members that its goals can be realized. Without such faith, this town, this business, this friendship, ceases to exist.

But what I was beginning to realize, sitting there in that trucker's bar over a plate of meatloaf, was that faith isn't enough. One also has to have the courage to act. It's not enough to just profess your faith in some belief, in some envisioned goal. You also have to act, to behave as if that belief is true. And that's where it gets scary, because initially, the belief only exists in your imagination. It can become real, just like every other creation of man has become real, every building and every book, but it starts out as only a dream.

And once you take the leap, once you set sail, make a commitment, start acting on your beliefs, the journey isn't over. Your faith will be tested daily. To keep the belief alive, you need to keep sailing, to hold course, even when the going gets rough, even when the odds turn against you. Even when God lets Satan destroy your herds and kill your children and cover you with boils.

And so, for me, the question became clear: was I willing to start acting like this trip was worth believing in?

On the walk back to the motel, Richard was still quiet and sulking. I joked with him that maybe the gods were messing with us, liked they messed with Ulysses on his odyssey home.

"Yeah, maybe."

"We've got to show them that we're not going to fold, that we're going to forge on, defiant, even if it comes down to pushing the old Bug across the Delaware."

Richard laughed. "Do you really think we've got the intestinal fortitude to take on the gods?"

"Fuck, yes."

"Well, I'm glad that at least you feel that way. I was beginning to think that we were doomed."

I didn't think we were doomed at all. We were not at the mercy of forces beyond our control. I was beginning to realize that we were in a story of our own creation. And that our future depended, more than anything else, on our ability to keep creating it, regardless of what reality might throw in our way. Despite today's new batch of trouble, I was feeling oddly elated, mysteriously powerful. When we got back to the room, I called Mars to tell him that we wouldn't be in Fargo tonight.

# 9

## THE OUTHOUSE THEORY

The next morning I woke up early, around 6:30. While Richard slept, I took a quick shower and went downstairs to find some coffee. Off the lobby was the usual breakfast room: 10 pastel tables with an L-shaped buffet in the back corner. A few businessmen were scattered about. A big color TV was keeping us all company. I grabbed a couple mini-muffins and a box of Frosted Flakes then sat down to eat.

The TV was tuned to the local morning news. The woman newscaster was going for that "I could be from anywhere" accent and appearance without quite achieving it. She briskly plowed through the usual stories: a tragic wreck on the highway, a local family devastated by a raging house fire, shocking new evidence presented in a murder trial, alarming new suspicions about a popular drug. It was as if the city of Bismarck was getting the Job treatment. Despite the reassurance of telling us what's "going on today in our world," what I was seeing was a paranoid parable of a world beset by violence, tragedy, and corruption.

It occurred to me that television, be it the local news or a game show or a sitcom or a Discovery Channel documentary, is our modern society's way of telling its story. Long ago, cave people told their stories around the tribal fire, weaving the fabric of a mythical world behind the darkness, beyond the immediate. As the firelight flickered across their faces, these stories created a communal consciousness of the world "out there". By giving the unknown shape and substance, these stories gave those listeners the courage to face the darkness, to confront the beasts of the forest. These stories made them stronger, gave them life.

Today, television is our 21$^{st}$ century version of that same communal firelight. But instead of encouraging and empowering viewers, the stories I was hearing on the local news seemed to be sucking the life out of people. The implicit message was: don't move. Don't touch that dial; your only hope of survival is to never leave the house, never turn off the television.

I sometimes think that the primary goal of television today is to keep people watching television. America is turning into a country of two classes: the active and the passive. The actors and the audience. Those who do and those who watch. That can't be good.

I finished my coffee and got back into the game. Leaving the breakfast room, I stopped at the front desk to ask if they had a map of the good kingdom of Bismarck, figuring it might just come in handy. Sure enough, they did.

When I got back, Richard was still sleeping. Though it wasn't quite 7:30, I dug out the number for VW-R-US and called. They were in. As I was explaining our dilemma, Richard woke up.

"What are you doing?"

"I'm calling the VW place."

He wiped his hands across his face and dragged himself to the bathroom.

I did my best to explain our situation—the newly replaced fuel pump, the spraying gas, the bolt tightening. The guy listened patiently and asked me what year the car was. He seemed to think he could find a fuel pump in town without much trouble. "Bring it by. I'll take a look at it."

"We're in kind of a hurry to get back on the road. Any chance you might be able to look at it in, say, fifteen minutes?"

The guy laughed. The time crunch was a deal breaker. "I'm up to my ears until late tomorrow afternoon at the earliest." He recommended another place, which I jotted down on the back cover of the local phonebook. I called that number, went through the same drill and got a "maybe, later today. Call after lunch."

Richard staggered out of the bathroom brushing his teeth with his index finger. "Any luck?"

"VW R US can't do it until tomorrow."

"That sucks."

I could feel last night's surge of faith slowly subsiding like a tide, but I was determined. "I'm not giving up yet. Not while I still have a phone book and a phone."

"Maybe we can buy some tools and fix it ourselves."

"There you go. How about letting me make a few more calls while you go get some coffee? There's free breakfast just off the lobby."

"Sounds like a plan."

Richard left and I worked my way down the short list of mechanics in the yellow pages. Five calls in, an upbeat voice answered the phone, "New Light Auto. How may we help you praise the Lord?" I told him he could help me by replacing a defective fuel pump on '69 VW Beetle in the next two hours. "I do believe we can do that." I couldn't tell if he was delusional or if he really meant it.

"Are you serious?"

"If we can find a fuel pump at the parts store, I do believe I can install it for you this morning. Praise the Lord."

I wasn't quite sure what to make of his Christian effusiveness, but I didn't care. This guy was sounding like my personal savior. "Thank you. I'll be right over. I can't tell you how much I appreciate this. You've saved my day."

"I'm just a servant of the Lord. He's the one who works the miracles."

Whatever. I found the address on the map I'd gotten from the front desk, and headed downstairs to find Richard. He was sitting in the breakfast room, being lured onto the jagged shoals of despair by the siren call of the morning news.

"Richard. I found a place. Let's go."

"Really?"

"Come on. It's half a mile away."

He brought his coffee with him. I navigated while he drove. Minutes later, we pulled into a strip mall of auto repair shops. Amidst the grimy façades was one painted baby blue. A sign in bright letters shouted out: *New Light Auto Repair*.

"What is this?" Richard wanted to know.

"From what I can gather, these guys do the Lord's work on car engines."

Richard was immediately doubtful. "I don't remember anything about auto repair in the Bible."

"Remember Job?"

"Vaguely."

"He had a Bug. I think it was a 1400 BC model."

We went inside. The small front office was decorated with pictures of candy-colored cars mixed with images of an upbeat Jesus. A guy in his thirties was sitting behind a counter answering the phone, "New Light Auto. How may we help you praise the Lord?" He held up his index finger to say "Be right with you." He had a vaguely mullet-inspired haircut and a disturbingly clean, yellow T-shirt that read *Jesus is Driving*. When the call ended, he beamed us an exaggerated smile that felt like a searchlight. "Let me guess? You must be the passing travelers with the '69 Beetle?"

"That's us," Richard stepped up to the plate.

"Pull it around back and we'll take a look at it. Praise the Lord." He disappeared through a door and Richard gave me a doubtful look.

I reassured him, "It is not for us to question the good Lord's plan. Do as the man says."

"Fine. But I'm not praying."

While Richard went with the car, I stayed in the front lobby and phoned Mars, catching him before he left for work. I gave him an update, telling him that with any luck, we'd hit Fargo around noon. Unfortunately, he was working until three. As we were now in a major time crunch, it seemed we were going to miss him. "We'll probably have to blow through town." I guessed Mars could sense the disappointment in my voice. He advised me to focus my energy on moving forward. "Such trips are taken to test our souls."

I had taken Meg's CD player out of the car. To pass the time, I planted myself in a folding chair off in a corner and pulled out some Beethoven. Maybe the *Eroica.*

Beethoven's Third Symphony, known as the *Eroica* or *Heroic*, is about facing adversity. It was written during a time in Beethoven's life when he realized he was going deaf. His career as a composer and performer seemed doomed: What worse fate could befall a musician than not being able to hear his own music? But instead of giving up, Beethoven wrote one of his breakthrough works, a symphony that pushed the possibilities of music to whole new levels of expression.

The first movement kicks off with a hero theme that evokes a brave and gallant knight suiting up for battle, all shiny steel and white stallion galloping. This theme then proceeds to get battered by one musical hammer blow after another, leaving it bruised and bloodied, a barely recognizable vestige of its former self. At its darkest moment, the music sounds as if it is coming apart. Giving up. Then, gradually, the hero theme re-emerges, limping and bedraggled, but unbeaten. Victorious. It was the perfect soundtrack for this particular morning.


It took longer to fix the car than I had hoped. I went around back a few times to see Richard and a mechanic hovering around the Bug, but thought it best to stay out of their way. The kitchen already had too many cooks.

After Beethoven, I pulled out my notebook and took another shot at putting this experience on paper. After nearly two hours, Richard came and gave me a report. As he'd suspected, the fuel pump we'd waited a day for in Miles City was indeed defective. The spraying gas was not caused by a loose bolt or a leaking gasket, but by an overflow valve that opened when the fuel couldn't make it through the pump. It was a minor miracle we'd driven all the way to Bismarck. The mechanic had pulled it out and sent Richard up the block to the NAPA store for a warranty exchange. They had one left in stock. After popping it in, the Lord's mechanic (his name was Andrew) gave the car a quick roadworthiness check-up. "He noticed the missing heat shield."

"Hmm." I wondered what he thought of all the duct tape on the heat vents. "So what was his verdict?"

"He didn't see any reason why it wouldn't make it to Jersey and back. Praise the Lord."

"Praise the Lord." While Richard thanked and paid Andrew, I walked back to where the Bug was waiting, repaired and ready to go.

The moment reminded me of yesterday morning in Miles City. Then I felt the rush of victory, the joy and satisfaction of beating a foe, the visceral thrill that comes from winning. Today, I felt an entirely different emotion, a deeper and darker feeling: a realization that ours was still an old and leaky ship, that it could easily break down again, that there were no guarantees, that there was still a good chance we'd never make it to Jersey, that this journey of ours could easily end on a desolate shoulder of the interstate, in the middle of nowhere.

It was the humbling realization of mortality.

I knew we might not make it. But I also knew that, despite the fact that doubt never goes away, despite the fact that doom is always just around the corner, despite the fact that not all stories have a happy ending, I would continue on.

We stopped off at the motel to pay our bill and fetch our things. And then we set off for Fargo.

\* \* \*

It was high noon by the time we left Bismarck. With the Bug once again running, our attention shifted back to the hourglass. We were well into the fifth day of what was supposed to be a five-day drive and we weren't yet halfway across the country. Given our track record, getting to Jersey by Saturday was looking iffy at best.

But a lesser goal now seemed salvageable. I pulled out the map book and calculated when we'd be reaching Fargo. Due to our late departure from Bismarck, it was likely to be near 3 p.m., about the time Mars got off work. Maybe we still could stop, have a late lunch with him, then push on into the night, crossing Minnesota and maybe even taking a bite out of western Wisconsin. It seemed a shame not to at least consider the option. We'd come all this way, sidetracking to North Dakota for the express purpose of seeing Mars. If we weren't going to make our goal for getting to Jersey, maybe we could at least achieve this one.

"Hey, Richard. I've got a plan…"

Richard listened to my pitch. Eager to move forward, he was reluctant to stop for anything. But he agreed with my logic. Passing through Fargo when there was any hope of seeing Mars felt like a betrayal of the whole goofy mission. I think he also sensed my implicit commitment to driving non-stop afterwards. "What the hell. Why not?"

There was *one* small detail I'd neglected to mention. When I'd called Mars that morning, I'd told him we wouldn't be there. So he wasn't expecting us. As he was at work, I had no way of contacting him. Using the cell, I left a message on his home answering machine, hoped for the best, and shifted my focus to the passing landscape.

North Dakota, like much of the Midwest, is notable for its lack of obvious scenery. The land is flat, and at this time of year, the fields of grain are just getting started. To break the monotony, every fifty miles or so, we passed an immense plastic farm animal. A twenty-foot high Guernsey cow. A huge red bull. A mammoth pig, perched on a rise, gazing out at the interstate. Who put them there, or if they were intended as anything more than a humorous roadside diversion, I had no idea.

About a half hour into the ride, we came upon a stretch of eastbound Interstate 84 that was being expanded from two lanes to four. Until now, we'd been driving on the new, wider road. From this point east, construction was still ongoing, and the usable lanes narrowed to two. To our right, I could witness the road building process in reverse, an interstate deconstructed, each few miles revealing a deeper underlying layer.

First, as the four lanes became two, there was the newly finished concrete roadbed, curing in the late summer sun, blocked off from the active interstate by a phalanx of orange cones, getting ready for its coming-out party.

A few miles later, this concrete skin was stripped back to reveal a dense skeleton of reinforcing rods, lots of them, dozens of parallel rods spanning the width of a mere two lanes. The long thin rods were set less that an inch apart, raised off the graded gravel bed by what looked like triangular risers, tied at each end to a rod that ran perpendicular. They reminded me of strings on a very long guitar.

Next, we came upon crews of men assembling the rods, lifting 20-foot strands of steel off flatbed trucks, knitting them together with spools of wire hung from their belts. It seemed to be incredibly tedious work, with each short span of road requiring hundreds of rods to be wired onto risers and then knit to the previous section, days of work for just a few feet of road, proceeding at the pace of a glacier.

Beyond the work crews, the road in progress devolved to a bed of rust-colored dirt that a large yellow roller, with two massive steel cylinders for wheels, smoothed out like a lazy dinosaur making its nest. Another mile east, the gravel road crumbled and a convoy of dump trucks poured fresh dirt into neat, conical piles. The native ground, far less pure, had been leveled and covered with long sheets of tarpaper, which men with black mops sealed with hot tar, roofers minus the roof. After them, a backhoe tore into the topsoil, while a bulldozer leveled an already flat field of wild prairie grass. After that there were only a few surveyors' sticks with their orange ribbons. Finally, the edge of a farmer's field, with a rickety wood and wire fence demarking its boundary.

Seeing how much work went into the making of an ordinary road made me wonder about the people who built all the thousands of miles of roads that crisscross this country. The better part of the interstate highway system was built between the mid-1950s and mid-1970s, the immense contribution of a single generation. Who were these people? In elementary school, I'd learned about the transcontinental railroad, but not the history of road building. And yet, thousands of people must have spent a good chunk of their lives wrapping the country in these concrete and asphalt ribbons, their gift to future generations.

That got me thinking about work in general. For most adults, life is very much about work, be it building roads or raising kids or producing cable television shows. At least, I knew mine was. Work was how I spent a great deal of my time and energy. It was an activity that connected me to society at large. And perhaps for that reason, I considered it to be a big part of who

I was. I felt immensely fortunate to have a job that I enjoyed doing, that allowed me to make a decent living, that challenged me, and that even, at times, gave me the satisfaction of feeling I'd made some positive contribution to the world at large.

From what I could gather, Richard had quite the opposite attitude about work. He was living on unemployment, making a little side money by fixing computers and selling pot, both of which he would prefer to do for free. Over the past 20 years, he'd apparently had a string of short-lived jobs: microfilm processor, computer tech, taxi driver, truck driver, apartment manager— all of which he considered work for hire. Pure moneymaking. No desire to rise above entry level. I wondered why that was.

"Have you ever had a job you liked?"

"Why do you ask?"

"Just curious. Seeing all this road building got me wondering about work."

He thought a moment. "I liked truck driving for the traveling part. But the job part pretty much sucked. Which, I would say, also holds true for every other job I've ever had."

"So work, for you, has always just been about money?"

"Yeah."

"Servitude."

"Yeah."

"Have you had any desire to find a job doing something you actually liked doing?"

"No. Come on. Be honest. Doesn't a job *keep* you from doing what you like doing? Isn't that why they have to pay you? "

He had a point. "I think you can have both."

"That has not been my experience."

"What has been your experience?"

"Money corrupts. The more you have, the harder it is to honestly live by any kind of principles. Having a career, becoming part of the system, to me, is just an accepted form of prostitution, selling out your values for cash, allowing yourself to become someone you would never become on your own. To be pure, you have to be poor. In my opinion," he pronounced, becoming increasingly wound up, "All forms of business are ultimately motivated by one of two things: greed or lust. And I want no part of either." For Richard, this particular subject clearly pushed an emotional button.

"All forms of business are motivated by greed or lust?" That seemed a bit extreme to me.

"Every boss I've ever worked for has asked me to do something illegal or immoral. It's an inevitable part of the capitalist system, a natural consequence of making profit the ultimate goal. In the end, people don't matter, principles don't matter, not even the product matters. What matters is money. And whatever you have to do to get it, that's what you do."

Wait a minute. Let's rewind and review here. "Every job you've ever had, your boss has asked you to do something illegal or immoral?"

"Every single one."

"And what do you do when that happens?"

"I quit. I don't want any part of it."

"*Every* job?"

"Yes."

"Give me one example."

He came up with one immediately, "I used to have a job doing tech support. People would call up with computer problems and I was supposed to talk them through it. I'm fielding calls from people who could barely figure out how to turn the computer on. Which is fine. At first, I enjoyed it. I'd get into conversation with them, patiently talk them through the problem, try to make the whole thing a pleasant experience."

"So what's wrong with that?"

"Two weeks into it, my boss calls me into her office to tell me I'm spending too much time on the phone. My 'call time numbers' were unacceptable. She tells me, 'No call over five minutes.' Well, for one thing, that's crazy. You can't get somebody's network card up and running in five minutes. *Then* she says she wants me to start pushing upgrade parts, on-site service, and extended warranties. I say, 'Well, what if they don't need it?' She says, 'If they knew what they needed, they wouldn't be talking to you.' I went back to my cubicle, unplugged the headset, walked into her office, handed it to her and said, 'I quit.'"

"And you just walked out?"

"Yeah. I have no interest in spending my days asking people to trust me, then betraying that trust by selling them stuff they don't need. I just can't do it. I can't live with myself."

I was beginning to notice a pattern here. Richard took great pride in being a guy who didn't back down; who refused to be intimidated by power or by authority, be it his supervisor at work or some guy who wants to pick a fight or Father McSmithy. He saw himself as a person who would rather take a beating than… what?… compromise his principles?

"Don't you think there are jobs somewhere that don't involve cheating people, where you honestly provide some useful service, all on the up and up? Where integrity is an asset rather than a liability?"

"If there are, I haven't found them."

"Have you ever looked?"

"Never had an interest."

As far as I could tell, for Richard, work was a form of surrender, a capitulation to the system, a giving-in to The Man, the antithesis of freedom, integrity, dignity. In his story, the path to fulfillment was to opt out, to disengage, to make it on his own.

I couldn't argue that it wasn't a valid story, a story supported by a wealth of solid evidence. I couldn't argue that there weren't many jobs out there that sucked, that ate away at a person's dignity and self-respect, that damaged their health and well-being. Richard's stance was heroic in its way. He had led a far more hardscrabble life than I had. I had no doubt that Richard had faced far tougher obstacles in life, obstacles I couldn't even imagine, much less overcome. And through it all, he refused to put up with anybody's crap. He had stood firm. Taken his hits without flinching.

But his story also struck me as sad. Because it was a story that ultimately led to solitude, that justified hiding out. To me, being pure wasn't about being poor, it was about being alone. And that seemed a shame. The Richard that I knew was too good a person to waste his life hiding.

But what could I say that might make any difference? I knew there was no point arguing with him, because there was nothing wrong with his argument. Was there another way? I thought back to the day in Portland when he showed me his inner sanctum with all its cobbled-together computers.

"What about that computer group of yours?"

"What about it?"

"Didn't you tell me you had plans for turning it into something that generated some cash? Do some kind of consulting or something?"

My unexpected question clearly hit another nerve, a crack in Richard's righteousness, a vulnerable Achilles heal. He weighed his words before responding, "That is currently a source of contention within the group." He explained that the group had been in existence for almost two years. It had begun as a weekly get-together to share software and brainstorm about problems they were having with their computers. It evolved into an informal referral service, and word of mouth was generating a decent second income for a few of the members. One of them, a guy named Vince, wanted to turn the group into a legit business. Nothing huge. Just a dedicated phone number, business cards, set rates, maybe an ad or two. Richard nixed the idea. He wanted nothing to do with money, preferring the purity of untainted labor to the corrosive effect of cash. They had an argument that ended with Vince walking out.

"That was maybe two months ago. He hasn't been back since."

"And is everybody else O.K. with that?"

"Not really."

"So what are you going to do about it?"

"I haven't figured that out yet."

Content versus context. Here was Richard faced with the problem of Vince. According to the story he seemed to be living in, Vince was the bad guy, the Black Knight, the envoy of the evil Kingdom of Money. Richard battles with Vince and sends him into exile. End of story. But is it? Clearly, the issue was not entirely resolved. There was a deeper problem here. The warning light was still blinking on and off somewhere in the back room of Richard's mind. The Vince-as-embodiment-of-evil story was not entirely working for him.

I could also see the outlines of another story. A story about King Richard and the citizens of Inner Sanctum. But how to tell it? How to get Richard to see in himself the person I sensed he could become?

Then I remembered what he had once done for me.

"Remember back in Miles City, we were talking about why you invited me along on this trip?"

"Yeah."

"Well, I had my own list of reasons for saying yes. And one of the biggest reasons was that I felt I owed you."

"Owed me for what?"

"Well, long ago, back when we were doing those one-act plays in high school, you saw something in me that, at the time, I didn't see in myself. You saw a talent. You laughed at the stuff I wrote. You encouraged me. You believed in me."

"I assumed you were always that way."

"No. Not at all. And I may never have discovered that about myself if you hadn't seen it and showed it to me. Over the years, I've come to learn how valuable a contribution that was. And I've always felt I owed you for that. So, thank you."

"You're welcome. But what does this have to do with what we were talking about?"

"Well, back then, and right now for that matter, I can see in you another kind of talent. You have a talent for... how can I put it? For bringing things to life. A talent for seeing possibilities. You did it with those one-act plays in high school. You've done it with this trip. You have a talent for transforming an idea into a reality, for hacking through the thicket of doubt to reach the clearing of deed. A talent for keeping the faith, for believing in something and getting other people to believe in it too. Are you aware of that?"

He chewed on that one for a second. "Yeah, I guess. I just wish it was a talent I could make more use of."

"Well, you can, and you should. And maybe a place to begin is with this computer group."

"How do I do that?"

"Well, you've got to open yourself up to the possibility that something you now think is impossible, is not impossible."

"Like what?"

"Like the possibility that work and personal integrity are not mutually exclusive."

"But I just told you, I don't believe that."

"I know. But at least a few of the people in your group do believe that. But they can't do it on their own. They can't do it with you digging in your heels, saying it can't be done. Maybe, just maybe, if you allowed yourself to let go of what you know is true and step into a new possibility, you could create something amazing. Maybe you could create a job that wasn't about compromise and corruption, a business that was driven by principles of honesty and integrity."

He thought about it, liking the idea but sensing a trick, suspecting that I was somehow rhetorically conning him into doing something he would later regret. "So what you're saying is that I should beg Vince to come back?"

"No. I'm saying that by banishing the guy just because he disagrees with you, you're doing a disservice to yourself. I'm saying that maybe the problem is that you're afraid he just might be right. And that would mean giving up your secure grip on the world as you see it. But if you could find the guts to do that, to jump in the pool, you're the one who would potentially benefit the most. Your world becomes a bigger and better place. And you have the talent to lead that whole group to a much bigger and better place. The promised land of emotionally fulfilling employment. Cash without compromise."

"You're so full of bullshit."

"Am I?"

He hesitated. "So what's the first step on this miraculous transformation you've got lined up for me?"

"Call this guy Vince. Apologize for being a dick. Invite him back and actually listen to what he has to say with an open mind."

"That's not my style."

"That's the whole point. Let go of your style. Embrace the possibility of an even better style. Have a little humility instead of having to be right all the time. I mean wouldn't it be great if you could be your own boss? Doing work that you actually enjoyed doing? Helping people out without ripping them off?"

"Not have to put up with anybody's crap."

"No. That never goes away. You'll still have to put up with people's crap. You'll have to put up with the customers' crap. You'll have to put up with the group's crap. Vince's crap. And they'll have to put up with your crap. That's the beauty of it: All these people, putting up with each other's crap, discovering that behind all their annoying habits and quirky dysfunctions and selfish propensities, they have something in common. Something bigger than themselves. And that allows them to connect. To find ways past the crap."

"The Outhouse Theory of Life," Richard dubbed it. "Beneath all the crap lies common ground."

"There you go."

"I like that."

\* \* \*

What Richard had dubbed the Outhouse Theory seemed to fit my (or anybody's) relationship to any community. Working for a living, raising a family, being a citizen of anywhere, entails dealing with other people. And inevitably, something about those other people—be it work habits, ambitions, lifestyle, values, ideas, politics—is going to bug me. From my perspective, they are (pick one): lazy, stupid, incompetent, immoral, offensive, insane, vengeful, sycophantic, greedy, consumed by uncontrollable lust, or flat-out evil. From their perspective, they're just doing their job, and I'm the one with the problem. Underneath all that, what's going on is that they are not playing along with my story. They're not following my script, my expectations of the way the world should work. Each of us ultimately lives in our own private reality. We have our own histories, our own genetic makeup. Every human being takes a unique journey through life. As a result, we each interpret the world in our own way. We live by different rules, have different habits, different tolerance levels, different things we put up with, different things we don't. We have different expectations of ourselves and of each other. We all live inside our own personal story. And that can make living together a bitch.

But that doesn't mean we can't live together. Being part of a group, be it at work, at school, in a family, or in a nation, means committing yourself to a higher purpose, to the "world" of that community, sorting through the tangle of stories until you find one that you can all agree upon, a common ground. It takes a small act of transcendence, letting go of a personal story and embracing a communal one. This, to me, is an experience akin to what people mean by "surrendering yourself to God," even being "born again."

Someone told me about a commencement speech that Mohammad Ali once gave at an Ivy League university. This was in his later years, after his boxing career was over, after Parkinson's disease made speaking a huge effort. As he walked onto stage, the gathered crowd was clearly nervous, bracing themselves for the experience of seeing this man, who was once so sharp-tongued and quick-witted, reduced to pathetically forcing out a few incomprehensible words. The whole thing suddenly seemed like a bad idea, an embarrassment all around. Ali stood at the microphone, waiting for the applause to die down. When it finally did, he just stood there, not saying anything, just looking out on all these Ivy League grads, the cream of the crop, America's best and brightest hope for the future. He leaned toward the mike and slowly, struggling with each word, spoke, "I just want to say one thing." And then he held out his right hand and extended his three middle fingers to form the shape of the letter M. "It's all about going from Me..." He paused. Then he slowly turned his outstretched arm so his three fingers were pointing skywards, forming a W, concluding, "...to We."

That was his entire speech. I'm not sure if the story is true or not, but if it isn't, it should be.


As we neared Fargo, my thoughts turned to Mars. I had seen even less of him in the past 30 years than I'd seen of Richard. In high school, he'd been a geeky guy before the days of geeks, with a fondness for higher mathematics, enigmatic literature, and depressing philosophy. Obscure, difficult authors; harsh, atonal music; and rarely-screened foreign films were his milieu. My mother once described him as "too intelligent for his own good." I'd admired his steadfast eccentricity, though it did occasionally drive me nuts.

The last time I saw him was just after college. I was living in Washington DC, when he came to visit during a winter break. There was a mild snowstorm, and he wanted to go to the Library of Congress to see some esoteric exhibit. I remember losing patience with his appetite for the arcane, saying something to the effect of, "Why bother? You'll only end up griping about what's wrong with it." We ended up doing nothing. He left the next day and I hadn't seen him since.

We arrived on the outskirts of Fargo just after 2:30. The interstate through town was under construction, and Mars had earlier given me directions for skirting the traffic. Just west of town, we diverted onto a country road that wound around towards where he lived. As we drove, my eye caught what I assumed at first to be two dark birds, spinning unusually elegant circles. Moments later, they headed toward us, drawing parallel lines of contrail: two F-16 jets.

We stopped to get gas and watch them as they reappeared from the north, not 1,000 feet above the ground, flying over our heads, then swooping straight up into the sky and disappearing again. The gas station attendant explained they were practicing for tomorrow's air show.

I cleaned off the Bug's bug-spattered windshield. A little girl, maybe 10, black, walked by, pushing her bike. She was the first African-American I could recall seeing since leaving Portland. I waved to her and she waved back.

Ten minutes later, we found Mars' street. His address brought us to a stark, newly constructed, eight-unit apartment building. We pulled up to a row of closed garage doors. We got out and searched for the front entrance. On the side of the building was a door that opened to a narrow hall with a row of mailboxes. Mars' name was on one of them, guiding us upstairs to his unit on the second floor. I knocked. No answer. He'd told me that morning that he'd be home from work at 3. It was now 3:14. As I had no work number for him, all we could do was wait.

While Richard and I sat in the Bug in Mars' driveway, I remembered that I hadn't spoken to Bill in Cincinnati since leaving L.A.

"What should we do about Bill?"

Richard looked at the map before responding. Sidetracking to Cincinnati meant driving south from Chicago through Indianapolis, a 200-mile detour. Then we'd have to find Bill's house and spend a couple hours hanging out. "I'd really like to get to Jersey sometime Saturday afternoon for the thing with my family. I don't see how we can do that and still go to see Bill."

Bill had also mentioned wanting to drive with us to the reunion, but I had no idea how we could fit him into the Bug. So I called him on my cell phone to deliver the bad news. He was home. I explained the situation, told him about our problems with the car, and apologized that it didn't look like we were going to make it to Cincinnati. He was disappointed, but understood, saying he'd try to find some way to get to Jersey on his own for the reunion on Sunday.

After that, we waited, both of us glancing frequently at our watches. After 45 minutes, there was still no Mars. Richard wanted to go.

"Let me try one more thing." It occurred to me that if I could get the main number for the college from information, they might have an operator who could redirect the call to his office number. It worked. A minute later I had him on the phone. After my earlier call, he'd assumed we weren't coming and decided to stay late to grade tests. "Give me five minutes."

Five minutes later, a white sedan pulled up, driven by a man I didn't recognize. Thirty years ago, Mars had been tall and gangly, with dark hair all cowlicks and a scrawny adolescent's goatee. Now he was as plump as Santa and buzz-cut gray. He climbed out of his car, a big grin on his face, spreading his arms in welcome, delighted to see these two apparitions from the past.

"Good to see you, Mars." I gave him a hug.

"Good to see you. I have to say, I rarely get guests passing though Fargo."

"Well, we're glad to finally hook up with you. It was looking pretty iffy there for a while."

"Did you get a chance to check out the town?"

"Just the drive here. Unfortunately, we're kind of pressed for time."

"Well, why don't I give you the 10-minute tour and then we can get something to eat?"

We piled into his car and drove around the nearby sights of Fargo, passing an austere building Mars called Norwegian Hall. "This is a town proud of its Viking roots."

"I didn't realize the Vikings made it this far."

"Oh yes." Mars told us about what he considered to be Fargo's one true tourist attraction: a full-sized Viking burial ship that had sailed all the way to Norway. "The man who built it, one Robert Asp, was a junior high guidance counselor who was obsessed with the theory that the Vikings got here before Columbus. To prove that it was possible, he wanted to build an authentic longship and sail it back to Norway. So he did the research and drew up plans based on a burial ship that had been dug up somewhere in Scandinavia. He and his brother went into the forests up north and cut down their own oak trees. He hauled them back to Fargo, rented an abandoned potato warehouse downtown and converted it into a shipyard."

"When was this?" I asked.

"In the early seventies. It took him six years to build the ship. When it was finished, he took it for a maiden voyage in Lake Superior. A few months later, he died."

"In the ship?"

"No. I think he had leukemia."

"How did the ship get to Norway?" Richard wanted to know.

"A couple of years later, a group of his relatives recruited a crew and sailed it from Duluth, through the Great Lakes, across the Atlantic, 6000 miles to Norway. It took 72 days."

"In a Viking burial ship?"

"In a Viking burial ship."

And here I thought a week in the Bug was an adventure. "How did it get back to Fargo? Did they turn around and come back?"

"No. I think they shipped it somehow. Unfortunately, that's about it for tourist attractions. I've heard tell that outside town there's a sidewalk with Ted Nugent's handprints. But I can't vouch for that, as I haven't actually seen it."

The ten-minute tour over, Mars took us to what he described as Fargo's only decent Mexican restaurant. "As you can see, I've learned to enjoy eating, and like to take every advantage of the few pleasures Fargo has to offer."

For once, we had a full-out feast. Fajitas. Chimichangas. Chicken mole. As we settled into the food, Richard steered the conversation towards the personal. "So Mars. You seem to be doing pretty well for yourself."

"Don't let looks deceive you. The life of a math professor is far from the paradise it may appear to be." It was good to see that Mars hadn't lost his flare for self-deprecation.

"Do you get to do any research, or is it all classes?" I asked, trying to pin down some specifics. He said a good chunk of his time was dedicated to students, most of whom were farm kids still struggling to adapt to the big city environment of Fargo. Every few semesters, one would emerge who actually showed an interest. The rest were just doing time, putting in their hours to collect the required credit.

The upside was that he occasionally got to travel to math conferences. Rome. Berlin. Kyoto. "I even went to Russia once." But he always ended up back in Fargo. I asked him why he hadn't moved somewhere else, and he replied, "Don't think I haven't tried."

The conversation turned to what he described as his one true passion in life these days. "You've heard of High Pointers?" We both confessed that we had not. He explained that High Pointers are a loosely knit group dedicated to the goal of reaching the highest point in all 50 states. They rarely, if ever, got together. They pursued their objective on their own, recording their results by the honor system. "What would be the point of lying?"

Mars had already been to the highest point in a handful of states, a humble accomplishment in the Midwest that required more driving than climbing. In pursuit of ever-higher altitudes, he had traveled extensively throughout the western half the United States and was intimately familiar with the most obscure of back roads. Richard, who had also done his share of back road exploring when he lived in Salt Lake City, pulled out the map and the two of them spent a good half hour asking, "Have you ever been here?"

"So how many highest points have you been to in the Rockies?" I eventually asked.

Mars just shook his head. "Unfortunately, none." He explained that, due to his excessive weight and poor physical condition, his every effort in the more vertical states had ended in failure. Mountain climbing was out of the question. Steep and winding trails weren't much better. Many times, he'd driven for days to face a 1,000-foot hike, only to quit halfway up the trail. This didn't seem to bother him. On the contrary, it gave him an excuse to go back another day, exploring another back road route in the process.

The conversation next turned to the subject of wives and children. I showed Mars a picture of Esmé, and Richard told him about Meg and Kevin.

"I don't know if you heard or not," Mars confessed, "But I was briefly married myself."

"Was?" I asked.

"To a woman from Iceland. I met her at one of my conferences. Her specialty was calculus. She moved over here with me."

"When was this?"

"About five years ago. The divorce only became final last month."

"I'm sorry to hear that. What happened?"

Mars explained that after they'd been married and living in Fargo for two years, he discovered that her semiannual visits back to Iceland weren't entirely motivated by homesickness. She had boyfriend in Reykjavik. When Mars found out, he confronted her. She pled guilty, but refused to give him up. For the next two years, they attempted to iron this wrinkle out of the fabric of their marriage, to no avail. One day she just disappeared.

Richard asked if he was at least happy now that it was over, and he said no, "But not as unhappy as I was two years ago, and for me, that's progress." Currently, he described himself as alone, discontent with his lot in life, and unresolved as to what to do about it. "But now at least I know that things can be worse."

After the meal, we went back to his apartment, a spacious, two-bedroom place filled with a library of books. Though he'd moved in months ago, he was still only half unpacked. Not that there was much to unpack. He owned minimal furniture, few clothes, and little decor. "Two dishes and two thousand books."

We spent the next hour talking, mostly about another of his current pursuits, which also happened to provide regular excuses for getting out of Fargo: his endeavor to locate the source of the Mississippi River.

The Mississippi rises north from the Gulf of Mexico, roughly dividing the country into east and west. At the same time, it is also one of America's great unifiers, connecting place to place, north to south, a watery highway of commerce and ideas. Lewis and Clark traveled it briefly as they made their way from St. Louis to the mouth of the Missouri. The Mississippi continues north from there, defining eastern Iowa, then separating southern Minnesota from Wisconsin before taking a turn to the northwest, splitting Minneapolis/St. Paul into two cities.

From there, it continues up into the center of Minnesota, weaving through lake country until it finally peters out altogether. Apparently it has no precise source, no deep hole bubbling up from the underworld. It just gets smaller and smaller until it vanishes. Despite the efforts of local promoters to claim this field or that mud hole as the Official Headwater of the Great Miss, the truth (according to Mars) is that they are all wrong. "It's a debate, that's been going on for over a century. " True to form, Mars' real interest seemed more in disproving existing theories than coming to any definitive conclusions of his own. The cantankerous math professor in him liked the idea that America's dividing line did not end in a point.

I noticed that it was getting near 7 o'clock, and reminded Richard that if we were going to make it through Minnesota tonight, we needed to get started. Having driven from Fargo to Jersey many times himself, Mars shook his head at our naïve ambitions.

"Two days. It takes two full days. Believe me."

"We can do it."

"Well, then. You'd better get started."

We said our good-byes. He handed us a pile of business cards to pass out at the reunion and promised to stay in touch. Then he went over to one of his many bookshelves and pulled out a slim volume published by a French group called the Oulipo Laboratory. According to the back cover, they were dedicated to "the possibilities of combining mathematics and literature" through the use of "self-imposed restrictive systems." Like a short story in which no word contained the letter "e" .

Why? Why not?

All in all, the perfect memento.

# 10

## A DOWNPOUR OF DEMONS

We left Fargo at just after 7 p.m., several hours later than we'd originally intended. The summer sun was just beginning to sink towards the horizon as we crossed the Red River into Minnesota. Up ahead, darkening purple clouds gathered like a meteorological herd of buffalo.

With our visit to Mars behind us and the side trip to Cincinnati cancelled, our sole focus now was getting to Jersey, hopefully in time for Richard's family reunion on Saturday.

"When on Saturday is the get-together with your family?"

"It's in the afternoon. I think it starts around one."

It occurred to me that Richard had barely mentioned this event since it came up in passing back in Portland. What little he had told me—that he hadn't been home in 14 years, that he rarely spoke to his mother—suggested that it carried more than a little emotional significance. I was curious to know more. "Who is going to be there?"

"From what I've been told, everybody. My three sisters. My brother. All their many kids. My mom. A few of my uncles."

"And you haven't seen any of these people in 14 years?"

"No. A lot of the kids, I've never seen."

"So you're like their legendary Uncle Richard."

"Yeah, I guess."

"Do they all live in south Jersey?"

"No. My brother's flying in from Florida. A sister and her family are driving down from upstate New York. My two uncles—my father's brothers—are coming from Pennsylvania."

I hadn't realized until then just how big a deal it was. The entire extended family getting together. People flying in from out of state—wedding and funeral stuff. I wondered if Richard saw it this way. He didn't seem to—but how could he not? What was really going on here?

"Sounds like a quite a to-do."

"Yeah."

"Why did you go back there 14 years ago?"

"My sister's wedding. And then, I was only there for a day or two. She has three kids now that I've never even met."

"Before that, did you go back there much?"

"Not really. Just the one time I lived back there in the early '80s."

"Did you spend any time with any of your family then?"

"I spent a little time with my older sister. That's about it. We'd gotten fairly skilled at avoiding one another."

From the sound of it, after he'd been thrown out of high school and left home, close to thirty years ago, he'd avoided his family for all of his adult life. I recalled what he'd said about feeling 'less than' and about his father's abuse.

The unspoken details flew around us inside the car like a shadowy spirit. I hesitated, wondering whether or not to press on with the conversation, whether or not to pry into something that wasn't my business, wasn't my life. I figured if he didn't want to talk about it, he wouldn't. But if he did, maybe I ought to at least give him that opportunity.

"What do you think has kept you away for all these years?"

He looked out at the road like there was something up ahead that he couldn't quite get into focus. "I don't know. Maybe too many demons."

I didn't say anything.

Richard went on, "The last time this much of my extended family was together was at my father's viewing."

"What was that like?"

"Strange. He'd died while he was at work. Massive heart attack. Completely out of nowhere. The night before, he'd seemed fine. His usual unpleasant self. Three days later, we were all in a funeral home for his viewing. They had him laid out in an open casket. All of us kids stood in a line while friends and relatives consoled us. I remember my mother was a wreck. My sisters were in shock."

"How were you?"

"My most distinct memory of that evening was of feeling nothing. Being conscious of feeling nothing. That's what made it so strange. I wasn't sad to have lost him, but I wasn't glad that he was gone either. I just felt nothing. Everybody was upset and crying and everything, and I was just standing there, blank."

"Why was that?"

"I suppose whatever love I had for the man had been buried

under a powerful anger, built up from years of his abuse."

"What kind of abuse?"

Richard's reply was calm and matter of fact, "He used to beat me with a leather belt. On a fairly regular basis."

"What for?"

"Who knows? Staying out too late. Talking back to my mother. Getting a C in Algebra. Pretty much any excuse."

"He'd just get pissed off and start hitting you?"

"He'd get pissed off and take me into a back bedroom."

"Did he hit your brothers and sisters too?"

"No. Just me. The next three kids were girls. You don't hit girls."

"Did your mother know about it?"

"Everybody in my family knew about it. It was very hard not to know about it. They'd all be sitting at the kitchen table in the middle of dinner while it was going on."

"And nobody did anything? Your mother never said anything?"

"What could she do?"

"Tell him to calm down? Knock it off? Stop hitting you?"

"No. She never did anything like that. She pretty much acted like it wasn't happening. Maybe she was afraid of him, too. Maybe she thought he was right. Maybe she thought I deserved it." His pause before saying that last sentence gave it a reverberation that hinted at something more. Like he'd wanted to say something else, but didn't.

"Did *you* think you deserved it?"

"You don't get 'disciplined' for nothing, right? I must have done *something* wrong."

"Like what?"

"I don't know. Not measuring up to some standard somehow. Letting them down. Being a general disappointment."

"Do you still feel that way?"

Richard paused to ask himself that question before responding. "No." He let the word hang in the air a moment to hear how it sounded, hear if he believed it himself. "It's taken quite a while, but I think I've finally stopped beating myself up."

I wondered if he'd ever had this conversation with anyone else. "Have you ever talked to anyone in your family about this?"

"I talked about it once, briefly, with one of my sisters."

"What did she say?"

"She remembered a few instances. She just figured I'd done something really wrong."

"How did she feel about your father?"

"I don't know. I don't know how she felt about me, either." Another long pause, while he weighed how much more he wanted to say. "A few years ago, my mother wrote me a letter, basically to tell me what was going on with the family, asking me how I was, that sort of thing. At the end of it she wrote a sentence or two where she said she was sorry about the beat-ings."

"That's the only time she ever mentioned it?"

"Pretty much."

"And you never mentioned it to her?"

"God, no. Until I got that letter, I think I had pretty much pushed the whole experience into some back corner of my brain. Like it was no big deal: 'Daddy hit me. Boo hoo.' In the course of my life, I've met many people who've experienced far worse abuse. I figured, who am I to complain? But that letter kind of shook me up. It made me realize how much that whole experience had affected me, still affects me. It was something I needed to deal with. Because it wasn't going to go away."

"Which is partly the reason for this trip?"

"Basically, yes. And then there's this whole confluence of events. Like planets lining up. This year, I'm the same age as my father was when he died. Kevin is about the age I was when I left home."

"And what's the significance of that?"

"Well, so far, I've turned out all right. I didn't turn into my father. I'm still alive. I've made it though a lot of bullshit and I'm still here. I did it. The only thing I have yet to do is go home. Go back to face the demons."

So there it was. Out on the table. I had my suspicions, but until that moment, I hadn't realized just how much this trip meant to him. And why it had taken him 30 years to summon the courage to make it.

I think one of the hardest things for anyone to accomplish in life is to resist repeating the sins of their parents. They are so imbedded in our genes and in our upbringing, so tightly woven into the fabric of who we are, that not repeating them is all but impossible. It was a battle Richard had apparently been waging all his life. This battle to not become his father. And he had won. Now he was finally ready to return home.

I wondered what he was expecting.

"What are you going to do when you get there? Is there anything specific you're hoping to do?"

"I'm not sure, really. For one thing, I hope to get an opportunity to talk to my mom and at least put the cards on the table. Not to blame anybody. Just to acknowledge that what happened

happened. If only to help her understand where I've been for the past 30 years. As for everybody else, I just want them to see that I'm O.K.—as opposed to the fucked-up deviant I could be."

And we left it at that.


We drove southwest along I-94 towards Minneapolis/St. Paul, through rolling green pastures marked by the occasional weathered barn and isolated farmhouse. Ahead of us loomed a massive, dark violet bruise of storm clouds. To either side, the sun's sharp, red-orange light illuminated the west face of anything standing, like an arc light from heaven, creating a scene of otherworldly intensity, made all the more brilliant by the long, dark shadows cast to the east.

Through the rearview mirror, I could see the sun setting like a fallen king, dying in a blaze of glory on some apocalyptic battlefield, surrounded on all sides by mournful backlit gold and scarlet clouds—loyal warriors gathering around to witness his last gasp. Up ahead, the eastern sky had grown even darker, a roiling mass of deep gray, black, and blue, descending like a heavy blanket that would soon envelop us.

The ominous landscape, mingled with Richard's story of his father's viewing, recalled the tale of how Meriwether Lewis met his end. He, William Clark, and the other 31 members of the Corps of Discovery survived their three-year trek across the Louisiana Territory and made it back to civilization remarkably unscathed. For all the daily life-threatening dangers they encountered, from grizzly bears to raging rivers, from freezing blizzards to strange diseases, not one of them had died.

Three years after their triumphant return, in 1809, Lewis

succumbed to a lifelong battle with depression and committed suicide. He went crazy one night and shot himself.

Death is life's greatest mystery. We all know it's coming, but few of us have any idea when or how. We humans are supposedly the only species that goes through life conscious of the inevitability of our own death, and this awareness is frequently cited as one of the roots of religion. The theory goes that in order to live with the terrifying knowledge of death, humans need a counter-balancing belief in an afterlife, in a soul that somehow survives to live on in a spirit world, or to return, reincarnated in this one.

I recalled a conversation I'd had when I was 15 with one of my most radical-thinking friends, a guy who, even at that tender age, could see through the bullshit in just about everything. For some reason, we were talking about what happens to you when you die. I confessed that I was beginning to suspect that when you die, you just die. You don't wake up at Heaven's Gate or in some spiritual waiting room. You don't drift around as a ghost or get transferred to a newborn's body. You just die. Fade to black. The end.

My friend adamantly disagreed, "That can't be true. I couldn't go on living if I believed that." So I asked him what he did believe. And he said he wasn't sure, "But this can't be all there is. There has to be something else. You can't just *die*."

Years later, I remember having a similar conversation with a woman in her twenties, another person I took to be an open minded, far-from-conservative thinker. She, too, firmly believed that life doesn't end when you die.

I asked her what then, in her opinion, survived the passage, "Do your senses survive? Do you think you can still see and hear?"

She thought about it for a moment, then said, "I guess."

"But aren't your sense organs part of your body? Don't they die when your body dies? I mean, how could they not? What would they connect to?" It made perfect sense to me. "Or do you think you still have hands and feet? A mouth so you can talk and eat? Do you still eat?"

"I don't know. Probably not."

Once she started squirming, I knew I was on a roll, "Do you think your brain still works? Do you have memories? Thoughts? Do you think you can still experience emotions? Enjoy anything?"

"I would hope so."

"But if your body is gone and your brain is gone, what's left? Do you think your soul has phantom body parts? If so, why do you even need a body?"

She didn't say anything at first, trying to process this sudden attack upon her comfortable relationship with death. Finally, she looked over at me and asked, "You know what your problem is?"

"What?"

"You think too much."

Of all the things she could have said, she had to say *that*. When I was 14, I was driving with my dad, and we were listening to the radio. A commercial came on for a new fitness center, which at the time was a novelty. It had a jingle that kept repeating the line: "You think too much. You think too much. You think too much." The implication was that you need to focus on your body more.

I remember being mildly outraged. "What a bunch of meatheads! How can anybody think too much? The problem with most people is that they don't think enough!"

My dad didn't say anything. His silence rendered his reaction all the more memorable.

I guess, in that respect, I haven't changed much. I still think too much. And I still think that when you die, you die. But for some reason, that doesn't scare me. I wondered why.

"What do think happens to you after you die?" I asked Richard.

"What?! Where do you come up with this stuff?"

"I'm just curious. It's my whole spiritual journey thing, you know. Cut me some slack. What do you think happens after you die?"

"I think you just die. It's like going to sleep."

"No afterlife? No disembodied soul?"

"No."

"And the prospect of that doesn't terrify you?"

"No. Why? What do *you* think happens to you when you die?"

"Same. I think you just die."

"So, why are you asking me this?"

"I was just thinking. A lot of people seem to have a hard time accepting the finality of death. I wonder why we don't."

"Because a lot of people are living in delusion and refuse to accept reality."

"What delusion is that?"

"The delusion that life can't possibly end, that unlike all the other living things on earth, we're somehow special, we get to cheat death."

"And you don't buy that?"

"No. I don't think we're all that much different than any other creature on this earth. Fleshy bags of guts and bones."

"You don't think any part of you continues on after you die?"

"Maybe your memory in other people's minds. Maybe the handful of good deeds you've managed to accomplish. That's about it," Richard pronounced, as usual the untroubled traveler on the post-religion highway, "What do you think?"

What did I think? Richard's take on death was not that far from my own. Light goes on, light goes off. But, coursing down this twilight road, I was again getting that faint suspicion that there was more to it, that I was missing something. "I'm not really sure. I see myself as kind of a cereal bowl."

"A cereal bowl?"

"Well, some kind of bowl. I see myself as a container. During my life, the container gets filled with all this stuff, stuff accumulated over the years from the Bazaar of Belief, from the culture, from other people, from you, from Mars. Life is about filling the bowl of your being. Arranging it. Organizing it. Seeing how much you can cram in. Tossing out old stuff to make room for new stuff. That collection of stuff in my bowl is me. That's the essence of who I am. My body is not me. My body just contains me. It's the bowl. And when my body dies, when the bowl breaks, all that stuff that was me is still there. It all came from outside of me to begin with. It passes in and out of me my whole life. I was just its caretaker for a while."

"You think you're a cereal bowl?"

"More like a flower vase maybe. Or like a junk drawer."

"You know what your problem is?"

"I think too much."

"Exactly."


I took over driving just west of St. Cloud. The looming storm had evolved into actual rain. It started out as a few negligible sprinkles, but quickly accelerated to a genuine downpour, with visible sheets of water whipping up the interstate like waves, appearing in the feeble beams of our headlights for a blinding instant before whacking into the windshield like a giant's slap. To keep things interesting, the car began to hydroplane, slipping uncontrollably into the next lane before regaining its grip on the road. The Bug's aerodynamics, not to mention its tires, were barely up to the task. The wipers did their merry little dance, swaying happily back and forth in sync as if they were frolicking in some pastoral Bavarian sun shower. Whoever designed them clearly had never experienced a Minnesota downpour. I found myself gripping the wheel with both hands, mono-focused on the 20 visible feet of road ahead.

Worse than the rain was the wind. It had slowly intensified from a slight southern breeze to a full bore, 40-mph gale. The rain was blowing sideways. I had to steer the car at an angle to the road, into the wind, like a helmsman tacking a sailboat, just to keep going straight. The trees, made briefly visible by intense flashes of lightning, were whipping the air like epileptics. Every so often, the odd trash bag or discarded sheet of newspaper would flick into my field of vision like an insane bird caught in a tornado.

A semi pulled up to our starboard side, mercifully offering a brief shield from the gale. Unfortunately, between the low visibility and the tendency of the car to hydroplane, I was only doing 40 miles an hour. The semi, far more prepared for such weather, quickly pulled ahead. The moment its rear cleared the car, the sudden re-exposure to the wind shoved the Bug a full lane to the left.

This was starting to get dangerous. There were too many variables in this equation. One false move on my part, one more gust like that last one, one car swerving out of control ahead of us, and we were crash test dummies in a tin can. It was time to speak up. Sound the alarm.

"It's getting a little windy."

Richard hadn't noticed. He looked up as a bullwhip of rain slapped the windshield.

"This is nothing. I've been in much worse than this."

My inner back seat driver begged to disagree: We're not exactly in an 18-wheeler here, Superman. Despite your unruffled confidence, your track record has been a few clicks shy of stellar. So your lack of concern isn't exactly calming me down. And my right arm is starting to go numb from keeping your ice skate of a car on course.

In my mind, a safety video was running at full volume. Far more people die in car accidents that die from shark attacks, snakebites, lightning strikes, airplane crashes, and terrorism combined. It is not irrational, wimpy, or unmanly to acknowledge you've reached the outer limits of safety. It's just stupid.

The rain was coming down in solid sheets. This was Noah rain. Rain from a wrathful god. By now, I couldn't see 10 feet in front of me. I had to physically wrestle the steering wheel to stay on course.

"I'm pulling off."

"Why?"

"For one thing, I can't see and I can barely control this car. For another thing, I need to pee."

"Fine."

When a blurry sign suggested an upcoming exit ramp, I went for it. I leaned forward, squinting to make out any hint of the off ramp. When the lane seemed to widen, I eased right, hoping I wouldn't mistakenly drive off the road. By this point, we were going maybe 20 mph.

Up ahead, I could faintly make out some orange cones and gambled that they divided the interstate from the ramp. I aimed to the right of them. I still couldn't see a ramp. Then, maybe 100 yards ahead and slightly up, I saw what appeared to be a blinking red light, cutting through the storm like a lighthouse beacon. I steered toward it, rising up the ramp. At the top, as I slowed to a stop at the light, the rain let up long enough for me to get some bearings. To the right appeared to be a strip mall, closed for the night. To the left an overpass led across the interstate to the green and white fluorescent glow of what I hoped was a gas station.

There was no other traffic in sight. I turned left and made for the glow. It was a gas station. There appeared to be a roof over the pumps, so I pulled under it and stopped. When I opened my door, the wind caught it and snapped it out of my hand, like a storm cellar door in a twister.

"Jesus."

A knocked-over trash can swayed like a wounded dog on the pavement between me and the door to the mini mart. The wind picked at it like a pack of starved rats, disembowling food containers and empty wrappers and wildly running off with them in their teeth.

Richard was impressed.

"It *is* kind of windy."

Indeed. Now that I wasn't battling it, the weather seemed comically over the top, almost fictional. Another of the mythical beasts we needed to defeat before making our way to Ithaca.

Instantly drenched, I sprinted past the ravaged trash can. Inside, the mini mart was a haven of white light and calm, empty except for a teenage girl behind the counter wearily paging through a gossip magazine.

"Damn," I said to her, rubbing my hands together, "Got a little weather going out there, huh?" She shrugged and went back to her magazine.

I paced the aisles to warm up and dry off. The brightly lit rows of snacks struck me as a testament to man's ever more ingenious ways of turning corn into junk food. I eventually found a pack of peanut butter crackers and a bottle of water. In a back corner was a rack of Minnesota postcards.

Richard had come in and was wandering the other end of the store. I heard him ask the girl how far we were from Minneapolis.

"Hour. In good weather."

This didn't bode well for our plan. We'd hoped to at least make it into Wisconsin tonight. I could see Richard was doing the same calculation in his head.

"So what do you want to do?" I asked Richard.

"I'll drive for a while. Let's go until midnight and see where we're at."

Normally, I would have been happy to pack it in here and now, but there was the mission to consider, the goal of getting Richard to his reunion. At this point, it was beginning to seem more important to me than it was to him. And I was not about to let a little bad weather get in our way.

From inside the bright security of the store, the wind and rain were still raging like the climactic scene in a Wagner opera. But what the hell? I paid the girl and followed Richard into the downpour. Cue *Ride of the Valkyries*.

This time, Richard drove. The downpour had not slackened. Visibility was near nothing, the wind cranked up to hurricane force. Though Richard wouldn't admit it, I could tell he was battling as much as I had been. We crept along, rarely making it to 50 mph. An hour later, we were only halfway to Minneapolis.

To my mind, the risk of wrecking the car was outweighing the benefit of putting miles behind us. That would be a disaster. That would end all hope of getting to Jersey.

"Look, Richard, this is stupid. Let's bag it, get a little sleep and hit the rode at dawn."

"I can go another hour."

"What's that going to buy us? Forty miles? Is it really worth risking getting into an accident?"

"We're not going to get into an accident."

"Richard, it's the people who don't think they're going to get into an accident that get into accidents. Nobody's driving around, thinking, 'Gee I'm going to get into an accident here. I better just keep on going. Don't want to miss my meeting with fate.'"

It was not easy to play Felix to Richard's Oscar. It was somehow contrary to the spirit of adventure and guy-ness.

"Look, if you're scared, we'll get off."

It was a middle-school dare.

I looked out at the torrent, barely able to discern the lane line in the road, as if we were drifting in a dark river. The wind was bucking harder than ever. There were no other cars in sight. This was nuts.

"Fine. I'm scared. Let's get a fucking hotel room."

"Fine. I'll get off at the next exit."


We drove another five miles before reaching what appeared to be an exit. Again we inched towards what we assumed was a ramp. At the top, there were no hotels in sight, only another gas station/convenience store.

"What do you want to do?" Richard asked.

"Let's go in and ask."

We carefully made our way around pools of uncertain depth and eased into the flooded parking lot. Richard pulled up right in front of the door, but we still got a quick cold shower before making it inside.

Unlike the last store, this one was inhabited by a half a dozen fellow travelers taking shelter from the storm. I asked the guy behind the counter if he knew of any nearby hotels. He didn't. I asked if he had a phone book. He did. There was a large, local map taped to a wall and we tried to figure out where we were relative to the dozens of hotels in the phone book. We appeared to be in Albertville, a suburb twenty miles west of Minneapolis. I used my cell phone to call a Best Western with an Albertville listing. The sleepy night clerk told me he was one exit up. Go left off the ramp, right at light, two blocks to a stop sign, turn left, he was on the right about a quarter mile. Couldn't miss it.

So back we went into the unrelenting storm.

It took us another 10 minutes to make it to the next exit. When we got off the ramp, the Best Western was nowhere in sight. But a Traveler's Inn was staring right at us.

"Let's just go there."

"But what about the Best Western?"

"Screw it. Let's just get this over with."

So Traveler's Inn it was. Richard navigated us through puddles into the parking lot. I grabbed my bag from the back and ran inside. The first thing I noticed as I hit the lobby was the distinctive smell of curry.

It triggered a warning light in my weary brain: the Patels.

Having spent my share of time on the road working various reality TV shows, I have witnessed the slow transformation of low-budget motels across America. In the last decade, many have been bought up by Indians. India Indians. That curry smell immediately triggered a set of visceral connotations: peeling wallpaper, plumbing fixtures that come off in your hand, paper-thin towels, chairs with one leg missing. It's as if their first move after buying the motel was to strip it of anything remotely valuable and replace it all with crap you couldn't give away at a yard sale. Wafer-thin pillows made from taking the stuffing from actual pillows and splitting it into four. Used shower curtains that come with half the grommet holes already ripped. TV remotes that are bolted to the night table. And phones that can't be unplugged. I've spent many discontented nights in these motels, accumulating an enduring resentment at this utter disregard for customer comfort and for the implicit assumption that I'm going to steal every loose object in the room.

Normally, I would have left and gone somewhere else, just on principle. But I was so relieved to be out of the car, and so dead tired, that I couldn't bring myself to walk away. How bad could it be?

The front desk was behind bulletproof glass, another classic touch. There was no one behind it. I banged on it a couple times until an old woman in a sari came through the curtains. At the same moment, Richard entered behind me.

"Can I help you?"

"Do you have any double rooms?"

"Yes."

"How much?"

"Ninety-nine."

"Ninety-nine dollars? You're kidding me?"

She glanced out the front window at the rain and then at Richard, standing sopping wet behind me. "Ninety-nine."

She knew she had me, and so did I. "Fine. Ninety-nine."

The woman ran my credit card and slid a guest registration card through the slot in the glass window. I filled it out with an unintelligible scrawl and slid it back.

"Check out time is eleven."

"We'll be out of here before sun-up."

She slid out a plastic key card and retreated behind the curtain. I scowled as I took it and turned away.

"What's wrong with you?"

"I just hate these cheap shit, rip-off motels."

"OK, then."

I went back out in the rain to fetch my bag and headed to the room. It wasn't that bad after all. But, for whatever reason, I was now feeling too wound up to sleep. I turned on the TV and caught the tail end of yet another Lakers vs. Nets game.

When Richard didn't appear, I looked out the window and saw him outside, sitting in the car. Doing what, I couldn't tell. He stayed there for a good 20 minutes, finally coming up to the room just as the game was ending.

"More basketball?"

"It's almost over."

He went in to take a shower. I fell asleep before the game ended.

# 11

## ON THE NTH DAY OF CREATION

Richard woke me up before dawn. He was already dressed and eager to get moving. "Miles to go before we sleep..." The clock bolted to the bed-table read 5:05.

I stumbled into the shower without saying a word. By the time I got out, Richard was already gone. I gathered the few things I'd brought up to the room, put on yesterday's shirt, grabbed the room key and headed downstairs. The *Free Breakfast!* coffee pot had yet to be turned on. Another elderly Indian woman sat expressionless behind the security window at the front desk. I slid my key under the protective glass. Without so much as making eye contact, she flipped through her file, found my credit card slip, and slid back a receipt. No "How was your stay? No "Thank you." Nothing. It made me wonder what sour story she was living in.

By 5:20 a.m. we were back on the interstate. Richard gripped the wheel and grinned, "This is a good sign."

"What's a good sign?"

"The sun's not even up and we're already moving." The rain had stopped, but the road was still wet in the faint beam of our headlights. Richard's haste turned out to have a realistic goal: to get through the Twin Cities before rush hour. "I can't stand city traffic." Today was Friday and the rest of the world would soon be driving to work. We were maybe 10 miles west of Minneapolis and so far there were few cars on the road.

As we came upon the city in the pre-dawn light, I realized it was the first major urban area we'd been through. No disrespect to Bismarck or Fargo, but here were tall glass buildings, concrete interstate ravines, early morning buses, trains whisking business travelers to the airport.

A short bridge took us across a river to St. Paul, and were it not for a small sign, I would not have remembered that this inconsequential creek was, in fact, the Mississippi, hardly the mighty river it would become a few hundred miles south, but nonetheless, the Ole Miss, the psychic divide between east and west. With so little time and so many miles left, I hoped it also divided bad luck from good.

A few miles further east, the city dissolved into countryside just as the sun made its first appearance on the horizon ahead. We crossed the St. Croix River—at this latitude much more imposing than the Mississippi—and entered Wisconsin.

The landscape had changed since we'd last seen daylight back in North Dakota. The endless open prairie had become rolling green hills, broken up by patches of leafy trees. Dairy cows, gathered around waterholes, chewed on carpets of dewy grass. There were postcard farmhouses with classic red barns. In the blazing golden light of sunrise, a soft mist rose up from every-thing, evaporating off ponds, off trees, off dew-wet rooftops, like a spirit rising up to heaven. It was a classic morning in America.

Once we were safely clear of any threat of rush hour traffic, Richard began yawning uncontrollably, his pre-dawn burst of energy already fading.

"You all right?"

"I'm fine. This is just not my optimal time of day."

By now, I was fully awake and more than happy to drive. "I could use some coffee. Let's pull off at the next exit and I'll drive for a while."

The next exit was another 20 miles. We got off to find a lonely gas station with a half-hearted convenience store. I went inside to get coffee while Richard topped off the gas tank. For a mini-mart, the place was curiously bare, the shelves sparsely stocked with an odd collection of dusty canned foods and fading plastic toys. In the back corner was a rotating metal rack that held a few trucker hats and a thin assortment of maps and postcards.

Or, more precisely, postcard. The rack was empty, except for a single, poorly composed, underexposed photo of dairy cows, bearing the greeting: *HELLO FROM WISCONSIN, America's Dairyland.* Of all the images that could be taken of a state, I wondered how this one had ended up on a postcard. It was so bad, it was good.

I poured myself a cup of coffee and found the old reliable pack of peanut butter crackers in the snack aisle. A thin, unhappy woman sat behind the counter, filing her nails. To stir up a conversation while I was paying, I asked if her shift was starting or ending. She looked up at me with weary eyes and snapped, "My shift never ends."

I smiled, took my change and didn't ask what she meant by that.

Back at the car, Richard was sitting in the passenger seat.

"Don't you want any coffee?"

"No. Later."

He seemed exhausted. "You get any sleep last night?"

"I don't need sleep," he said, half asleep.

"Suit yourself."

The old Bug started, first try. I shifted into gear, swung back onto I-94 and steered southeast towards Eau Claire. A mile down the road, Richard was in the land of Nod.

It was still early, not yet seven. Without the distraction of a radio or conversation, my mind went wandering. Off to the right, hovering over a field of just-sprouting corn, was another of those long, self-propelled sprinkler systems I'd first noticed back in the deserts of eastern Washington. A long water pipe was raised 15 feet in the air by a row of triangular towers, each spaced roughly 30 yards apart. At the base of each tower were wheels that somehow slowly moved the long pipe across the field, sending down a gentle, controlled shower. *Pivots* were what Richard said they were called. Because of last night's rain, these pivots were shut down, standing motionless and tall, like monuments to irrigation.

I'd read that irrigation was one of the primary catalysts of early civilization in Egypt and Mesopotamia. Agriculture had gotten people to give up the hunter/gatherer life and settle down onto farms, anchored by the roots of whatever crops they were tending. But it was irrigation that turned those handfuls of loosely connected family farms into civilization. That's because building a serious irrigation system required a much larger, more organized society. The benefit was a dependable supply of water. More food could be grown with less work. But getting all these unrelated people to live and work together meant resolving a new set of problems: how to organize the labor, distribute the food, protect property, provide security, and settle arguments so people didn't keep killing each other. The solutions to these problems eventually gave rise to a new world order: palaces and temples, laws and commerce, slaves and kings, armies and empires. All, to some degree, the unintended consequences of irrigation.

And here we were, several millennia later, still coming up with new and improved ways for getting water from where it is to where we want it. I wondered who had dreamt up the idea for the pivot? Was it a sudden brainstorm, an inspiration that came to some quirky inventor one morning while he was watering his lawn? Or did it take years to develop; the combined effort of an R & D taskforce holed up in cubicles on the seventh floor of an office building in Peoria, their final proposal slowly emerging from countless PowerPoint presentations, CAD drawings, and team meetings; their initial energy thwarted by bureaucracy, office politics, professional rivalries, and the dread of being unemployed once they'd finally agreed upon an optimal design? In brief, how did the pivot come into being?

That got me pondering the idea of creation. Explaining creation—how all these plants and animals and mountains and oceans got here, how *we* got here—is another big part of most religions. The Bible opens with Genesis: God creating the world in under a week, starting with dividing light from darkness to create the first day and ending with the creation of the first human. Creation myths were the centerpieces of all early religions. Sumerian and Egyptian, Greek and Roman mythologies were rooted in stories explaining the origins of everything from the world itself to specific flowers and trees. When I was a kid, my mother waxed poetic over roses in bloom or idyllic mountain scenery, wondering aloud how anyone could doubt that there was a God after seeing such beautiful examples of his handiwork.

Western religions generally claim that things came into being because someone or something called God (conceived as anything from a nebulous cosmic force to a large, white bearded man on a throne) created them, either in an initial burst of inventive energy or as an ongoing process in some heavenly workshop.

But God did not create the pivot. There was no pivot in the Garden of Eden. It did not descend from heaven. No one claims a naughty wood nymph was transformed into a giant sprinkler system.

Science, on the other hand, offers its own ideas about creation. Science would say that things come into being as a result of natural evolution. After the Big Bang blew its tight ball of primal matter into a gazillion tiny pieces, stray atoms evolved into elements and the stars formed as all this free-floating stuff congealed around one lucky speck. Things came into being because their constituent parts found it easier to stick together than to break apart. Life on earth was the outcome of a similar series of random events, environmental flukes, and genetic mutations, each building on the last, simple things evolving into ever-more complex things, all in the absence of either a design or a goal, all without the aid of a Creator's hand.

But evolution did not create the pivot either. The pivot is not a product of nature's forces randomly banging against each other. Nor is it the inevitable result of physical laws.

So how did the pivot come into being? Who, or what, created it?

I would say it came from an idea.

"Idea" is one of those words we use without thinking too much about what it means. Whole books can, and have, been written about the idea of Idea, dating back to at least Plato. Ideas categorize things and qualities of things: apples and oranges, red and blue. But ideas can also conceive things that don't, or didn't originally, exist in nature: good and evil, bricks and mortar, computers and pivots.

Throughout the past 3,000 years, countless individuals have pondered new and improved ways to irrigate crops. Some of these ideas sprang from observations of nature, some from combining already existing ideas that no one had thought to combine before, some were pure leaps of the imagination.

The idea for the pivot evolved from this long chain of ideas, each theoretically traceable to a single individual. No doubt, like any invention, it had bugs that needed to be worked out. But with each new problem, someone came up with a new idea. And sure enough, here today is this thing, the pivot, created by the human imagination. My point is this: I believe that human beings possess the ability to bring things into being. Creation is not an exclusive power of either God or nature.

And that leads to another question: free will. Can humans come up with their own ideas? An all-knowing, all-powerful God would certainly know our fate. Therefore, our future is predetermined, and we are powerless to change it. God's plan for us is set. Interestingly enough, science has it own version of this same idea. In a perfectly mechanical universe, every action, every movement, everything we think and do can be explained by a set of physical laws of nature. If we can identify and measure the causes, we can predict the results. We can determine the outcome by plugging the right numbers into the right formula. Free will is an illusion. We are all slaves to the laws of genetics, biophysics, psychology, whatever.

I don't buy it. Our destiny is not determined in advance by fate or divine will. We are not wholly subject to physical and psychological forces beyond our control. We have the power to create things that did not exist before we created them. It is this power that makes us free; that gives us the ability not only to perceive reality, but to create it, to bring new things into being.

But where does this power come from? How did we get it? I don't know, but I suspect that our creative power ultimately comes from our ability to connect with other human beings. Without a shared language, without an inherited communal knowledge, without an ability to learn and to teach, we would be as powerless as any animal to conceive ideas and create new things.

Though this creative power could not exist without the communal mind, we each experience it as individuals. We each inherit a cultural legacy, shaped by all the people who came before us. As individuals, we have a choice of what to do with this inheritance; whether to ignore it, squander it, preserve it, break it, fix it, or to somehow make it greater for our having been its keeper.

It goes back to my cereal bowl idea. In a sense, every individual can be seen as a repository—a temple. We are the temporary keepers of the treasure. For our short lives, we are the incarnation of humanity, inheritors of the rich wealth of culture created and passed down by our ancestors, custodians and protectors of our small piece of the kingdom. Each of us is a unique individual manifestation of a vast WE that was here before we were born, and will be here after we die.

Near noon, Richard woke up just as we crossed into Illinois. Our plan was to take the shortest possible route east. That meant getting to Route 80/90, which cut across the top of Indiana and Ohio. There were two ways to get there from here. The safer, but also longer, route was to avoid Chicago, taking I-39 straight south, picking up I-80 in LaSalle. The other option was to take I-90 east out of Rockford and cut through the Chicago suburbs, running the risk of hitting traffic. The upside was that route was at least 30 miles shorter.

Richard wanted to go the long way. "Believe me, traffic out of Chicago is insane. I know. I used to drive a truck through here all the time."

My in-laws live in Chicago, and I've driven through these suburbs more than once myself. They were far less insane then Los Angeles. And besides, it was the middle of the day. We could be on the other side of Chicago in an hour. If we were serious about getting to Jersey by tomorrow, we had to cut every corner.

"We can handle this," I countered, "Let's not tip-toe around the lair of the beast. Let's drive right through it."

"I can't handle that kind of traffic."

"I'll drive."

"You've already been driving for six hours."

"I don't mind. What else have I got to do?"

"Fine. But if we get stuck in traffic, we're making it up tonight."

"Courage, my friend. Our ship is strong and our course is true."

"You worry me with that crap."

I grinned and exited onto the I-90 towards Chicago.

We made it past O'Hare Airport just fine. But then we hit the fork where I-90 merges with I-94, heading south along Lake Michigan, and our 65 mph pace ground to a near dead halt. Four lanes of solid traffic, painfully inching forward without leaving first gear: accelerator, brake, accelerator, brake.

"How can there be this much traffic?" I was mystified, "It's one o'clock in the afternoon."

"Tollbooths."

"Tollbooths where?"

"All along this road for the next twenty miles. Some brilliant politician figured out a way to pump people for quarters. Never mind all the gas and time that's being wasted in the process."

"There's got to be some other way."

I grabbed the map, braced it on the steering wheel, and as I inched the car forward, found the page. I-90/94 went south for another 15 miles, skirting the western edge of downtown Chicago before splitting again. At our current 2 mph, that could take forever. The only obvious alternative was turning around and trying some convoluted route that at least tripled the distance and risked us getting lost. "We're screwed."

"This stretch is legendary with truckers. Big John called it Fate's Freeway."

"Fate's Freeway?"

"Yeah. He used to say that this freeway is like fate. You can't escape it. You try to drive around it, but then boom, you're somehow right back on it again."

"Why didn't you tell me this back in Rockford?"

"I guess I forgot. That's part of the legend. The victims forget the pain. You get stuck on this thing in a semi loaded with perishable fruit that has to be somewhere on a hard deadline and you swear to God, 'Never again.' Then two months later, you're back on Fate's Freeway, cursing yourself for getting lured in again."

There did seem to be a disproportionate number of trucks on the road. Every third vehicle was some variety of long-hauler: semis, flatbeds, tankers, and car carriers. We'd get caught between two of them and the sun would all but disappear.

"How long did you drive a truck?" I asked to get my mind off the present.

"On and off for about six years."

"What was that like?"

"It was great. It's got that whole outlaw/cowboy/nomad thing going for it. You're always in transit, always moving, rootless. There's no routine, no nine-to-five. You'll be asleep at two in the afternoon and driving, wide awake, at four in morning. It's like you're unmoored from the rat race. Though God knows, you're in a whole other rat race. Always on some insane dead-line, always eating away at these never ending miles, calculating your route to hit cities at some time of day when you won't get killed by traffic, trying to line up your next load over the cell phone so you don't go empty too long. It's a brutal game. There's a lot more to it than you'd think."

As we slogged our way past Chicago, he gave me a crash course in trucking, pointing out how semis shift the placement of their rear axle to more evenly distribute weight, how empty flatbeds are actually bowed up in the center, how tankers deal with sloshing half full tanks, the protocols of weigh stations. "One time, we got stopped for driving a hundred pounds overweight and we had to unload these crates by hand in a parking lot. I had to sit and wait with them while Big John dropped off the rest of the load and came back to get me, like ten hours later."

"Sounds like it suited you."

"It did and it didn't. It was an adventure. Kind of like the Army, I guess."

By 2:30, we were still creeping south at a snail's pace. I was getting stiff from the nonstop driving, and hungry from having only eaten a pack of crackers for breakfast. Up ahead, I saw what appeared to be a rest stop built on an overpass, with windows gazing down on the river of traffic. A banner read: *Take a Break, Chicago!*

"Let's stop to get some gas and eat."

"Sure."

It took another 10 minutes before we made our way to the exit ramp. It was the first time I could remember speeding up to get off a freeway. Twenty miles an hour felt like soaring.

The rest stop was dreary at best, one of those 1950s bright ideas in modern design that had soured into a grim reminder of how wrong we were about the future. There was a spacious open center area with a weathered red-and-brown linoleum floor and a wall of large, aluminum frame windows that overlooked the interstate. What had been envisioned as an amazing view of the steady stream of Chevys and Fords zipping by like the pace of progress, turned out to be a depressing spectacle of too many cars in too little space. Most people sat away from the window, preferring to avoid spending their meal break gazing down on traffic, a brief respite from a fate they would soon enough return to. Several dozen fellow travelers were scattered at tables in the empty center of the room, under dusty banks of fluorescent lights. Along the far wall, the usual suspects stood in a line-up: Burger King, Pizza Hut, Taco Bell. Inner city youth with bad skin, world-weary eyes, and cheery uniforms handed out slices of limp pizza, sad hamburgers, and paper sacks of fries. Richard wasn't hungry. "I'll go fill up the tank and meet you outside."

He left, and I bought a cheese steak and a Coke. I quickly ate half and tossed the rest, stopping in a small gift shop to pick up an Illinois postcard for Esmé. Oddly enough, they only had postcards for Indiana.

I bought one with a picture of a barn in the background, overlaid with smaller images: a windmill in the center, a small state capitol building in the lower right, and a cardinal in the opposite corner. I also found a mailbox, and remembered the book of stamps I still had in my wallet. I bought a pen, addressed cards from the last four states, and mailed them off to Esmé.

A large clock over the exit door informed me that it was past three. Out in the parking lot, I found Richard half napping in the driver's seat, with his bag of almonds in his lap.

"So what's the verdict?" I asked.

"As I recall, the traffic lets up just ahead. I was looking at the map. I bet we can make it across Ohio tonight."

"Can't wait."

Richard took over behind the wheel. Half a mile south, we passed through the final tollbooth, and the traffic mercifully started moving again. We crossed into Indiana and headed due east on I-90. Once we were clear of Gary, it was back to smooth sailing. I pulled out the map.

"You really think we can get all the way across Ohio?"

That was another 400 miles: seven or eight hours, barring any breakdowns, traffic snarls, or acts of God. Somewhere in Indiana, another time zone crossing would take away another precious hour, meaning we'd be driving until at least midnight. Eighteen hours of driving in a single day. But hey, we were on a mission. Whatever it takes.

The road ahead was wide open, the weather near perfect, and the old Bug was running like a champ, without so much as a hiccup since North Dakota. Even the taped-up heating system seemed to be cooperating.

The passing Indiana countryside was flat, open farmland. Nowhere near as endless as North Dakota, nothing as immense as Montana, or as dramatic as Idaho. Mostly just farms that you could see in a single glance, broken up by fences into family-sized chunks. Weary, I took another shot at listening to music on the CD player. But the car noise still overwhelmed the feeble volume. So I closed my eyes and slipped into sleep.

By the time I woke, we were in Ohio. The summer sun was going down. The scenery had become Early Modern Interstate Corridor, walls of trees and barriers of concrete intended to separate the cross-country traffic from the locals. The landscape along the interstate had been stripped of all clues as to who might live here or what their lives might look like.

I glanced at my watch and calculated that we were into our 15th hour of driving.

"You still think we can make it across Ohio tonight?"

"I'm happy to just keep going," Richard replied, now back in full truck driver mode.

Pulling out the map again, I estimated that crossing Ohio was roughly a four-hour drive. Pennsylvania was another five. I had no desire to be in the car all night and even less to land in Jersey at the crack of dawn, puffy-eyed and stiff from lack of sleep. Barring disaster, a good night's rest, combined with another early start, would still get us there fresh and in time for Richard's reunion with his family.

"Why don't we get through Ohio, get some rest, then tackle Pennsylvania first thing in the morning? That puts you in Jersey just in time for the party."

"Sure. But let's at least get across Ohio."

"Sold."

We made our way past Cleveland and Akron without seeing the slightest hint of either. From the interstate, the Rust Belt was a long row of innocuous oak trees and sound barriers. By 11:00, the road was dark and empty and even Richard was getting tired. We were maybe fifty miles from the Pennsylvania border.

"Youngstown is coming up," I noticed from a passing sign. "What say we get off there and call it a day?" The old Bug had somehow endured a 900-mile stretch. I would call that a miracle. "I think we may actually pull this trip off."

"I told you this was a good car," Richard said, happy to be on the rebound.

"Oh, me of little faith."

We took the first Youngstown exit and followed the signs towards town. A few miles up the road, we came upon a Best Western and got a room. We were both exhausted, and it was past midnight by the time we got settled in. Richard was asleep before I had a chance to ask him when he wanted to get up.

Then a curious thing happened. I was in the bathroom, brushing my teeth, looking at my haggard face in the mirror. I was feeling a sense of satisfaction that after all the doubts and setbacks, we were now (knock on wood) half a day's drive from our destination.

Then I remembered that this trip was also supposed to be—was *primarily* supposed to be—a 21st-century spiritual journey. How far had I come with that? And how far did I still have to go? Had I found any answer to the question I'd started off with? What did I believe in?

I looked at myself in the mirror and went over what I'd come up with so far. I believed I was part of something greater than myself, part of a human community that came into existence long before I was born and that would survive, hopefully, long after I passed away. I believed I was the heir and embodiment of this legacy, this tradition, and that it was something akin to what I had once called God.

But so what? What did that have to do with how I lived my life?

The moment I asked that question, I experienced a sudden and entirely unexpected flash of clarity. It was as if a stage-hand from the dark wings of my unconsciousness had rushed, unannounced, onto a brightly lit stage, interrupting the actor who was about to brush his teeth. Attention everyone! May I have your attention? I have an announcement here!

The audience hushed.

"There are three sacred tasks."

Huh? What?

"There are three ways to connect to this greater whole. Three sacred tasks."

The surrounding stage had gone dim as the spotlight focused on the intruding stagehand, catching his breath, waiting for my reaction. It was the strangest experience, standing there staring at myself in the motel mirror, suddenly enveloped in this glow of clarity, hearing a voice in my head that didn't sound like me, that spoke not with my usual ponderous pondering, but with a certain authority. Here is a gift. Don't question it. Accept it.

So I shut up and listened.

The first task is to learn. The legacy we inherit does not come to us automatically. It is not encoded in our genes. We must venture out and find it. We must educate ourselves. Open ourselves up to the wisdom of others. Listen. Observe. Read. Practice. Embrace experience with humility and respect. The more we learn, the more connected we become.

The second task is to teach. Just as it is important to embrace the knowledge passed down to us, it is equally important to pass it on to those who do not yet have it, to our peers, to the next generation. Teaching, in all its forms, is one of the greatest gifts we can give, because through it, human life transcends death.

The third task is to engage. To connect with the world outside yourself and make it somehow better for your having been alive. It is not enough to learn what there is to know and pass it on like a fire brigade handing off buckets of water. You need to engage, to participate in the grand drama of life on earth. Turn off the TV. Get off your ass. Speak up. Tend to the world as you would a garden. Nurture the things that enchance life. Weed out the things that diminish it.

It is our sacred task as citizens of the human community to engage with life, to revitalize tradition, to contribute, to make better. That could mean building a bridge, writing a book, improving a recipe for apple pie, refusing to perpetrate an injustice, or healing a wound. This third task is not just for the smart or the talented or the powerful. Each of us is unique.

We each have knowledge, talent, and power that no one else has. Each of us has the opportunity to make humanity better for having lived in us.

To learn, to teach, to engage: that is what God expects from me.

I laid down my toothbrush and shut off the light.

The motel room was dark. The vividness of my bathroom epiphany instantly vanished. I was back in the regular world. Making my way past Richard, I sat down on the far bed and looked out the window. Most of the view was blocked by the top of a tree that was illuminated by an unworldly orange glow from a sodium vapor street-lamp. The leaves ebbed and flowed in the invisible airwaves, caught in the tide of the night sky.

What had just happened? My mind (as you can tell, if you've made it this far) has a tendency to wander off into thickets of thought, picking its way towards some hoped-for clearing like an explorer wading through a jungle. Usually, thinking requires effort. Diligence. It's an odd experience for me to have ideas just pop up, fully formed.

"Three Sacred Tasks" sounded like something out of a New Age self-help book. Did I really want to go there? Did I really want to open myself up to that brand of self-important pretension?

To learn, to teach, to engage: weren't these all things everybody did anyway? What was so sacred about them?

As I've said before, my generation (for that matter, every generation that came of age after 1972) has been accused of being overly ironic, of refusing to take anything seriously, of holding our principles at arm's length, safely disengaged from full commitment, keeping anything we might dare to consider "sacred" safely encased in "quotes." Here we are now, entertain us.

I suppose that this reaction is, in part, a defense mechanism. Not only has religion taken a beating of late, but so has any kind of truth. Nothing is sacred anymore. In a world of Seinfeld and Howard Stern and Eminem, professing belief in *anything* (at least in anything beyond unfettered freedom of speech) only opens one up to ridicule and accusations of hypocrisy. We live in a post-truth universe, where nothing is accepted without question, where no idea is sacrosanct.

Who can blame us for having a certain reluctance to openly declare what we believe? We have all personally witnessed yesterday's self-evident truth being picked to shreds on this morning's talk show. We have all had the disheartening experience of embracing some new bit of wisdom, with a child's excitement and enthusiasm, all but breaking into song about it, only to be laughed off the stage. If we hold anything sacred, we tend to keep it private, safely tucked away from the rolling eyes and sarcastic remarks of the quick-to-mock, irony-armored culture we live in, not wanting to be mistaken for some kind of delusional dimwit or proselytizing kook.

But ultimately, what we do with our lives has to be based on something, on some vision of the world, on some set of beliefs, whether we're conscious of them or not. If we keep our values at a safe distance, hesitant to fully and openly embrace them, we become tentative, weak, uncertain, stepping carefully—always braced for retreat. If there is no belief that we are willing to declare and defend, there is no way we can summon up clarity and courage when such virtues are needed. If we cannot believe in anything strongly, we cannot be strong.

What we of the ironic generations have discovered is that no truth can be guaranteed by scientific proof or logical argument, especially the kind of truth we rely upon to get us through life. I'm not just talking about God. I'm talking about family, country, career, home, diet, lifestyle. Embracing any of these is ultimately an act of faith.

The point of this trip, for me, was to discover if there was anything in my post-religious, post-modern, irony-encrusted life that I hold sacred—and if so, what I could do to bring those beliefs into my daily life, to translate them into actions.

To learn, to teach, to engage: these were things I did already. But seeing them in this new light gave them a resonance I had not felt before: a new meaning, a new power, a way to shine a spiritual light upon the mundane goings-on of my daily life, upon the interactions I had with my family, my friends, with the people at work, with the larger world around me, with myself.

And I'd be willing to call that sacred—without quotes.

# 12

## OLD MAN MOUNTAINS

"Time to get up."

An eager Richard already had his jacket on and packed bag in hand. My sleepy eye searched for the clock and found 6:15. A thin, mist-filtered light sniffed around the window curtains. The night had passed in a blink.

"Give me a minute."

"I'll be outside."

I got up and rubbed my face. It was Saturday, the final leg of the journey. I trudged over to the bathroom and felt for the light. In the mirror, my face was puffy and my hair upended.

In the fog of a weary morning, the bright revelations of the previous night were now only a faint glow. *The Three Sacred Tasks*. What were they again? To learn, to teach…. What was the other one? Oh, right, to engage.

I smiled at myself and took a moment to feel their warmth again. It reminded me of camping. You stay up late gathered around a campfire, soaking in its heat, entranced by its flickering flames, made all the brighter by the fact that they're surrounded by darkness. There's something magical about sitting by that fire. Something spiritual.

But in the morning, the world returns. You climb out of your tent, alone, grabbing for another sweatshirt in the cold, wet light. You walk over to the fire pit, which has faded to charcoal and ash, hoping to find a few bright embers still alive. And sometimes you do. Sometimes there's just enough that, with a little care, you can get the fire going again.

That's how it seemed to me that morning, as I held my hands out over last night's thoughts. I could still feel their heat. Their promise. A campfire somewhere deep in my soul that I knew I could return to and reignite whenever I needed it. And that felt good. Like I was finally getting somewhere.

Ten minutes later, I was outside. The parking lot was swaddled in gray mist. A few semis were stirring on the road by the motel. The Bug was already purring. Richard was sitting in the driver's seat, chowing down almonds.

"Want some?"

"No. Any chance we can get some coffee?"

"Sure, if you can find any at this hour."

"There's always coffee somewhere."

I stowed my bag in the back and climbed into the passenger seat, while Richard packed away his almost empty bag of nuts.

"How are you feeling this morning?" I asked him.

"I'm feeling great. Slept like a rock. How about you?"

"I'm good. Glad to get some rest. Car start OK?"

"First try."

I looked at the map and discovered that last night, in my eagerness to get off the road, we'd somehow missed the turnoff for I-76 South, which runs from I-80 to the Pennsylvania turnpike like the lower leg of a knocked over Y. Rather than backtrack, it made more sense to find a southbound surface street that would, in theory, eventually hit the 76. Richard didn't seem to care.

"Just tell me where to go."

"Let's find coffee, and we can ask directions. It looks pretty simple. We just need to find a big street that runs south." I glanced at the position of the sun to figure out which way south was. "Can't miss it."

It only took driving a few blocks to find the inevitable Stop N Go. Richard filled his road mug and I bought coffee and a pack of crackers. I found a postcard with an Ohio map and a smattering of clip-art: the state flower (red carnation), the state bird (cardinal), the unusually shaped, two-pointed state flag, and a few tourist icons (a covered bridge, a bi-plane, and curiously, for a state with no ocean coast, a lighthouse). *Ohio, the Buckeye State.* I wasn't sure what a buckeye was. Some kind of nut, I think.

I asked the guy behind the counter how to get to 76 South. He shrugged. "I'm not from around here."

Hmm.

Where would he be from if not from around here? Did he commute from miles away to work the morning shift at Stop N Go? If he commuted, wouldn't he at least know the surrounding roads?

This is not an isolated phenomenon. It is one of the mysteries of modern travel that, more often than not, convenience store clerks—unlike the gas station attendants of old—seem to have no idea where they are. Whether it's some elaborate ruse, or if they really are this mind-numbingly unaware of places that are only a few blocks away, I can only guess. Maybe it's somehow a side effect of the job, a byproduct of working in a generic environment that contained no reference to its geographic surroundings beyond a stack of local newspapers (and not even that, if *USA Today* had any say in the matter). Maybe working here had turned them into generic citizens, residents of nowhere, unable to perceive the unadvertised world, the universe as not seen on TV.

I slowly backed away from the counter. Out front, Richard was gassing up the Bug and talking to a guy wearing a faded-yellow, cotton-brim hat with a fishing lure stuck into it. The guy was making dramatic directional gestures with both arms, like he was flagging an airplane into a gate. "Two blocks south, hard left at the light, go about two miles and you'll see the sign."

"Hi." I walked up to them. The guy turned and shined a Cheshire grin at me.

"Hey, there. I'm Clement."

Clement was wearing a tackle vest. When he talked, his head jerked with an odd twitch as if there was a small creature trapped inside his skull struggling to get out.

"I was telling him about our trip," Richard explained, "He said getting to 76 South is a piece of cake."

"Two blocks south. Hard left at the light," Clement repeated for my benefit.

"Thanks. You off fishing this morning?"

"Nope. Going to Home Depot. Got a blocked-up toilet."

I was beginning to wonder if I had woken up in the Twilight Zone. Richard put the nozzle back and got in the car, "Nice to meet you, Clement. Thanks for the directions."

"Have a safe trip," he said.

"Good luck with that toilet of yours."

"Thanks. I may need it."

We bade goodbye to Clement, who didn't seem in any hurry to be anywhere, and drove away. Two blocks south, hard left at the light, Clement's directions proved to be spot-on. What he'd neglected to mention was that the interstate entrance was closed for construction. A police car was parked at the top of ramp just to make sure no one missed the message.

Richard pondered the situation.

"Crap. What do you think that cop is doing there?"

"Blocking the ramp."

"I bet you he stops us because we have out-of-state plates."

"What? Why?"

I remembered Richard's secret stash of pot in the glove compartment, then flashed on what a battered Bug from Oregon must say to an Ohio State Trooper. At seven in the morning. With nothing better to do. Fruit ripe for the pickin'.

"Maybe we should just ask him how to get to the next exit?"

"Fuck, no. Never give a cop an opening. Especially a State Trooper. Those guys are the sharks of the road. Always on the prowl for fresh meat. We'll find it ourselves. Don't look."

Richard drove past the patrol car with his eyes locked straight ahead. The moment we were clear of the overpass, he glanced up into the rearview mirror. We turned at the first light and worked our way east on a street that seemed to run parallel to the interstate. I found this abrupt shift into criminal-on-the-run mode a shade troubling.

"That was fun."

"I just don't like cops." He kept glancing back in the rear-view mirror. "This is Ohio. Remember Kent State."

"I think that was the National Guard. Thirty years ago."

"Same difference. It's an us-against-them world out there. Ignore it at your own risk."

Up ahead, a sign for I-76 brought our brief flight from the law to an end.

We crossed the border into western Pennsylvania at just after seven. It was turning into a clear summer day, with one exception. Wherever the road crossed a creek or a small river, a thick cloud of fog rose up off the water. It did not disperse into the surrounding atmosphere, but ascended into the sky for at least 100 feet, following the river in either direction like a gauzy cotton curtain.

I wondered how a caveman would have reacted to such a sight. Back in the shrouded eons of prehistory, nature must have been a mysterious and powerful force. On one hand, it provided humans with everything they needed to survive: food, clothing, and shelter. Mother Earth. But it also had a downside. It was dangerous. It was filled with things lurking in the shadows, hurtling down from the sky, sneaking up from behind, roaring out of nowhere, biting, burning, poisoning, crushing, freezing, drowning, ripping the life out of you without so much as a second thought. In other words, not something to be messed with. The dark forest and the wild sea must have been both tempting and terrifying. Nature was a presence that demanded respect, and primitive religion became mankind's way of dealing with it.

Today, thanks largely to 500 years of science, the mysteries of nature have been replaced by a myriad of time-tested theories. As far as explanations of nature go, the sacred texts of western religion have been, for the most part, replaced by scientific textbooks. In many areas, nature has shifted from being the master of the human race to its servant, and in the process, it's been stripped of the awesome power it once had over the human imagination.

Half a mile ahead, I could see another curtain of fog hanging in the morning light, rising up over the trees. Richard was looking at it too.

"Have you ever seen anything like that?" I asked him.

"You mean that mist coming off the river?"

"Yeah. How it just hangs there. Like a curtain."

"Hmm. It is kind of weird."

"I wonder why it doesn't dissipate?"

"It must have something to do with the air temperature or the humidity."

A natural phenomenon that once inspired awe and wonder, that once may have even suggested the presence of a supernatural power, is now shrugged off. There's no mystery left. Even if we can't explain it, we have a scientific faith that someone can, that some professor at some research lab has written the definitive paper, captured the unknown in a series of formulas that just require plugging in the numbers, turned the mysterious into the mundane.

As we passed through the fog curtain, it once again occurred to me that I was missing something. My spiritual ramblings of the past few days had led me to a place I hadn't expected to go, to some acceptance that religion wasn't all baseless baloney, but that there was something to it after all. For me, religion was an acknowledgement that I was part of something greater than myself. That "something greater" was the whole of human culture: past, present, and future.

But was that enough? In most religious traditions, that "something greater" was more than just mankind. It encompassed all of nature, everything in the universe. It connected believers not just to their fellow man, but to all of life, to the universe in its entirety.

I'd missed that part.

Which got me wondering: Is there still any spiritual benefit to be had from nature? For many people, Richard included, nature was the pathway to the spiritual. It was when they were hiking up a mountain or through a forest that they felt most connected to the universe. Most spiritual. For them, God was embodied in nature's forces.

So what was I missing?

I decided to ask Richard. "Do you think there's anything spiritual about nature?"

"How do you mean?"

"I don't know. Walking in the woods. Growing a garden. Staring at the stars. Is there something spiritual in that kind of experience?"

"Hmm. I guess. I get something out of seeing the trees change with the seasons. Plants popping up."

"There you go."

"I grew a couple of tomatoes last year. That was kind of cool."

How far the mighty have fallen.

Science has armed us with a power unlike anything the Earth has ever seen. We now have countless ways to subvert nature, harness its forces, dominate wherever we dwell. To survive, few of us have to wander into the dark forest or set off upon the wild sea. Few of us have to hunt for our supper or tend to the fields—and those of us who do are usually well armed to ensure that the odds are in their favor.

We have distanced ourselves from direct confrontation with

the natural world. The link between the thing we consume and its original source in nature is convoluted at best. There are so many middlemen between a grain of wheat and a Big Mac, so many complex processes between a field of cotton and a pair of Levi's, that few of us can even make the connection. Nature has become something we visit on vacation, or at the zoo, safely locked away in a cage.

In many ways, that's a good thing. I'm delighted not to have to wrestle with nature on a daily basis. I like my supermarket and my department store, my central heating and my clean bathroom. But I can't believe that mankind's conquest of nature hasn't come at a price. Excuse me for getting all National Geographic here, but it's hard to deny that in our relentless pursuit of science's manifest destiny, we have destroyed entire species, upset endless ecosystems, sucked the earth dry of one resource after another, stomped across the pristine wilderness in our giant corporate hiking boots, oblivious to all the damage we've done and continue to do. And that can't be good. In the end, we are still as dependent on the Earth as we have ever been: for the air we breathe, the food we eat, the clothing we wear, the home we live in.

The Bug made its way up into the Appalachian Mountains. I remembered driving along this turnpike as a kid on vacation and being amazed by these rounded green peaks, hovering over us on either side of the road like sleeping giants, lifting us up to vistas of the vast valleys below. But this morning they struck me as small, more ancient, and more worn-down than the mighty Rockies, more quaint than awe-inspiring. Old men mountains. Not unlike myself.

A hundred and fifty years ago, this area was the wellspring of a new economic era. This is where America first discovered oil — not Texas or Saudi Arabia, but Titusville, Pennsylvania — a discovery that defined a century, changing the way Americans live in a hundred different ways, not the least of which was turning a cross-country journey from a year-long ordeal to a five-day diversion.

"Did you know that the first oil well was in Pennsylvania?"

"I've never seen any oils wells in Pennsylvania."

"That's because they're all gone. Tapped out years ago. Kind of makes you realize that the earth isn't a bottomless pit."

"I heard somewhere that in fifty years there won't be any oil left anywhere," Richard added, "In three or four generations, we will have sucked the entire earth dry and burned God only knows how many trillion gallons of oil and gas. Tell me that ain't gonna come back to bite us on the ass."

Mankind's relationship with nature has been turned on its head. Once humans worried that nature might destroy them; now we worry that we might destroy it. Between resource depletion, vanishing wilderness, global warming, species destruction, population booms, garbage piling up, and pollution seeping out, a day of reckoning is not hard to imagine.

Sure, sure, it's not all doom and gloom. Nature has a way of renewing and repairing itself. There are many concerned organizations and responsible corporate citizens watching our backs, keeping an eye on the scale of economic checks and balances. It's even true that some parts of the environment are better off now than they were a few decades ago. I don't see as many sooty smokestacks and green-goo run-off pipes. Los Angeles has less smog and cleaner oceans. Last time I sniffed, even the Jersey Turnpike smelled better.

But if the rest of the growing global economy ever develops America's insatiable consumer appetite, trouble can't be too far off. For every well-meaning environmentalist toweling off an oil-soaked penguin, there's a gung-ho entrepreneur more than happy to gun down an endangered rhino. For every environmental law passed, there's somebody finding a new way to get around it.

I thought back to Richard's comment about sucking the earth dry, and realized that driving along this turnpike, burning another tankful of gas, made us as culpable as anyone else. "We're not exactly innocent ourselves."

"Hell, no. Never said I was. But at least I'm not driving some eight-cylinder, gas-guzzling SUV, blasting the AC and towing jet skis. I may not be Henry Thoreau, but at least I'm not Homer Simpson." I suppose there's some consolation in knowing that, however bad we are, there's always somebody worse—even if he is only a cartoon character.

Out the window, I saw an Amish buckboard, clip-clopping along a narrow road that paralleled the turnpike. A bearded man dressed in black, wearing a wide-brimmed hat, sat beside his white-shirted son, who was holding the reins to the single-horse rig. An Amish driving lesson.

Maybe they've got it right. Maybe keeping things simple is the way to go. Get out of the whole frigging, consumption crazy rat race. Live up in the hills on soybeans, brown rice and organic vegetables, composting and conserving, seeking some self-sustaining, give-and-take balance with nature.

"Do you think the Amish may be onto something?"

"What do you mean?"

"Keeping life simple. Living close to the land. Opting out of the last hundred years of gadgets and gizmos."

"No. Not really."

"Why is that?"

"You can't escape the world."

"Why not?"

"Because no matter how far you run, the world is still there. Knocking at your door. Coming through the TV. You can't escape it. You can only pretend it isn't there. Pretend you're somehow free of all the bullshit."

"But what's wrong with pretending?"

"What's wrong with pretending is that the only person you're fooling is yourself. You can seal the door all you want, but the world still finds a way to seep in." I couldn't help but notice the duct tape over the heat vents as Richard continued, "I read somewhere that the Amish are some of the biggest drug dealers in Pennsylvania. Part and parcel, dude. It's all part and parcel."

"I've never heard of any Amish drug dealers."

"Don't quote me, but that's the word on the street."

"So what's the alternative?"

"To Amish drug dealers?"

"No. To retreating from the world?"

"Look the world straight in the eye. See what the fuck is going on. And deal with it."

"Yeah, but a lot of what's going on is way bigger than anything you and I can have any effect on. We're just little pawns in some vast global chess game."

Richard turned his head from the road and stared at me with bug-eyed alarm. "You're the last person I'd expect to hear talking like that."

"What do you mean?"

"You've been in my ear this whole trip about how you've got to stop sitting on your ass and become an active presence in the Bazaar of Belief or whatever the hell you call it. You're the one who says, 'Have the conversation. Who knows? You might learn something. Or you might teach somebody something.' Or you might even help the world start to untangle the mess we've gotten ourselves into. That's what you can do. Even if you are just a pawn. It all starts with somebody. "

Learn. Teach. Engage. I hadn't even mentioned it to Richard, but somehow, he'd heard it anyway. I guess another benefit to telling other people what you believe is that, if you ever forget, they'll be happy to remind you.

"You're absolutely right, Richard."

"Damn straight, I am. So don't go getting all Amish on me. I need you to get me through this weekend."


Just after 11:00, we began to see the first signs of the north Philadelphia suburbs: Pottstown, Valley Forge, Norristown. When I was a kid, these places were the farthest reaches of the known world, distant towns where second cousins lived. Beyond them was a world inhabited by nobody I remotely knew, the unknown universe. Now, after being so long gone, these familiar names felt like lighthouse beacons—landmarks signaling that I was on the outskirts of familiar ground. Home.

I pulled out the map. "How should we make our grand entrance?"

"What do you mean?"

"Well, we've got some choices."

The Pennsylvania Turnpike ends at the Delaware River,

where a bridge connects to an artery of the Jersey Turnpike: a convenient, if dull, route. The alternative was to get off just before the bridge and head south along Route 13, through the town of Bristol, where we could make our crossing on the more interesting and familiar Burlington-Bristol Bridge. Richard thought it was a great idea. It would take us through Burlington and then south along the river, through the string of towns where he and I grew up.

As we approached north Philadelphia, the sooty city began calling out to us: billboards for local radio stations and Atlantic City casinos, chemical tanks with faded oil company names, brick factories with peeling advertisements painted on the leeward side.

We took the last exit. I fished out the turnpike ticket and we paid our toll. Route 13 dropped us straight into the heart of Bristol, a working-class town most notable (to me) for being the namesake of the *Bristol Stomp*, a local dance hit from the '60s that I doubt made it far outside of Philadelphia: "The kids from Bristol are sharp as a pistol, when they do the Bristol Stomp."

The town was a mix of older row houses, covered with asphalt siding made to look like bricks; and newer duplexes, sheathed in aluminum siding made to look like wood. There were corner taverns with neon signs, and mom-and-pop markets that weren't 7-Elevens.

"Did you know I was born here?" Richard casually commented.

"You're kidding?" I thought he'd been born in South Jersey. He pointed to a side street that ran beside a used car lot. "We lived about three blocks up that way."

"I had no idea. How old were you when you moved?"

"Four. My parents bought a house in Edgewater Park." Edgewater Park was a South Jersey tract development built in the late

'50s on old peach orchards, adjacent to the original Levittown.

"Do you remember living here?"

"Little things. I remember the house. I remember I had a blue, toy dump truck that got stolen. I remember I cut my hand and got four stitches. My dad carried me down the stairs when we went to the emergency room. That's about it."

"The formative years."

"Yeah. Funny what sticks with you."

It seemed another of this trip's odd coincidences that we would end up on this particular route, retracing the trail of Richard's family saga.


Bristol's most infamous landmark was a chemical plant called Rohm & Hass. I remember, as kids, driving past it and holding our noses to keep out the rotten egg smell of sulfur. Back then, the plant was always surrounded by yellow and green-gray clouds of God-only-knows-what foul emissions. Today, as we passed it on our way towards the bridge, it appeared to be considerably cleaned up. No smoke stacks or yellow clouds. Evidently, the good people of Bristol had finally taken a stand. Or at least somebody had. I found that reassuring.

The Burlington-Bristol Bridge was another childhood memory. A drawbridge with only one lane in each direction, it seemed ancient and on the verge of collapse, even when I was a kid. Its roadbed was made of interlaced steel plates that caused car tires to hum nervously, adding a soundtrack to support the visual impression of impending disaster. The center section, which was maybe 500 feet long, was suspended between two towers. To open the bridge, this entire center section of road lifted up. Last time I'd crossed it, the toll was a nickel. In a quarter century, it had gone up to a whopping $2, but only for westbound traffic. So we entered Jersey for free.

Though Richard hadn't been here in a decade and a half, he hadn't lost his mental map of the place. We quickly weaved through Burlington and on to the road that led through the necklace of small towns where we'd grown up.

The first was Beverly, not much more than an intersection and a block-long main street. What few stores had been there were now mostly shuttered or converted to second-hand shops. An old guy sat on a folding chair in front of one of them, staring off into space. A little girl on a pink bicycle wobbled tentatively along the sidewalk, turning up a side street.

Just beyond the center of town was St. Joe's, where Richard had gone to elementary school. "Want to stop?" I asked.

"What the heck?" The parking lot was empty. Richard parked the Bug in the shade of an ancient oak tree. To our left stood the church, its steeple and tan bricks bright in the Saturday sun. The yard around it was freshly landscaped with spring flowers and recently mowed grass.

To the right was a two-story elementary school, boarded up and encircled by a chain link fence. The building appeared to have been abandoned for several years. A few windows were broken, and weeds grew untended in the yard behind the No Trespassing sign. It was news to me that it had closed down.

"So the place finally went out of business," Richard said, a little nostalgic as he walked along the fence. "I started going here in the third grade."

"Why the third grade?"

"That's when it opened. That was the third grade, right there."

He pointed to a window in the back. It was too dark inside to see if there were any traces left of a classroom.

"My first year here, there were only three grades. So we were the oldest kids. Every year after that, they added a grade. So there was no fourth when I was in third, no fifth when I was in fourth. No older kids to pick on us. We were always the oldest. I never had to deal with upperclassmen until high school."

"Was that good or bad?"

"I don't know. It was kind of nice, I guess, always being on top."

"Why do you think it closed down?"

"Who knows? Not enough nuns."

"Or not enough Catholics."

We got back into the car and continued south until we crossed the Rancocas Creek into Riverside, where I'd grown up. Riverside was maybe a square mile in size, with its own high school, hospital, and cemetery. When I last lived here, it also had at least a dozen churches, counterbalanced by at least a dozen bars.

I hadn't been back in quite awhile. I'd lived here until I was eighteen. My parents moved away twenty years ago, and after my grandmother died, so did most of my extended family. The last time I was in Riverside was probably ten years earlier. I happened to be in Jersey over Memorial Day weekend and brought Esmé to see Riverside's annual parade.

We drove by the old Watch Case Building. A hundred years ago, it was the centerpiece of town, the world's largest manufacturer (or so I've been told) of metal cases for pocket watches. Around the time of the First World War, it was brought down by a new idea in timekeeping called the wristwatch. The market for watchcases followed the market for pocket watches down a declining slope to economic oblivion. For a while, the company tried to make use of its machine tools by shifting into other kinds of metal work, but never quite found a new niche, and eventually shut down. For all of my childhood, the Watch Case loomed empty and unused, home only to rumors of a new tenant who never seemed to arrive. But now, it appeared to be coming back to life. The brick had been sandblasted and the broken windows fixed. A sign in the front announced the *Coming Soon* of retirement condos.

Just beyond the Watch Case, across a set of railroad tracks, was downtown. City Hall, a fire station and a post office stood around the intersection of Pavilion Avenue and Scott Street. Beyond were two blocks of depression-era, brick and stone storefronts. When I was a kid, there was Red's Barber Shop, Rider's Meat Market, Grant's Five and Dime, and Stecker's Soda Shop. All gone. Rider's Market (owned by my uncle) had gone out of business years ago. Grant's became a thrift shop. Reds retired. People were lured to the new malls and shopping centers that were springing up outside town to serve new tract housing developments. Downtown Riverside faded, but somehow hung in there on life support.

Thirty years later, it was still hanging in there, open for business, but far from prospering. The bank and jewelry store were almost the same as I remembered them. Other storefronts had been reincarnated with new names. People were on the streets. But they weren't the Riversiders I'd expected—the pale and graying faces of old timers. Today, the faces on the streets were several shades darker.

When I was a kid, Riverside was predominantly second- and third-generation European: German, Polish and Italian. Apparently, since I'd left, a new wave had arrived from, of all places, Brazil. There were a Portuguese market and a bar, flying the green and yellow Brazilian flag.

Though I suspected that longtime Riversiders probably had a different opinion, it seemed to me a healthy sign. Where else in the world could a town shift its culture so dramatically in less than a generation? America's great strength has always been its ability to embrace change, to welcome new eyes able to see new possibilities, to accept that, in the end, we're all immigrants.

It made me think of the many places on earth where some ethnic minority digs in their heels and pulls out their guns; where religious zealots, backed into a corner, would rather blow themselves up than open their eyes, clinging to a crumbling past rather than embrace an emerging future. That isn't the path to life. That is the road to death.

What is true for an individual is no less true for a small town: getting too set in its ways, clinging too tightly to some idea about how the world ought to be, tuning out anything foreign, only leads to isolation, to a disconnect from an ever-changing world. Who knows where the Brazilians will take Riverside? But I'm sure it won't be backwards.*

At the end of Pavilion Avenue, we came to St. Pete's, a Catholic parish whose four brick buildings took up an entire block: the church I'd attended as a kid, the "old church" where my parents had been married (long ago converted into a community hall), a rectory where the priests lived, and the elementary school,

---

* In 2006, Riverside made national headlines when it passed an ordinance that banned hiring or renting housing to illegal immigrants. In response, most of the Brazilians moved away, and the town, at last report was sliding back into cultural and economic stagnation.

where I'd spent nine years of my life.

We stopped and got out of the car. Unlike St. Joe's, the school at St. Pete's seemed to be thriving—thanks, perhaps, to the Brazilians. It was a three-story, red brick block of a building, bordered on two sides by an asphalt schoolyard. The front entrance was made of white, carved granite, with twin arches rising above two sets of no nonsense, aluminum and glass doors—an odd mix of medieval and modern.

This was where I'd learned to read and write; to add, divide, and multiply; to name the presidents of the United States and pick out the countries of the world on a map. This was where I came to inherit the legacy of Western culture.

This was also where I'd come to know religion, where I learned about one particular version of God. I could remember receiving my First Communion and going to confession every Friday to recite my meager list of sins to the priest hidden behind a screen. I could remember shifting impatiently on a wooden pew through many a mass and rosary and Stations of the Cross. I could remember Confirmation, the Catholic rite of passage, where we spent months rote-memorizing a catechism of our beliefs: "What do you believe?" "I believe in God, the Father Almighty, maker of heaven and earth…"

I had abandoned all those carefully memorized beliefs long ago. For many years, I had resented having them crammed into my brain; regretted getting an education that was more about closing off than opening up to the world around me. But standing here today, I felt no regret. This is who I was. This was how I had gotten my unique perspective on the vast pageant of human culture. Had I not gone to this school and come to know this particular religion in the way I did, had I not embraced it with innocent belief, felt its majesty and power, my appreciation for religion and spirituality would not be what it is. I would never have been able to make this journey.

Bob Dylan once said something to the effect that a good folk song never loses its truth. That's what makes it good. But it's not enough for a folk singer to just sing it. A folk singer's job is to find some way to make that song mean something to the world today, to sing it in a way that people can hear it.

I say, "Amen to that."

Richard was leaning against the car, eager to get going.

"Had enough?"

"Yeah."

"It's getting late. I've got a family reunion I'm supposed to be at."

"Let's go."

And so off we went.

If you asked me now if I believed in God, I would be hard pressed to say no. My belief is something that I doubt any organized religion would endorse. I cannot hold up any book (except perhaps this one) and say, "Here. This is what I believe." I do not know of any church where I would feel at home.

But I do believe that what people call God refers to something real. It is not just a delusion of the masses. The God that I believe in gave humans the power to transcend their animal instincts and create civilizations that would not otherwise have existed. The God I believe in is a story that transformed the world, an unseen force that binds us to the rest of humanity, living and dead, to the rest of life on earth, and to the mystery that is our universe.

I would even go so far as to say that this God of mine makes demands. To learn, to teach, to engage. To be aware of and re-spect the world around me. To acknowledge that there are things greater than myself and to be humble in their presence. And even, on occasion, to offer up my services in God's name, like saying yes to an old friend who asks me to drive across the country so he can go home.

# 13

## AND IN THE END

R ichard dropped me off at my parents' condo. I thanked him and wished him luck with his family. The next night, I drove to a house in the Pines that my friend Paul had borrowed for our ersatz high school reunion. Amazingly, everybody who said they were going to come did, and then some. Bill and his wife drove all the way from Cincinnati. We sat around the pool for hours, drinking beers, eating hamburgers, reminiscing about the past and catching up on almost 30 years. It was what a high school reunion ought to be. A celebration of the youth we'd shared.

Richard arrived in the old Bug with his younger brother. He had a big grin on his face as his went around giving out hugs and handshakes. "Long time, no see. How's it going dude? This here's my long-lost brother."

Eventually, I had the chance to ask him how the family get-together went.

"Fucking unbelievable. It was like I had never been gone.

I spent half the night talking to my aunts, my uncles, my sisters. Turns out my brother smokes the same kind of weed I do. This morning I sat at the kitchen table, talking to my mom for like three hours."

"So it's all good?"

"It's all great, man. Thanks."

"For what?"

"For making the trip. For letting me air out my last bit of emotional baggage and leave it on the road where it belongs. It's been a long fucking journey, but I feel like I'm finally home."

"Thanks for inviting me."

And that was it.

The next day, I flew back to Los Angeles and picked up right where I'd left off. I tried describing the trip to a few people, but a brief retelling rarely seemed to do it justice. So I decided to try writing it all down.

A few weeks after I got back, I sent Richard an e-mail to ask how things had gone after I'd left. He replied the next day:

> Now that's all over, I realize that the reason I had to go back there was so I could leave the pain where it originated, rather than carry it around. I left it in front of the house where I grew up, where I sat for an hour, overcome by the emotion of what it was like to grow up there. I left it on the Pennsylvania Turnpike as I drove back west, forcing myself to sob bitterly at the misfortune of my youth. After that, there were no more tears. Just acceptance. And a possibility for growth that had been thwarted time and again by the ghosts of the past.

I wrote him back, to praise his courage and thank him for the privilege of allowing me to be his traveling partner. I also asked if the drive west had gone more smoothly than the drive east.

He replied that the old Bug had run perfectly until... *I hit Iowa, where the transmission seized up. Turned out it was leaking fluid all along. That's why the car was so hot. Go figure.* True to form, he found a local expert. Two days and $200 later, he was back on the road—*already planning to go back next year.*

That pretty much sums it up. The trip may be over, but the journey never ends.

## About the Author

DAN JACKSON is a producer, writer and director of non-fiction television. He lives in Los Angeles with his wife, daughter and dog. *Old Bug*, written over three years of early mornings and days off, is his first book.

**End Run Press** is a small publishing company that relies largely on word of mouth. So if you enjoyed this book, don't be shy. Tell a friend. Give a gift. Write an online review. Consider yourself our field rep.

To learn more, or to send us your feedback, please visit
**www.endrunpress.com**